MEDIEVAL LONDON

ℭHowe Bꝛute buylded London / ⁊ called this londe Bꝛytayne / and Scotlonde Albyne / and walys Camber.

ℭ London.

The earliest printed view of London, showing Old St Paul's, the Tower, London Bridge, Ludgate and the church of the black friars, from the Chronycle of Englonde *printed by Richard Pynson in 1510.*
(By courtesy of Goldsmiths' Librarian, University of London)

MEDIEVAL LONDON

Timothy Baker

PRAEGER PUBLISHERS
New York · Washington

BOOKS THAT MATTER

Published in the United States of America in 1970
by Praeger Publishers, Inc., 111 Fourth Avenue,
New York, N.Y. 10003

© Timothy Baker 1970

Library of Congress Catalog Card Number: 73-112018

Printed in Great Britain

Contents

Illustrations

Preface

Medieval London, strictly speaking, should have a more cumbersome title. The story begins in the Dark Ages, after the retreat of the Roman legions, and continues throughout the Middle Ages, which conventionally are held to have started with the Normans and to have ended in 1485 with the defeat of the last Plantagenet, Richard III, by the first Tudor, Henry VII. Such dates are sign-posts rather than turning-points, and here the medieval scene is assumed to have lasted for another fifty years, until the Reformation.

'London', too, has no precise limits. It embraces the land within the Roman wall, as well as the suburbs which spread outwards during the Middle Ages to the Bars, which mark the limits of the city today. It also covers the extension along the riverbank as far as the abbey and palace of Westminster, where there grew up a political centre, nourishing and nourished by the commercial capital. Across the river Southwark and Lambeth are included, as offshoots of London and Westminster. To the north-west Clerkenwell, although beyond the Bars, has so much to link us with the medieval city that it can hardly be left out.

There is no modern general history of medieval London, although chronicles, dating back to Anglo-Saxon times, and the records of the corporation, some of which have been printed, form the basis of many specialized works. By far the richest narrative source for the city in the Middle Ages is *The Survey of London* by the Elizabethan John Stow, first published in 1598. An edition by C. L. Kingsford, with valuable notes, was published by the Clarendon Press in 1908 and is now being revised; an edition in Everyman's Library, with an introduction by H. B. Wheatley, was revised in 1956 and reprinted in 1965. At the end of his *Survey* Stow added a translation of the earliest description of London, written by William Fitz Stephen about 1180. Fitz Stephen's *Description* has also been printed as an appendix to *Norman London* by F. M. Stenton (Historical Association leaflets, nos. 93 & 94, 1934). H. A. Harben's *A Dictionary of London*, published by Herbert Jenkins in 1918, is a good gazetteer for features of all ages in the city itself, although in some instances corrected by E. Ekwall's *Street-Names of the City of London* (Clarendon Press, 1954).

Many relics are now in the London Museum and the Guildhall Museum, housed respectively in Kensington Palace and in future shop-premises in Bassishaw High Walk. The collections will be amalgamated when the Museum of London has been built in Aldersgate Street. Other antiquities, with treasures from much further afield, are in the British Museum. Although the museums have produced many monographs, none has an up-to-date catalogue of all its London finds from the Dark Ages or the Middle Ages. The London Museum's *Medieval Catalogue*, issued in 1940 and reprinted in 1967, is the fullest survey of the different types of object which have been found.

Essential as guides to buildings or remains on their original sites are the two volumes on London by Professor Sir Nikolaus Pevsner in the series *The Buildings of England*, published by Penguin Books; Volume I, embracing the Cities of London and Westminster, was revised in 1962; Volume II, covering the outer areas (among them Lambeth, Southwark and Clerkenwell), published in 1952, is now being revised. Pevsner's books, like most of those on London's architecture, are concerned with all periods. Many buildings are the subjects of short guide-books, which are most easily bought on the spot; official guide-books, published by the Ministry of Public Buildings and Works, can be obtained from Her Majesty's Stationery Office, and publications by the Corporation of London are obtainable at the City Information Centre. More detailed modern authorities include *A History of St Paul's*, ed. W. R. Matthews and W. M. Atkins (Phoenix House Ltd., 1957) and *A House of Kings* [Westminster Abbey], ed. E. Carpenter (John Baker, 1966), each of which describes the history and organization of its church, and the article on the Tower of London in *A History of the King's Works*, ed. H. M. Colvin (H.M.S.O., 1963). Post-war excavations are recorded by Professor W. F. Grimes in *The Excavation of Roman and Medieval London* (Routledge & Kegan Paul, 1968). Additions to our knowledge of all aspects of London's history are regularly made in the *Transactions of the London and Middlesex Archaeological Society* and the *London Topographical Record*.

Space does not permit individual thanks to all those who deserve them. The book is heavily indebted to the research of historians and archaeologists, the courtesy of owners and curators, the skill of Cassell and Company's editorial staff, and, above all, the patience and help of my wife.

CHAPTER ONE

The Rebirth of London

If the towns of southern England were to be obliterated by nuclear war and, a generation later, wandering survivors were to seek a new site for settlement, they would probably not choose London. The destruction of the Thames's embankments would cause the flooding of hundreds of square miles. High tides would cover what were once marshlands, to east and west of the Roman city, for the melting of the polar ice-cap has raised the high-water mark by some fifteen feet over the past two thousand years. Westminster would disappear and the slopes on which London itself was built would be left more isolated than when they first attracted man.

In spite of the wide flood-plain, London exists because of the river. The Romans needed to bring their ships as far as possible up the estuary and unload them at a point from which men and goods could be dispersed into the country. For some two miles along the northern foreshore, from what is now the Tower of London to Waterloo Bridge, a firm gravel terrace arose from the mud, opposite a lower outcrop on the south bank. Here, where the Thames was still tidal, although shallower than today, a bridge could be built and a ford may already have been in use.

The northern terrace rose to two small hills, Cornhill in the east and Ludgate Hill in the west. These are now crowned by Leadenhall Market and St Paul's Cathedral. 'When ye have sought the City round, yet this is still the highest ground' says a plaque from Panyer Alley, overlooking the steps which lead from its old home to the new Cathedral Place, a few yards north of St Paul's; Cornhill, by reaching sixty feet just east of the Royal Exchange, in fact out-tops Ludgate Hill by some two feet. Between these twin hills ran the Walbrook, a stream which still flows underground from the former marshes around Finsbury Circus and whose passage under Cannon Street makes the road dip to the west of the station. Here, on Cornhill, Londinium was founded in the middle of the first century AD.

The Romans had chosen a strong defensive position, whose slopes have become less steep with the partial filling up of the Walbrook's valley and the reclamation of a strip along the Thames, now stretching a hundred yards inland. Centuries of refuse-dumping and of rebuilding have everywhere raised the street level, so that a cut made straight down below the present foundations would reveal layer upon layer of debris and ashes, each representing a stage of London's history. Today, when the ground is covered by buildings of all shapes and sizes, the contours are harder than ever to see. The site was also well drained, easily cleared and, backed by the higher plateaux of Highgate and Hampstead, a good stepping-stone towards the interior.

What suited the Romans was of no use to more backward peoples. The London basin, a saucer-shaped depression stretching from the Chilterns to the North Downs, repelled primitive settlers. Its heavy clay, which still defies millions of suburban gardeners, was covered with oak forests and matted, thorny undergrowth; the swamps along the Thames, which meandered sluggishly through the middle of the basin, were equally forbidding. Only on the chalky hills at the fringe and on a few gravel patches by the river could homes be made. Most of the gravel was hard to reach and could support only small, remote communities.

In the Middle Ages, when any explanation was better than none, men were told that London had been founded by Brutus, a refugee from the sack of Troy. Geoffrey of Monmouth, the Welsh monk who first set down this story, says that the original name, New Troy, was changed by King Lud, who reigned in the time of Julius Caesar. Despite London's undoubtedly Celtic name, perhaps derived from that of a man, there may not have been a single inhabitant on the slopes beside the Walbrook when the Romans came. Strong government, trade and a network of communications were needed to make the bridge-head of a tidal river into a city.

Londinium became the richest city in Britain, with perhaps twenty-five thousand people, and the fifth largest in the northern provinces of the Empire, which embraced western Germany and the whole of Gaul. All this needed the authority of Rome. Townsmen are specialists in a craft or profession, working for profit to meet sophisticated demands. They are packed together in a narrow space, so that only careful regulation can keep squalor and violence at bay. Sooner or later they come to rely on others for food and defence. If order collapses, they must revert to a more natural state, scratching a living from the soil.

When Germanic tribesmen overran Roman Britain, urban civilization died. The invaders were Angles and Saxons, from north-western Germany, and Jutes, probably from the Rhineland; eventually they all became known as Englishmen, although the Angles themselves settled farther north than London. For these peoples, a city was something to be plundered. They were warriors and subsistence farmers, unused to anything larger or more permanent than a wooden village. They too had their craftsmen, but these were individuals, who excelled in making personal ornaments and weapons for chieftains. The newcomers would have to change their way of life before London could revive. Should they do so, the site which had attracted the Romans ought also to attract the English.

As a result of grinding taxation, British town life had been decaying for at least a hundred years before the last legions retreated in 410. The Germanic conquest in the fifth century took a long time. It was the work of countless small bands, at first no more than raiders, which cut ever more deeply into the country and ended by settling wherever they could. Londinium, unlike Rome, may not even have been sacked. The cutting of communications would have had the same effect.

London's history is obscure for two hundred years, while the Jutes colonize Kent and rival Saxons carve kingdoms out of the remaining Home Counties. Under the year 456 an unreliable passage in the much later *Anglo-Saxon Chronicle* supplies the first reference to the post-Roman city: Hengest had defeated the Britons, who deserted Kent 'and fled with great fear to London'. Probably it was a rural slum, where walls and crumbling stone buildings still offered some kind of shelter. Grim's Dyke, the long earthen rampart which crosses the golf course at Harrow Weald, may be part of a boundary line, designed to keep the first marauders from settling within ten or fifteen miles of London itself. This, besides explaining the claims of medieval citizens to privileges over the surrounding countryside, would show that London resisted the invaders, preserving its identity in the Dark Ages as did no other British town

3

save Canterbury. Recent Iron Age finds, however, suggest that the dyke is much older; in this case the medieval area might represent an early kingdom, larger than Middlesex, held by the obscure Middle Saxons.

In the chaos of the fifth century, the story of medieval London begins. The break with the past was complete: the long Roman roads still converged there, but the symmetrical street-plan vanished and only the wall and the gates survived to shape the future city. The first large Saxon settlement nearby seems to have been farther west, on the gravel terrace of the Wandle, where a pagan cemetery has been discovered near Mitcham Station. A score of scattered finds, now in the London Museum, shows that soon afterwards the newcomers reached the city itself; there, perhaps peacefully, they mingled with a population that was far too small for the 330 acres within the wall, so ensuring that the hills beside the Walbrook would not revert to wilderness. No new London arose, phoenix-like, from the ashes of the old. A meaner settlement took shape, illuminated at first only by passing references which are separated by many generations. At least it can be said that the light grows clearer with time and has never again been put out.

The return of Christianity brings the first written evidence on Saxon London. In 601 Pope Gregory the Great nominated St Augustine as bishop there and told him to send a fellow bishop to York, with whom he was to share authority over any other sees. Presumably these two places were chosen because their imperial glory was still remembered at Rome. Chance and tribal politics frustrated the plan. On his way Augustine had been welcomed by King Æthelberht of Kent and had already founded a church at Canterbury. In 604 he consecrated his disciple Mellitus as bishop of London, which had passed with Middlesex to the East Saxons, under Æthelberht's overlordship. It was the king of Kent who built for Mellitus the church of St Paul, the forerunner of many which have dominated London from its western hill. This mission is recorded over a century later by the Venerable Bede, England's first true historian. Bede, who was chiefly interested in kings, bishops and the progress of the faith, may never have travelled farther south than York. In his monastery at Jarrow, near Tyne-mouth, he heard that London was 'a market-place for many peoples, who come by land and sea'. It might have boasted a cathedral and still have been no more than a hamlet. It is Bede who enables us to call it once again a city.

4

What did early Saxon London look like? The tide-level rose about nine inches every hundred years and the Walbrook, confined by the Romans to a width of perhaps twelve feet, probably resumed a broader, more natural course. Saxon colonization may have started on Ludgate Hill because Cornhill, the site of the Roman forum, still sheltered British families among its ruins. Possibly King Æthelberht's choice of a site for St Paul's was dictated by the existence of a church on the site of St Peter Cornhill, whose rectors in the Middle Ages were given precedence over others in the city because of their church's supposed Roman ancestry. According to tradition Æthelberht and succeeding overlords had a palace north-east of St Paul's, in Aldermanbury.

The palace and most churches must have been of timber, the humbler houses of wattle-and-daub, in other words of interlaced laths or twigs, smeared with clay. London has no local stone-quarries, so that the wall had been built from Kentish ragstone, quarried around Maidstone and shipped down the Medway and up the Thames. The use of this rough but exceptionally hard material preserved the wall and so helped to shape the medieval city. The Romans had also worked kilns on Ludgate Hill, where there was a patch of brickearth. The Saxons never made bricks and at first were quite unskilled in masonry; they could re-roof the gutted stone buildings with wood or thatch but it was not until the end of the seventh century that they managed even to rebuild a church in Roman materials (*see p. 20*).

Although Kentish overlordship died with Æthelberht, the see of London never rivalled Canterbury. This was because later East Saxon rulers returned to paganism, expelling Mellitus, and because London was awkwardly placed at the junction of several tribal kingdoms. Nature made it too valuable to be left to Essex, a faction-ridden minor power, cut off by the dense forests of Epping and Hainault. The bishopric, restored in 653, was soon afterwards sold by Wulfhere, king of Mercia, who had extended his sway from the Midlands over all his neighbours to the south and east. Soon however two East Saxon kings gave it to Earconwald who, to confuse matters further, was later called 'my bishop' by yet another southern English overlord, Ine of Wessex.

Earconwald left his mark by founding the nearby monastery of Barking, which acquired what was probably the first Saxon stone church in London. He retired to Barking in 692 but was buried in St Paul's. A bishop for the West Saxons had already been

5

consecrated in London by Archbishop Theodore and it was to Earconwald's successor there that Sebbi of the East Saxons came, after resigning his crown, to seek the monastic habit. Amidst this tribal warfare and missionary work, the tidal port was developing, unrecorded, at its own pace. The earliest reference is to human traffic: Imma, a Northumbrian nobleman captured by the Mercians in 679, was sold in London to a trader from Frisia.

Darkness again falls for over a century after Bede's death in 735. The future lay with Mercia or with Wessex, central powers which could expand in several directions at the expense of the cramped little kingdoms on the coast. For most of this time the Mercians dominated southern England and treated London as their town, while the rulers of Kent and Essex lingered on as sub-kings. A network of frontiers strangles trade; the more unified the nation became, the more important became links with the Continent. Offa of Mercia, who styled himself 'king of the English' and died in 796, made with Charlemagne the first commercial treaty in England's history. The emperor in one of his letters complains that merchants from the island pretend to be pilgrims in order to escape paying tolls; he also grumbles about the short length of English cloaks, so mentioning for the first time the island's famous textiles.

If cloth was sent abroad before 800, raw wool was probably sold in much larger amounts. No ports are named as outlets for this trade, which was largely the work of heathen Frisians, another Germanic people. These were hardy sailors who controlled the mouth of the Rhine and traffic up the river, as well as the passage of goods from the Channel into the North Sea. They had colonies in many Christian kingdoms, and made cloth and metal-work, but above all they were carriers, who brought wine from the south and furs from the north-east. From England they perhaps took corn as well as wool; more profitable than either may have been slaves, usually Britons but sometimes, as Bede shows us, the victims of a purely English feud. Already trade could conflict with morality. The Church, fearful for the souls of Christians under pagan masters, persuaded King Ine to ban the sale of English people out of their own country. This did not kill the traffic, nor was it intended to stop native Londoners from keeping slaves of their own.

London naturally attracted the Frisians. Bede's writings are not the only evidence of their presence there at least a hundred years before Offa, since similar tiny silver coins, *sceattas*, have been found on both sides of the Channel. London is the only town whose name

appears on these early coins. The Mercian kings themselves preferred the Midlands and vainly tried to degrade Canterbury and
York by setting up a third archbishop, at Lichfield. Offa, however,
was probably the builder of a Saxon chapel on the site of St Alban
Wood Street, near the traditional palace of London's overlords. He
also acquired the Kentish royal mint at Canterbury and struck the
first silver pennies, which now replaced the *sceattas* as England's
staple currency.

After a victory in 825, Egbert of Wessex briefly wrested London
from Offa's heirs and issued the first surviving penny with the city's
name (*Fig. 1 upper*). While Mercians and West Saxons fought,
both were overtaken by the Vikings. These northern pirates
hovered off the Thames at Sheppey in 835; year after year they
came back until, in 850, they first passed the winter on English soil,
on the Isle of Thanet. The *Anglo-Saxon Chronicle*, compiled from
earlier, vanished sources at the end of the century, says that there
was great slaughter at London as early as 842. Nine years later 350
ships anchored in the estuary, stormed London and expelled the
Mercian king. Londinium had died a slow death; the early Saxon
settlement ended in blood and flames.

Fig. 1 (upper) *Silver penny of Egbert of Wessex, reverse inscribed*
LVNDONIA CIVIT, about 825 (British Museum)
(lower) *Silver penny of Alfred, reverse inscribed with monogram of*
London, about 886 (British Museum)

The Viking onslaught, far from wiping London off the map for
generations, turned out to be a blessing in disguise. The English
peoples drew together to face a common enemy, Alfred and his

7

West Saxon heirs emerged as their champion and London became the backbone of the resistance. Men clung to the ravaged site, until the Mercian port became a national stronghold. All this is known mainly from the *Anglo-Saxon Chronicle*, itself a sign of Alfred's determination to foster national pride. In 871–2, when Wessex seemed about to succumb, the Danes wintered in London. Possibly they used it for many years as a base-camp, from which to pillage the south. Not until 886 did Alfred gain entry by force (*Fig. 1 lower*). He drafted in colonists from the countryside, presumably families which had lost everything, and repaired the still formidable wall. There were other Roman remains, perhaps more useful as quarries than as homes: in 889 the bishop of Worcester was granted an enclosure at 'an ancient stone building' in the city. London, while it has often come to terms with invaders, has never since been taken by storm.

The Vikings were now swarming all around Europe, ravaging the French and Iberian coasts and penetrating the Mediterranean from the west, pushing up the river valleys of Russia to reach the Black Sea and Constantinople in the east. Nowhere did the native, Christian peoples fight back more successfully than in southern England, no townsmen were tougher than the men of London. In 895, when the Danes were at Benfleet in Essex, the English army, picking up recruits as it swept eastwards through the city, surprised the enemy and retired within the wall with the captives and plunder. This, the first record of Londoners at war, was followed in the summer by a fruitless thrust against a Danish fortress on the river Lea some twenty miles to the north. The *Chronicle* records: 'Then later, in the autumn, the king encamped in the vicinity of the borough while they were reaping their corn, so that the Danes could not deny them that harvest.' London deserved Alfred's special protection, but its citizens were still half countrymen, working in the fields for their food.

London was drawn into the West Saxon orbit at the moment when the kings of Wessex were becoming kings of England. Alfred respected local feeling and entrusted London to the ealdorman Æthelred, who had emerged as ruler of unoccupied Mercia out of the chaos which had engulfed the old royal line. Æthelred married Alfred's daughter and loyally served the one remaining English dynasty. After 899 Alfred's son Edward the Elder continued to reduce the areas of Viking settlement known as the Danelaw, bringing them for the first time under a single king. The future capital was painlessly absorbed on Æthelred's death in 910, when

King Edward succeeded to 'London, Oxford and the other Mercian lands'.

Alfred's successors were always on the move, living off their estates and on the profits of justice and the food-rents which were owed by groups of villages. They had no proper capital, for the centre of government was wherever the king happened to be. He spent most of his time in the south country when not fighting to enlarge his kingdom, but Winchester, the historic heart of Wessex, remained the favourite seat. It was here, in the following century, that the treasury was to be fixed, when it became too inconvenient to cart all the king's wealth around in his wake. None of this affected London's future. Winchester lay on the Itchen, which meandered picturesquely for a dozen miles before reaching Southampton Water. London had the Thames estuary, muddy, fog-ridden, tidal.

The triumphant West Saxon kings founded many boroughs or fortified settlements on their lands, where plots were also acquired by the Church and by wealthy nobles or thegns. Royal boroughs were peopled by the king's tenants, free peasants and a few thegns who hoped to prosper through trade, paying rent for their land and tolls on their business, as well as performing services laid on them by the founder. A few boroughs had their own courts by the year 1000, but most were no more than meeting-places for courts of the surrounding district, the hundred or the shire. These embryo towns were divided into fenced holdings, called tenements, and surrounded by walls or earthen ramparts, beyond which stretched open fields shared out among the inhabitants. Every borough boasted a mint, although the dies from which pennies were cast were always cut at London; these were often changed, so that the king could charge local moneyers for the new dies. The borough was thus a stronghold, an administrative centre and a market. London, on a larger scale, had all these features.

The rights which were later claimed by these new boroughs were often clearer than those of London, which went back to the earliest times. At least we know that in the tenth century Londoners were uniquely well organized. Among the many Anglo-Saxon law-codes there is one in the name of Alfred's grandson Athelstan, who died in 939, drawn up by the bishops and officials or reeves who were responsible for London. Intended as a supplement to the general laws of the kingdom, it deals with a mysterious *frithsgild* or peace association and the members' efforts to safeguard their property.

Every man shall pay 4d. a year into a common fund, from which shall come compensation for stolen goods, and the members themselves are grouped in bodies of ten and then of a hundred. Here are the earliest English by-laws. The men who framed them, while apparently unique in trying to help themselves, end tactfully by saying that 'if our lord [the king], or any of our reeves, can devise any additional rules for our association, such suggestions shall not be unheeded. . . .'

London's prosperity has always had its darker side. The opening resolution of the *frithsgild* orders death for any thief over twelve years old, who has stolen goods worth more than 12d. Another clause lays down that everyone shall join in searching for a runaway slave: 'if we can catch him, he shall receive the same treatment as a Welsh [i.e. British] thief or he shall be hanged'. The men of the *frithsgild*, although tight-fisted, were not exceptionally cruel. Their first decree merely repeated a law which applied to the whole kingdom, and it was the general law which ordered that a British thief should be stoned to death. Their concern about livestock, with compensation ranging from half a pound of silver for a good horse to 10d. for a pig, shows that the richest citizens were still farmers. These laws of Athelstan reveal Saxon London for the first time as an organized community. They also show how far it had to go.

Soon there was another association, the *cnihtengild*, perhaps at first made up of retainers kept in London to buy goods for their masters; we know almost nothing about it until Norman times, when it included most of the chief citizens. Order and growth have never been news. In the mid-tenth century, as in the reign of Offa, there was little to write about London. Peace at home and marriage alliances with royal houses abroad no doubt helped the flow of trade. History, obsessed with man-made havoc, becomes so dull that we catch a glimpse of the natural disasters which repeatedly struck. In 962 there were widespread deaths, presumably from the plague, and St Paul's was consumed in a great fire; the church, which must have been destroyed at least once before, by the Vikings, was rebuilt immediately, on the same hill-top. Twenty years later, the *Anglo-Saxon Chronicle* remarks simply that 'London was burnt down'.

Another bald statement provides the first record of a bridge, although many earlier ones must have existed. Between 963 and 984 a widow and her son were convicted of driving iron pins into the image of a man named Ælsie; the son escaped and was outlawed, the mother was taken and drowned at London Bridge. This wooden structure probably lay east of its famous medieval successor (*see p. 99*). A thousand years ago, when London was cursed with fires, pestilence, witchcraft and slavery, it pointed the way to the future. There was no other road-way over the Thames below Staines. The river was the source of London's wealth; the bridge became its symbol.

The bridge occurs again, in a law-code probably dating from the 990s. Here we first learn of sites, apart from those of churches, which are known today: Aldersgate and Cripplegate, two of the Roman gateways, which had to be guarded, and Billingsgate, probably named after a man, a wharf where ships drop anchor. Planks and cloth form cargoes, together with wine and 'fat fish' brought from Rouen; the fat fish may have been whales, prized for their blubber as well as for their meat, or porpoises, a delicacy known to the Saxons as sea-swine. Men from Flanders, Ponthieu, Normandy, the Ile-de-France, Huy, Liége and Nivelles all pay toll for displaying their goods, while traders from the Holy Roman Empire enjoy the same privileges as natives. These German merchants can buy wool and melted fat (tallow) and can stock each of their ships with three live pigs. They probably spend the winter in London, for at Christmas and at Easter they must provide two lengths of grey cloth and one length of brown, ten pounds of pepper, five pairs of gloves and two saddle-kegs of vinegar. We also learn that people carry hampers of hens and eggs on their backs to London's markets, where women selling cheese and butter twice have to pay tolls of 1d. in the fortnight before Christmas, perhaps because that was already the time for a shopping spree.

Nearly three hundred years after Bede's death, these laws at last bear out his claim that London was a 'market-place for many peoples'. Ironically, the Vikings now returned, their piracy again leading to an attempt at large-scale conquest. This time the English were weakly led by Æthelred II, remembered as 'the Unready' from the epithet *unraed*, 'lacking in counsel'. Neither heavy tribute—the notorious Danegeld—nor a massacre of Scandinavian subjects on St Brice's Day, 1002, saved Æthelred, who fled to his brother-in-law the duke of Normandy after the invasion of King Swein Forkbeard in 1013. For the first time, all England submitted to a Viking.

The kingdom's loss was London's gain, for the citizens' behaviour

stands out in twenty years of national humiliation. Swein and his
ally, Olaf Tryggvason, king of Norway, had sailed up the Thames
as early as 994, hoping in vain to burn down the city, and more
attacks had failed in the early winter of 1009. On the first occasion,
the *Anglo-Saxon Chronicle* proudly recalls that the invaders 'suffered
more harm and injury than they ever thought any citizens would do
to them'—a startling claim in an age which thought little of farmers
or merchants. In 1012 the chief Englishmen met in London to pay
tribute to the Danes, who slaughtered Archbishop Ælfheah of
Canterbury in their camp at Greenwich but allowed his body to be
carried into the city, where it was laid in St Paul's. Before the
century was out he had been commemorated in the first church of
St Alphage London Wall (*see pp. 159, 233*).

While the rest of England was yielding to Swein, his soldiers
were driven back from London and many were drowned in trying
to ford the Thames. Not until their king's flight did the citizens
temporarily submit. The conqueror's sudden death allowed
Æthelred to return in 1014 when, with his more robust son Edmund
Ironside, he faced Swein's son Cnut. Edmund's hopes of checking
the Danes in the Midlands were dashed by the news that the
English army would march only if helped by the king himself and
the men of London. Soon afterwards he joined his father in the city,
where he was at once hailed as king on Æthelred's death in April
1016. An elaborate siege started in May and the failure of a full-scale
attack, under Cnut himself, at last induced the Danes to accept
partition. Most unfairly the Londoners, not living in historic
Wessex, were handed over to Cnut and left to buy their own peace.
As the Vikings anchored in the Thames to exact tribute, Edmund
died and all question of further defiance died with him.

The whole northern world heard of London's strength. The
Heimskringla, a collection of Norse sagas written down in the
thirteenth century, tells in detail of a Danish failure to hold the city,
presumably after Swein's death. This story is the first to mention
'a great market town called Southwark' on the opposite bank and to
name the materials of which the bridge and nearby homes were
built; it may describe the very fight now represented by the finest
collection of Viking weapons in the London Museum. Æthelred,
allied with Olaf Haraldson, the future king of Norway, could
recapture neither London nor Southwark, where the Danes were
entrenched behind banks of wood and earth. The bridge, 'so broad
that two waggons could be driven past each other over it', was

dotted with the defenders' towers and would have to be won before ships could pass upstream to invest the city on the farther side. Olaf found the answer: 'great mats of willow and pliable wood, taken from houses made of wickerwork' were placed over the ships, some of whose crews reached the bridge, passed ropes around the wooden piles and rowed furiously away, dislodging the timbers and drowning many who stood on top, whereupon the Danes surrendered. The narrator then breaks into a song, which begins like the nursery rhyme 'London Bridge is broken down'; the Viking version, perhaps dimly linked with ours through centuries of children's games, is much the gorier.

Alfred's work lived on, for Cnut prized England above his other realms and soon confirmed the native laws. London, his early stumbling-block, was made to settle old scores by paying a seventh of the money which England provided towards paying off most of the Viking war fleet. As consolation, the citizens were now at the heart of a maritime empire, the strongest northern power of its day. One man's rule over Denmark, the southern tip of Sweden and, for a time, Norway, brought peace from the Baltic to the Atlantic. Cnut, with his European influence, also wrung concessions from the Holy Roman Empire and Burgundy for any subjects who travelled to Rome, whether for their pockets or their souls. It was probably now that Danish and Norwegian merchants were first allowed to stay in London for a year, instead of the forty days normally allotted to aliens. The king's Danish blood explains why his own compatriots could visit markets anywhere in England, while the Norwegians' trade was confined to London. Tradition plausibly ascribes to Cnut's soldiery the riverside settlement beyond the west gate, at St Clement's well, which was slightly north of where St Clement Danes now stands (*see p. 62*). Another Danish encampment lay to the north-east among the marshes of the river Lea, at Haakon's *eg* (island) or Hackney.

Londoners were asserting themselves in politics as well as in war. After Cnut's death in 1035 a council at Oxford vested the regency in his bastard, Harold Harefoot, since the legitimate heir, Harthacnut, was detained in Denmark. The seamen from London, whom the council heard with respect, supported this decision. Harold soon usurped the throne but died in 1040, whereupon Harthacnut succeeded in peace, only to drop dead two years later while drinking at a wedding feast in Lambeth. Even before his funeral the men of

13

London ensured the return of Alfred's line by acclaiming Æthelred's son Edward, whom Harthacnut himself had invited back from exile in Normandy. London's size and wealth, which emboldened it to ignore feeling in other parts of the country, were no substitute for royal tradition. It was at Winchester that Cnut and Harthacnut were buried and it was there that Edward the Confessor was crowned.

In the next twenty years London often saw meetings of the royal councillors, the *witan*, and was treated as the key to the kingdom. This is shown at the turning point of Edward's reign in 1052, when the half-Norman king vainly tried to prevent the return from exile of Earl Godwine of Wessex. It was to London that the earl sailed, after plundering along the south coast, and it was there, above the bridge, that the royal fleet lurked. The citizens, in league with Godwine, allowed him to occupy Southwark and to pass under the bridge. This bloodless victory forced Edward to accept the Godwines once more as his chief advisers and led to the expulsion of the Norman archbishop of Canterbury and other foreigners. More ominously, it frustrated the childless king's hope that his throne would pass in peace to Duke William of Normandy. London was thus largely responsible for the Norman Conquest. Fear of Godwine's pirate crews may have swayed the citizens in 1052, but they were later to show that they disliked foreign rule as such. Danes and Englishmen understood one another and could live side by side, so long as English customs were respected; men who spoke French were welcome only as traders.

Edward the Confessor, who must have loathed his richest city, was to prove its greatest benefactor. He abandoned the palace there for the marshes to the west, where he spent excessive time supervising work on an enormous abbey, in place of a monastery which had been wiped out by the Danes (*see p. 67*). The development of this desolate site into the fixed seat of England's government was to bring together great nobles, whose demands only London could satisfy, and remove the citizens from close royal supervision, so nourishing their independence. In fairness, all this should be traced to the Saxons. They did not found London, they merely breathed new life into what they had almost destroyed. At Westminster they began what was to be a new city, a complement but never a rival to the old.

Our earliest picture of any building in the area comes from the Bayeux Tapestry, probably English work executed well before the

Fig. 2 *Edward the Confessor and Westminster abbey church, from the Bayeux Tapestry, late 11th century* (British Museum)

end of the century: the king sits in his hall next to the abbey church, while a man climbs up to place the cock of St Peter on the central tower (*Fig. 2*). Edward died at Westminster on 5 January 1066 and was buried in his new church the next day. This, its first funeral, preceded by a few hours the abbey's first coronation, after Godwine's son Harold had been offered the throne. London's approval, although unrecorded, is borne out by events after Hastings. Rather than accept the Norman duke, the citizens rallied to the boy who had been passed over in favour of Harold, Edgar the Ætheling, the last male of Alfred's line. William's vanguard, approaching from Canterbury, was beaten back at the southern end of London Bridge. The Conqueror took his time, burning Southwark on his way west, crossing the Thames at Wallingford and advancing through the Chilterns. Cowed by this strength of purpose, Edgar's chief supporters sought terms at Berkhamstead, where William promised to be a good lord to the men of London. He plundered right up to their gates but entered with little or no bloodshed. On Christmas Day, anxious as ever to pose as Edward's legitimate heir, William was crowned at Westminster.

The new king, unsure of his hold, moved out to Barking Abbey and at once built a camp of earth and timber at the extreme south-eastern corner of the city. Before his death, this was to give way to the White Tower, which is still the nucleus of the Tower of London (*see p. 140*). It was meant to overawe the citizens, although it also shielded them from attacks up the estuary, such as those led by Swein and Cnut. Apparently as early as 1067 the Conqueror issued a writ, now the most terse but perhaps the most precious document treasured by the Corporation of London. Addressing the bishop of London, the chief municipal official or portreeve and all the burgesses, both French and English, William promised respect for the laws of King Edward and full protection for the citizens. His words have been taken as a sign that the populace already included many Frenchmen. At any rate there were no calamitous racial riots. This at first is surprising, in view of London's record and the prolonged resistance in other parts of England. In fact, while trade and industry are quick to react to a threat, they are also ready to make the best of an accomplished fact. Both the Normans and the Londoners knew where their real interests lay.

In William's time the Walbrook was still a dividing line, as it had been since the Romans founded Londinium. On each side there was a shopping centre, East Cheap and West Cheap (now Cheapside), a fish market, near London Bridge and in Friday Street, and a quay, at Billingsgate and at Edredeshythe (later called Queenhithe, after it had passed to the consort of Henry I). Self-government was a later, medieval, achievement, but its roots lay in Anglo-Saxon times, with thrice yearly meetings of all the citizens, the folkmoot, and weekly meetings of the husting court, whose business included the regulation of dealings with foreign traders. Even municipal divisions were based on the Walbrook, for there were twelve wards on each side of the stream, each with an alderman to preside over petty affairs at his local wardmoot. (*See Chapter Five.*)

London's growth in later Saxon times is shown by a more even balance between the eastern and western halves. Archaeology proves that the Saxons, originally clustered around Ludgate Hill, afterwards crossed to the slopes of Cornhill—moving in the opposite direction to the Romans. By 1066 the citizens' wood and wattle homes, covered with thatch and sometimes on two floors, had spread over most of the land within the wall. This does not mean that dwellings everywhere were close together. Although fairs and games were held on the levels outside to the north—the 'smooth fields' of Smithfield—there must have been a wide open space north-east of St Paul's, where the folkmoot gathered; the Tower too was built on empty ground. Apart from the cathedral and the fortifications, no Saxon building would have been big enough to impress anyone today. The patched walls, some church towers and, in a few cases, the churches themselves, are all that are known to have been built in stone. Even though it boasted St Paul's and at least thirty-two parish churches, London cannot yet have held as many people as it had in its Roman heyday.

If London in 1066 was but a shadow of Londinium, it was a metropolis by the standards of its day. Undeterred by political upheavals, trade had flourished for a century before the Conquest. Between the landing-places at Billingsgate and Edredeshythe lay a third quay, Dowgate, at the mouth of the Walbrook. Perhaps this was where the Rouen merchants had always unloaded their wine and fat fish, for they owned a wharf here under Edward the Confessor. If traders had come from what are now northern France, Belgium and Germany in the troubled reign of Æthelred II, still more must have arrived under Edward. Across the North Sea, Cnut's countrymen had grown used to bringing fish, skins, furs and tallow to London, the western end of the Baltic trade route. From the mouth of the Thames went wheat, honey and, above all, wool and woollen cloths; the slave-trade, increasingly frowned upon by churchmen, was now more evident in the west, where there were still plenty of Britons for the taking.

What remains of Saxon London? Most obviously, the layout and names of its streets. For over a thousand years the basic road-plan was simple: three long routes from east to west, one from south to north, and two shorter ones also leading north. The east-west line close to the river now survives in Lower and Upper Thames Street; parallel to it the line of East Cheap and Cannon Street led out through Ludgate towards Westminster; farther north again, and busiest of all, the line of Cornhill and Cheapside continued the highway from Colchester, which entered through Aldgate and left through Newgate for Oxford and the west. All three were crossed by the road which led from London Bridge up Fish Street Hill and Gracechurch Street to pass through Bishopsgate to the north; the other roads north are now represented by Wood Street, from Cheapside to Cripplegate, and St Martin's-le-Grand, which led to Aldersgate. Although the main thoroughfares used Roman gates, settlement has destroyed the Roman pattern within the wall. Apart from these, from many short alleys running down to the Thames and from some symmetry in the north-west on the site of a Roman fort, London became a warren of cross-streets, lanes, passages and courtyards. Over the years empty spaces were filled, the pattern spread further beyond the walls, and the alleys themselves grew darker as men built upwards and outwards. The Great Fire of 1666 did not produce a more rational system, as Wren would have liked, and even in the nineteenth century only two major passages were cut through the ancient maze: King William Street, from the rebuilt bridge to the Mansion House, and Queen Victoria Street, from the south-west to this same central point. It was not until after the Second World War that sweeping new schemes threatened the historic ground-plan, which still gives the city its unique character.

The street-names too, every one of which has been analysed, are often of Saxon origin; these evolved long before they were written down, however, so that the earliest instance is usually well after 1066. Only the bridge, five of the gates and a few churches actually figure in pre-Conquest documents. Every morning, trains disgorge thousands of city workers at Cannon Street station, a few yards east of the hidden mouth of the Walbrook, where the men of Rouen landed their cargoes a thousand years ago. The passengers step out into a street known by the 1180s as Candlewick Street, the home of the candle-wick makers. Many go straight along Walbrook, keeping some fifty yards east of the stream, which flows more than thirty feet underground; the name itself means 'stream of the Britons' and is London's sole reminder of the old population, whom the English called Wealas and who are now commemorated in Wales. Several of the roads which meet at the Bank bear more recent names, although Cornhill occurs before 1133, probably as a slope where crops were grown rather than as a thoroughfare, and Poultry was so called by 1301. Turning left, a short walk along this former poultry-market and then along Cheapside, from the Anglo-Saxon *ceap*, a market-place, leads to St Paul's, on the hill-top chosen by the Kentish overlord of the East Saxons. The way through the old western shopping centre passes entrances whose medieval names still recall trades or manufactures which must have been localized there before the Conquest: on the south Bread Street, on the north Ironmonger Lane, Honey Lane, Milk Street and Wood Street.

Similar pictures can be painted in most corners of the modern city. Many streets are named after the simple activities of early townsmen, some of the places after the men themselves. Perhaps the first Londoner to be so honoured is Coelmund, whose vegetable garden by the west gate was granted by the Mercian king to the bishop of Worcester in 857; his plot must have been very near Coleman Street, which first occurs in the 1180s although it now seems more likely that the street is named after a Celtic saint. A few post-Conquest immigrants, the Jews, the Lombards and the religious orders, have also left their mark, but since their coming there has been remarkably little change in the names of streets or lanes. Even now, when the lines themselves are at last being blurred, old names are tacked on to entirely new features. It has of course always been easier to rebuild and rechristen houses, but here too the past is often commemorated, perhaps with a guilty conscience. The Saxons' imprint has thus outlasted that of any later age and will probably outlast that of today.

What else survives? No complete buildings; little that is large enough to be called a monument; hundreds of smaller objects, especially weapons and coins. Pictures and plans of the Roman and medieval cities are common; some are on view in the London Museum, which makes no attempt to re-create the Saxon scene, although the Guildhall Museum shows the sites of some early churches, the folkmoot and King Æthelberht's palace. The only traces of thousands of pre-Conquest homes lie beyond the western wall. Four clay loom-weights and a cooking pot, now in the London Museum, show that a hut existed in the sixth, seventh or eighth century on a spot famous for good living since the Middle Ages, where the Savoy Hotel now stands; in 1963 excavations on the site of the Treasury revealed that there had been a large timbered hall there in the ninth century. The finest Anglo-Saxon churches are hidden in the countryside, where no one has felt the urge to rebuild or destroy. In London itself it would be astonishing if anything less massive than the Roman wall had been preserved above ground.

Curiously enough there is one exception, and that from the early Saxon period. Like many remains, it came to light after German bombs had destroyed priceless later treasures. The top of Tower Hill is dominated by the present guild church of Toc H, All Hallows by-the-Tower, sometimes called All Hallows Barking because of its early dependence on Barking Abbey. Reconstruction of the wrecked fifteenth-century church uncovered a Saxon doorway, some four feet wide and ten feet high, near the western end in what was the south wall of the very first nave; roughly squared whitish masonry is set in a section of rubble about twelve feet long and surmounted by a rounded arch of re-used Roman tiles, without a keystone. This, the oldest archway in London, was built in the dawn of English Christianity about 680, almost certainly by foreign masons such as those whom Bede says were brought over to work on churches in Northumbria. More Saxon walling surrounds a piece of tesselated Roman pavement at the bottom of the stairs leading to the crypt. There are also two square pieces of a carved cross-shaft, which fell near the Saxon arch during the air-raids, and half of a circular cross-head, found in 1951 under the nave. The cross-head dates from about the year 1000 although the shaft might be a little later. It is well worth arranging in advance to see these and other treasures in the crypt, which is a museum of the history of the south-eastern corner of the city.

Apart from All Hallows by-the-Tower the only Saxon remains on their original site are in the crypt of St Bride's, in Fleet Street. The church is on the west bank of the Fleet and so lies beyond the Roman wall, which crossed the drier slope to the east, half-way up Ludgate Hill. It falls within the historic limits of the city only because these were pushed westward to Temple Bar in the Middle Ages. Before the Conquest it was a suburban church, showing that life was spreading outside the wall while there was still plenty of space within. Here too rebuilding after the blitz uncovered a series of early churches. These are illustrated in the crypt itself by plans. Beneath the restored masterpiece of Wren we can wander among Anglo-Saxon foundations about three feet high and outlining a rectangular nave, a chancel and a rounded east end, or apse, later extended by the Normans. Although hard to date, at least part of this lumpish grey masonry belongs to the earliest period of stone church-building. A side passage along the north wall leads past the site of a Saxon burial, and a glass show-case in the former nave contains, among medieval relics, a curved piece of stone from a Saxon font. This is the only place in London where we can see for ourselves the area covered by a Saxon building.

Both Saxons and Vikings are famous for their sculpture, not so much on buildings as on free-standing crosses and slabs. London boasts very little, but the Guildhall Museum has one treasure which makes up for the loss. This is a tombstone, probably quarried at Bath, dug up with a skeleton in 1852 on the south side of St Paul's churchyard. It is now displayed next to a painted plaster-cast. Along the narrow left-hand edge of the slab, which once stood 1 foot

Fig. 3 *Stone tombstone from St Paul's churchyard, about 1040*
(Guildhall Museum)

$10\frac{1}{2}$ inches high and 2 feet $4\frac{1}{2}$ inches long, a runic inscription commemorates Toki, perhaps a minister of Cnut who was buried in the 1030s (*Fig. 3*). The face portrays a fantastic and semi-abstract animal caught in writhing tendrils, described as a lion and a serpent or, more recently, as a stag struggling with a dragon. It is in the Ringerike style, called after a quarry in southern Norway but perfected under the influence of the delicate foliage of Anglo-Saxon manuscript illumination. Toki's tombstone is born of two cultures, fused in southern England under Cnut. It is the finest Viking antiquity in the British Isles, with few rivals in Scandinavia itself.

The British Museum displays two fragments of a longer, thicker slab, used for covering a Viking grave. The larger piece has an incised quatrefoil design, intended as a cross, in the Ringerike style. These too come from the city, perhaps St Paul's churchyard, and belong to the eleventh century. Less important finds include part of a recumbent slab of about 1000, now in the Guildhall Museum, and

21

D

a circular cross-head of purely native workmanship, now in the British Museum; the first comes from the churchyard of St Benet Fink, formerly in Finch Lane, the second from that of St John-the-Baptist Walbrook, whose site is covered by the southern end of Bucklersbury House.

One other curious survival, from Saxon or perhaps from Roman or even pre-Roman times, is London Stone. This apparently meaningless chunk of limestone, the rounded end of a longer piece, lurks behind a grille in the wall of the Bank of China on the north side of Cannon Street, a few yards east of the station. The bank occupies the site of St Swithin's church, which was gutted during the Second World War; the stone was embedded in the south wall of the church at the end of the eighteenth century, having previously stood deep in the earth by what is now the station's entrance. If the stone is connected with the Roman palace which lies beneath the station, it is odd that it should be made of limestone from Clipsham, in Rutland, where no early quarries are known; if it is part of a Saxon monument, perhaps a cross-shaft, it is equally odd that no more precise name should have survived. London Stone, whatever its origin, is the most ancient object visible in the streets, for it is mentioned over a century before the Norman Conquest. Medieval buildings are often said to have been near this landmark, and many citizens took their name from it. In 1450 the Kentish rebel Jack Cade struck the stone with his sword, to impress on the crowds that he was now their master. Although, as the baffled Elizabethan Stow points out, the stone did not mark the centre of the city, it came to symbolize the heart of London, just as Hyde Park Corner or Piccadilly Circus does today.

The British Museum, the Guildhall Museum and the London Museum contain many smaller finds from pre-Conquest London—pagan and Christian, Continental, Anglo-Saxon and Viking. No single book could furnish a proper guide to these collections, which are always growing and are now being rearranged; soon, it is hoped, they will be given detailed, up-to-date catalogues. A few objects, however, can make clear the importance of London even in the dimmest period of its history. All of these were found in or near the city itself; the fifth- and sixth-century pagan cemeteries at Mitcham, Ewell and Hanwell are excluded, since they lie too far away.

Pottery can be a valuable pointer to trade. Among the earliest finds, from the sixth to seventh century, is a decorated cup of Frankish type. Later specimens include examples of Rhineland ware from the village of Pingsdorf, near Cologne; this was superior to the coarse, gritty work of most Anglo-Saxon potters, and was often imported with wine from the ninth century onwards. Lead glazing, introduced about 900, found its way to the chief centre of native pottery, at Stamford, whose own ware spread over the eastern Midlands to East Anglia and London. The tiniest fragments and most uninspiring vessels thus help to build up a picture of far-flung business, as is shown by a map next to some examples in the Guildhall Museum.

Bone-work, finer yet more durable than pottery, brings us still closer to everyday life. Large pins, combs—for weaving and personal use—spoons and knife-handles, although often intricately carved, show how little basic designs have changed in a thousand years. Trial-pieces, bits of bone scratched with patterns, recall the experiments of apprentices or the boredom of idlers. The London Museum even displays a kitchen grater, as well as four circular counters, used for backgammon or some such game, and two chessmen (*Fig. 4*), while the Guildhall Museum has an unusual sword-pommel. The chessmen are particularly interesting, since

Fig. 4 *Bone counter from Newgate Street and chessman from Westminster, probably 11th century* (The Trustees of the London Museum)

they are early bishops. When chess reached Europe from India, via the Moslem world, it had very different rules, and the pieces included an elephant with a howdah on its back. As a war-game,

23

which the best strategist won, it automatically appealed to the fighting nobles of the north. The elephant was strange to them but the points of the howdah resembled those of a bishop's mitre, so that the piece gradually changed its character. London's two 'bishops' were found at Westminster and in the City Ditch; like the round gaming pieces, they are labelled Viking for want of fuller information and may in fact date from after the Conquest.

Metal-work, of course, survives more plentifully. Personal ornaments and horses' trappings make up much of the collections. Here and there, some item reminds us of people about their work: the Guildhall Museum's slender, pointed styli, used for writing on wax tablets, or two ninth- or tenth-century chatelaines, from which dangled the keys carried by the lady of the house. Nothing brings closer the Anglo-Saxon shopkeeper than the remains of an early eleventh-century jeweller's stock, found in Cheapside and now also in the Guildhall Museum; the pieces—brooches, rings, beads and ear-rings—are all of pewter and many are unfinished, perhaps because the owner fled or was slaughtered in one of the Danish attacks.

Caches of money are sure signs of danger and can be traced back to a quantity of *sceattas*, the minute silver coins which preceded the penny, dredged up from the Thames, where they had lain since the middle of the eighth century. Most of these coins are now in the Department of Coins and Medals at the British Museum. Nineteen such hoards have so far been identified within a twenty-five-mile

Fig. 5 *Silver-gilt sword-pommel from Fetter Lane, about 800* (British Museum)

radius of London, accounting for one in six or even one in five of all those in England. Since London was by no means the most ransacked city, it must have held wealth undreamed of elsewhere in the kingdom.

Fig. 6 'The London Bridge Hoard', probably early 11th century
(The Trustees of the London Museum)

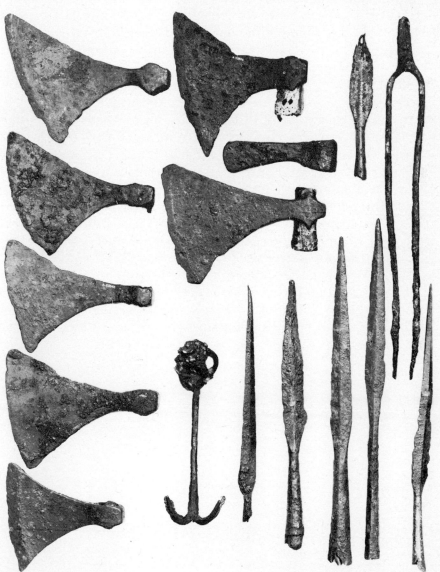

The commonest of all pre-Conquest finds are weapons. There are many heavy iron swords, wielded throughout the period by a warrior aristocracy, and battle-axes, widely used from the eighth century onwards. Still more plentiful are spear-heads, used by the humbler soldiery, although none of the wooden shafts has been preserved. A solitary wooden sword-hilt, rescued from the Thames and now in the London Museum, reminds us that the smith worked hand in hand with the carpenter. The British Museum has some much costlier pieces: a broad iron knife, beautifully inlaid with silver, which was found with coins of Æthelred II, and an earlier knife-shaped sword or scramasax, inlaid with copper and bronze. Nearby is a unique silver-gilt sword-pommel of about 800, found on the site of Monotype House in Fetter Lane (*Fig. 5*); one side is patterned with four swirling snakes and the other with a spread-eagled beast, outlined in a sulphide of silver called niello. Of about the same date is the Palace of Westminster sword, with its yellow bronze hilt, dug up in Victoria Tower Gardens and now kept in the Jewel Tower.

'The London Bridge Hoard', in the London Museum, deserves special mention, since it forms a single group: seven battle-axes, one smaller woodsman's axe, like those in the Bayeux Tapestry, six spear-heads, a rare grappling-iron, of the sort recorded in sea fights, and a pair of smith's tongs (*Fig. 6*). All these were found in the foreshore, near the north end of Old London Bridge, and probably belonged to a Viking warship of the early eleventh century; perhaps her master sailed up the river with Swein or Cnut, only to fall foul of the Londoners. Such rusty but still vicious weapons speak more vividly than the chroniclers of the stormy world into which London was reborn.

CHAPTER TWO

The London of
William Fitz Stephen

The Normans gave London many features that we should expect to find in a city. Already Edward the Confessor had brought Norman masons to work on Westminster Abbey and had found an expensive answer to the lack of local quarries by using fine, white stone from Caen. Under William and his sons the skyline grew more varied, with the White Tower in the east and two more strongholds, Baynard's Castle and the Tower of Mountfitchet, in the west; still farther west, past the bend in the river, Westminster Hall became the nucleus of a new palace next to the abbey. St Paul's and most of the parish churches were rebuilt on a grander scale. Religious houses were to loom large in the medieval scene, because of their wealth, power, architectural splendour and civilizing influence. Before the Conquest there had been none nearer than Barking, save the obscure bodies of priests which served St Paul's and St Martin-le-Grand, and the monks at Westminster. Within months of William's entry St Martin-le-Grand was loaded with privileges. The first of many new houses was founded at Southwark in 1106 and near Aldgate in the following year. At about the same time the earliest hospital, St Giles-in-the-Fields, was set up by the western highroad out of Newgate. There was probably a prison on the east bank of the Fleet, north of the road out of Ludgate, by 1130. London's oldest surviving buildings are Norman (*Fig. 7*).

London also grew rapidly as an international port. Foreign rulers demanded foreign luxuries; repeated Channel crossings by the king and his barons gave more protection to travellers; order at home encouraged people to risk journeys. Enterprising Norman merchants must have seen London, with its northern links, as a better centre than any town in the duchy; there are no statistics but

27

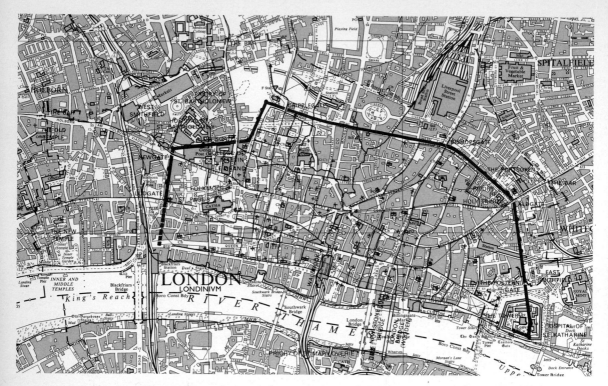

Fig. 7 *Map showing the main features of Fitz Stephen's London, super-imposed on the street-plan of the modern city* (Crown Copyright Reserved)

enough names to suggest that there were hundreds of French-speaking settlers. Norse influence, still strong immediately after the Conquest, dwindled as the Baltic trade passed to the Hanseatic League, so that by the 1120s Germans were the chief foreigners. Called at first 'the men of Cologne', they too were eventually allowed to trade anywhere in England. In 1157 they already had part of the site which they later held rent free, as the Steelyard, and which is now covered by Cannon Street station.

Other strangers were more exotic. The king, who could stay at Westminster or the Tower, no longer needed the royal 'soke', a large area between what is now the Guildhall and the Mansion House. Part of this, around Ironmonger Lane, was colonized by Jews, a hated minority existing on royal sufferance but undoubtedly adding to the city's wealth. After 1100 Jews also settled in the provinces but never so thickly as in London, where they could hope for protection from the garrison in the Tower; until 1177 a plot outside Cripplegate was the only place in the kingdom where a Jew might be buried. Two quasi-monastic orders, the Knights of the Temple (the Templars) and the Knights of the Hospital of St John of Jerusalem (the Hospitallers), reached England in the early twelfth century. Although they, too, were to spread throughout the land, they made their headquarters beyond the western wall, the Templars at Holborn, from which they later moved southward to the Temple, and the Hospitallers at Clerkenwell. For all foreigners, except new religious orders seeking solitude, London was the strongest magnet.

Prospering citizens inevitably demanded more say in their own affairs, as well as in those of England. William the Conqueror was followed by three other Norman kings, his strong-willed sons William Rufus and Henry I and his more amiable grandson Stephen. In 1130 Henry I allowed the Londoners to choose their own sheriff and to assess and collect their own taxes, paying a lump sum of £300 a year, known as the farm; these privileges, although later withdrawn and amended, were unique in England and a milestone on the road towards self-government. Stephen, whose reign was largely passed in civil war, received decisive support from London. Wealth had brought self-reliance and political power.

Norman London, like Saxon London, grew bigger over the decades, but it did not grow smoothly. Fire and tempest had always been more familiar than invading armies. The menace must have increased with time, as the last Roman buildings fell into ruin and gave way to rickety structures of timber, plaster and thatch. There was in fact no single city, forever expanding, but a series of re-settlements, proof of human tenacity and the natural advantages of the site.

The Normans literally laid the foundations of a more lasting city, but their contribution was only a beginning, limited to castles and churches. It was a hundred years after the Conqueror's death before the first efforts at town-planning were made, which included a ban on thatched roofs and an insistence on stone party-walls. How desperately some regulation was needed is shown by the monotonous record of fires, which broke out in 1077, 1086–7, 1092, 1098, 1100, 1132 and 1135–6. In the first of these, according to the *Anglo-Saxon Chronicle*, 'London was burned down . . . worse than ever it had been since it was founded', in the second St Paul's and the richest part of the city were consumed, in the third a blaze swept westward from London Bridge, through the cathedral and beyond the walls to Aldwych. Storms could be just as bad. On 17 October 1091 a south-easterly gale flattened over six hundred houses, destroyed the bridge and whisked away the wooden roof of St Mary-le-Bow; a foreign visitor, hearing of this nine years afterwards, tells of rafters hurled over fifty feet, and a later English writer says that beams twenty-six feet long were buried in the earth so that only four feet could be seen.

Apart from natural disasters, very little is known of the Norman city. Neither London nor Winchester is in Domesday Book, not because they were excluded from the survey but probably because the clerks were faced with so much information that they never managed to include it in the fair copies which deal with most of England. The Guildhall Library's series of Letter Books, in which anything of municipal interest was currently recorded, do not begin until almost two hundred years later. Monastic chroniclers, mainly relying on hearsay, are supported by very few business-like records: a list of the urban properties of the monks of Christ Church, Canterbury, around 1100, and the *cnihtengild*'s gift of all its land to Holy Trinity priory, twenty-five years later, help to fill the gap with the earliest references to many famous sites.

One interested foreigner was Hugh, abbot of Flavigny in Burgundy, who was sent to London within a few weeks of Rufus's death. After telling all that he had heard about the fearful storm of 1091, he remarks that London is a spacious and populous city. He is chiefly fascinated however, by the many dogs, 'as short in body as they are quarrelsome and fierce in nature', which prowl around St Paul's at night, ready to bite any lone passer-by who is feeble or without a stick. At last it was decided to slaughter the pack but, on the night that should have been their last, all the dogs are said to have fled, freeing the city for ever.

Henry of Anjou, who succeeded Stephen in 1154, was by inheritance and marriage the lord of an empire much larger than that of the Normans, stretching from the Scottish Marches to the Pyrenees. As duke of Aquitaine he controlled the rich wine country around Bordeaux, which became the main supplier of what was now the chief drink of England's ruling class. The earliest description of London was written about 1180, nine years before his death. Henry II was the first of the Plantagenet kings—often subdivided into Early and Later Angevins, Lancastrians and Yorkists—who were to rule England until the end of the Middle Ages. Strictly speaking, therefore, the London of Henry II was not Norman. It was, at any rate, very like the Conqueror's city, only bigger and with some grander sights. Settlement was still uneven and houses were flimsy. The citizens, in spite of their efforts, did not yet fully govern themselves. Changes in the next thirty years, however, were to leave their homes less at the mercy of a chance spark or a strong gale. Self-government, too, was to come within a generation. If no one had written until around 1200, we should have no first-hand account of the Norman scene. As it is, we are shown a city which has outgrown its buildings and institutions, and which is about to break out of its chrysalis.

Among the foreigners who were lured to London after the Conquest was a well-born merchant from Rouen, Gilbert Becket. Gilbert became portreeve of his adopted city and grew so rich that his Norman wife is said to have given their son's weight at every birthday in money and kind to the poor. The boy, Thomas, had been born in 1118 at his father's house on the site of the present chapel of the Mercers' Company in Ironmonger Lane. His career, as boon companion to the young Henry Plantagenet, as chancellor, archbishop and martyr, belongs to the history of England. The see of Canterbury has been filled by many better men and by several who have been put to death, but none was remembered so long or so widely as Thomas Becket—thanks to the power of the Church in the twelfth century, to his own personality and, in part, to the fact that he was a Londoner. Until the Reformation, Thomas of London, as he had called himself, was possessively venerated in his birthplace. Countless pilgrimages were made to his shrine at Canterbury, one of them immortalized in Chaucer's *Canterbury Tales*. Londoners would dearly have loved to have Thomas's tomb in their own city; as it was, thousands of them from all classes rode or walked to Canterbury. They showed their devotion by bringing back pilgrims' badges, many of which can be seen in the museums today (*see p. 209 and Fig. 8*).

One of the first contributors to the cult of Becket, which was to stretch as far as Iceland and Sicily, was his clerk, a fellow Londoner named William Fitz Stephen. Pride in London's most famous son was linked with pride in the city itself. As an introduction to his *Life of Becket*, Fitz Stephen devoted a few pages to the urban scene in which both men had grown up; his *Description of London*, in Latin like all the other histories of the time, has long outlived the work of piety which followed it. Perhaps Fitz Stephen would not have minded. It was unthinkable that anyone should then write

31

Fig. 8 *Leaden pilgrim's badge of St Thomas Becket from the Thames at Dowgate, mid 14th century* (The Trustees of the London Museum)

about everyday life, when there were stirring deeds to be related and morals to be drawn. London was not a fit subject for a saint's biographer; it crept in all the same because Fitz Stephen could not contain his local patriotism.

In the Middle Ages, climate was held to have a powerful effect on human nature. Fitz Stephen was born too late to have seen the storm of 1091 or even the freak ebb tide which, one October day in 1114, allowed people to cross the Thames on foot east of the bridge.

He begins by praising the mildness of the weather, which is neither so soft that men are enslaved by lust nor so harsh that they become brutalized. The matrons, he says elsewhere, are very Sabines, in other words they are as chaste as the legendary victims of the Roman soldiers. These and similar exaggerations, like the story which gave London a lineage satisfyingly older than that of Rome, at least show how deeply a Londoner could feel for his birthplace.

London, an earthly paradise to Fitz Stephen, must also have seemed so on a fine day to anyone gazing down from the wooded slopes of Highgate or Hampstead or across the Thames from the Surrey hills. After miles of unbroken countryside and halts at villages which were no more than collections of hovels, he would see the city, a rough rectangle, its southern side stretching for a mile along the river. The shape was still determined by the Roman wall, pierced by six named gates inherited from Londinium, although Fitz Stephen says that the riverside wall (which was not in any case a defensive work) had long been washed away. Apart from the three Norman castles and St Paul's, the houses were interspersed with at least 98 churches: Fitz Stephen's figure—13 monasteries and 126 parish churches—includes the suburbs. The beautiful silhouette of towers, battlements, pinnacles and occasional spires belongs to the later Middle Ages, but there were already imposing buildings to break the pattern of the roofs. Something of this fairy-tale aspect was soon to appear in the earliest, formal attempts to depict London: the common seal, which dates from John's reign (*Fig. 9*), and a slightly later drawing by the monk and historian, Matthew Paris (*Fig. 36*).

This panorama covered much more than the 330 acres within the wall. A wooden bridge, soon to be replaced by one of stone, led to a settlement at Southwark, clustered around the recently founded priory of St Mary Overie. The Thames itself was crammed with shipping of all sizes, from barges and tiny rowing boats to rounded, clumsy-looking cogs with an average crew of twenty-three. These cogs, which increasingly relied on sails rather than oars, were now replacing the sleek Viking ships; they could hold much bigger cargoes, although they were rarely more than two hundred tons before 1300. There were many anchorages and wharves but the safest havens were indentations in the river bank: Billingsgate to the east of the bridge, Dowgate at the mouth of the Walbrook, Queenhithe below St Paul's, and the mouth of the Fleet. On every landward side beyond the walls there were rows of houses, with

33

Fig. 9 *Obverse of the common seal of the Corporation of London,
designed in the early 13th century, from a 17th-century copy*
(Guildhall Museum)

spacious gardens and trees. Although these outskirts were mainly
inhabited by townspeople, the nobles were already leaving their
cramped lodgings within the city for mansions nearer the royal
palace. The longest and grandest piece of ribbon development
stretched along the gravel strand towards Westminster, by now a
busy suburb. Here the abbey and palace reared up from the flat
plain, making the vista even more impressive in the west than did
the Tower of London in the east.

From the distance, London and its outskirts were still patches in
a sea of green. The Middlesex forest pressed close to the northern
ridges, filled with game, deer and wild boar. A traveller, coming
down the slopes, passed through corn fields, fertile 'like the plains
of Asia'. There were meadows, orchards and a vineyard which had
probably been planted since the Normans' coming. From what are
now Highgate Ponds a stream—in Anglo-Saxon a *burna*—ran
through a *holh* or hollow, whose steep banks gave it the name of the
Holborn; this hollow may still be seen from Holborn Viaduct,
looking north up Farringdon Street. A highway from Newgate,
west-north-westward from the city, crossed the stream by the

present Viaduct; below this bridge the water became tidal and was known as the Fleet, from the Anglo-Saxon *fleot*, a creek, flowing straight down to the Thames and sheltering small shipping. West of the Holborn, the Tyburn flowed from Hampstead through what is now Regent's Park, where it has been dammed to form the lake, into the marshy levels around Westminster; still farther west and well beyond the built up areas, the Westbourne, part of which is now the Serpentine, ran from the same source to join the Thames at Chelsea. These streams, in their way, were as vital as the Thames, since they brought fresh water to the expanding medieval city. In 1180, if the church bells were not ringing, the first sound which would have met the traveller from the north would have been the clack of watermills, which Fitz Stephen thought very pleasing.

Early Londoners must have relied more on the little Walbrook, most of whose course lay within the wall and which could hardly have been seen from far off, and on nearby springs. The most famous springs, Holywell, Clerkenwell and St Clement's well, became favourite meeting-places for students and other strollers on summer evenings. At Holywell, near several other springs about three-quarters of a mile to the north-east, a nunnery had been founded about 1140; at Clerkenwell, north-west of the city and a few yards east of the Holborn, another had been founded at roughly the same time and there the Hospitallers soon afterwards built their main English house; St Clement's, on the increasingly busy road to Westminster, had long been associated with the Danes. Between Clerkenwell and Aldersgate, the nearest city gateway, lay the flat, sometimes marshy ground of West Smithfield, where horses were sold (East Smithfield was beyond the Tower). Here too, although Fitz Stephen does not say so, lay a large pond, the Horsepool, at which animals were watered; another pond, where a woman was drowned in 1244, lay a little to the east, by the church of St Giles outside Cripplegate.

After passing through the gates, a traveller would find the stone defences less dominating than they appeared from far off. He would lose sight of them altogether among the alleyways, for the occasional open space and wide thoroughfares like East and West Cheap contrasted with narrow, winding passages. Officially a street should take two loaded carts or sixteen armed knights riding abreast, as distinct from a lane which was often less than six feet wide. In either case a man had to pick his way with care, since even hard surfaces might be slippery with filth or beset by pot-holes.

The houses were usually of wood and built in terraces, the ground floors being booths or workshops, with counters opening on to the street, the upper floors being living space. There was much elaborate carving and plenty of paintwork, especially red, black or blue, which helped to make the houses inflammable. It was a colourful but very crowded scene, destined to become more crowded as the Middle Ages wore on.

Most visitors to London would not have been so interested in education as was Fitz Stephen, a man of letters. There were schools attached to St Paul's, St Martin-le-Grand and the priory of Holy Trinity, Aldgate, as well as independent teachers. On saints' days, the pupils met at church to recite and debate in public, wrangling over points of grammar and ready to confound their friends, or even their elders, with 'Socratic wit'. Fitz Stephen tells of the audiences' delight, although not of how many could follow the arguments. Every schoolboy spoke Latin, in which were taught the three liberal arts of the *trivium* (grammar, rhetoric and dialectic or logic); he might then pass on to the *quadrivium* (music, arithmetic, geometry and astronomy).

London was never the intellectual capital, nor did the kingdom boast the most famous schools in Europe. A pupil who advanced beyond the *quadrivium* to study law, divinity or medicine might enter the household of a learned prelate or attend one of the cathedral cities in the provinces; by 1180 he could go to Oxford, then emerging as England's first university. The best scholars were wanderers who nearly always went to Paris, supreme in law and in the increasingly popular dialectic, the art of philosophical disputation; often they passed on to Chartres and Orléans, farther south to Montpellier and Salerno for medicine, or to Bologna, Paris's one rival in law. In spite of London's limitations, however, it had a relatively high rate of literacy. Ambitious merchants could not afford to despise education, as did many of the nobility.

Travellers could not pass through the gates after sunset, and must often have been desperate for lodgings. Accommodation in London itself was scarcer and more respectable than in the more raffish suburbs, particularly Southwark, over which the city had no control. There were plenty of people selling drinks but perhaps not yet any proper inns, since there were only three in London a hundred years later. A visitor might pass the night as the guest of a monastery or, if he could afford it, stay in a private house. Fitz Stephen, as a native, presumably never faced this problem, for he praises the citizens for their open-handed hospitality. The reception of paying guests was in fact common; to judge from later efforts to stifle competition, it was also lucrative.

One rather unexpected institution, which Fitz Stephen thought the acme of civilization, was the public cookshop. It was used both as an eating-place and as a kitchen, where servants were sent to fetch food. It was always open and could feed any number of people, as well as suit all purses and palates. This famous place lay by the river and among the wine-shops, perhaps close to the vintners' quay near the mouth of the Walbrook.

Anyone who could afford it spent what would now seem excessive time and money on meals. Meat, game and fish, the only food mentioned by Fitz Stephen, were preponderant. Pork, the general favourite, was plentiful in an area where swine could live on the mast of the oak forests; venison could still be brought home by the huntsman and, like game and hares, was much more common than it is today; rabbits, on the other hand, were introduced by the Normans and, as 'conies', carefully protected in warrens. Fish, or shell-fish, had to be eaten on Fridays and during Lent. Salmon were plentiful, Westminster Abbey being entitled to one tenth of every catch, and so were trout and eels; sturgeon, later reserved for the mayor, were sometimes found, and porpoises continued to be a delicacy. Vegetables were more limited, headed by the onion and the leek (the Anglo-Saxon gardener was called a leek-ward), with the native cabbage perhaps not far behind. Common fruits were apples, pears, plums, cherries, sloes, quinces, strawberries and mulberries; much present-day garden produce, including goose-berries, raspberries and black-currants, was unknown before Tudor times, as were tropical fruit, while oranges and lemons were costly imports. Dark rye bread was far cheaper than white bread made from wheat; pastry provided a great deal of the bulk which later came from potatoes; comfits and sweet bakery, especially with an almond flavour, were popular; the sweetness came mainly from honey, since sugar, another import, was an expensive medicine.

Few people now could stomach medieval cookery—particularly its more ambitious dishes. Most of our knowledge comes from recipes and accounts of the later Middle Ages but even in 1180, when French influence may already have started, food was mushy and complicated. Cummin, orpiment and other long-forgotten spices, with exotic names recalling the Eastern trade, would prove overpowering laxatives, as tourists can still find out. There was no

37

clear distinction between sweet and savoury: blancmange was to start as a luxury of meat or fish boiled in sweetened almond milk, with additional sugar and salt, and even oysters were recommended with a sugary sauce. Everything was chopped or ground, seasoned and coloured, beyond recognition. London's commerce must have given exceptional scope for adding something extra; egg-yolks, green parsley and blood were among the ingredients used for colouring, but none were so prized as saffron, from the nearby crocus-fields of Essex. Food was messed up partly because little livestock could be fed through winter, and because transport was slow, so that salted and overkept flesh needed disguising; partly because cooks, like most specialists, made an elaborate mystery of their art; partly because people's teeth fell out, thanks mainly to their diet. Above all, forks were not used at table until after 1600, so that food had either to be eaten in lumps with the fingers or scooped up with a spoon.

Large and heavy meals were washed down copiously with alcohol. The traditional tribal drink had been mead, made from fermenting honey with water, to which herbs could be added to produce metheglin; this had largely disappeared under the Anglo-Saxons, although local cider and perry, perhaps equally old, were always drunk. By Norman times the popular drink was what the Saxons called beer and the Danes ale, made from water and malt, usually barley malt; the result was sweet and thick, for hops, while useful for keeping beer, were much more common in Germany and the Low Countries until the fifteenth century. Although London brewers used the Thames, their beer was probably safer than plain water. Wine remained expensive, even after the Conquest, and spirits were unknown. Then, as now, rarity in itself made things desirable. While the English nobility drank the wines of Bordeaux, Becket, on an embassy to France, took as a present two waggons laden with casks of beer; his hosts, says Fitz Stephen, admired a drink that was wholesome, clear, of the colour of wine and of a better taste! At home, many writers thought that far too much was consumed; apart from frequent fires, the only fault that Fitz Stephen recognized in London was 'the immoderate drinking of fools'.

Fitz Stephen tells us nothing of the port, beyond echoing Bede's words that merchants came from every nation under heaven. He also says very little of how and where Londoners earned their living, save that vendors, craftsmen and labourers had their customary places, which they took up every morning. These men worked a long day, divided according to the hours of church services and beginning around 6 a.m. with Prime, after which came Terce, Sext, None, Vespers, Compline, Matins and Lauds. Since daylight saving was important, the daytime services were rather more than three hours apart in summer and fewer in winter. Some compensation for working from dawn to dusk was provided by whole holidays on certain saints' days, of which there were several in most months.

Everyday shopping could be done within the wall. Larger livestock were bought outside, to the north-west, where there was 'a smooth field in name and in reality'. Here, every Friday unless there was a major festival, horses were paraded. A horse then had much the same appeal as a car has today—a man's wealth could be judged from his steed and his virility from the way in which it was handled. No social scientist would be surprised to learn that the noblest visitors mixed with citizens at these shows, to look or to buy. Every kind of horse—ambling nags, unbroken colts, chargers and beasts of burden—was on view. Fitz Stephen himself was so infected with excitement at the furious races, under the boy jockeys, that he could hardly believe that there was no such thing as perpetual motion. In a less fashionable part of the ground the peasantry gathered, with farm implements, pigs, cattle, sheep and mares, often big with foal and used for pulling ploughs or carts.

The races at Smithfield were noisy and savage affairs, where spurs and whips were freely used. Even the youngest spectators enjoyed violence, for at Shrovetide the boys brought fighting-cocks to school and spent the morning watching them struggle in the classroom. Another Shrovetide entertainment was some kind of ball game, played in the nearby fields between rival schools and between the tradesmen of different crafts, while the city fathers looked on, re-living their own youth. This game, so familiar to Fitz Stephen that he does not bother to describe it, probably resembled modern football rather than hockey. It may have sprung from a fertility cult, when two gangs of villagers struggled for the head of a sacrificial beast or some other symbol of the life-giving sun, which would make the crops grow. Fitz Stephen is the first to record any kind of football in England, although the game for which the English have become so famous was already known in France. The fact that it was played by the young Londoners before Lent further suggests that it came from abroad; under the Saxons, this had been a sombre time of shrift, and it was only after the Conquest that the carnival spirit appeared.

Football needed so little equipment that it was a poor man's sport; it was also relatively tame. On Sundays in Lent young men on horseback, perhaps mainly from Westminster, rode into the fields, while the citizens' sons rushed out of the gates with shields and lances. These were supposed to be only sham fights, for the iron heads were taken off the weapons of the younger boys; courtiers attended, if the king happened to be near, and those aspiring to knighthood seized the chance of some practice. There must always, however, have been a dark under-current of rivalry between the London youths and those who were marked out by birth for the envied career of arms. On at least one occasion the contest became a dangerous battle.

There were several other outlets for pent-up energy. At Easter a tree-trunk was embedded in the Thames, within sight of the bridge, and contestants, each on the prow of a rowing-boat, tried to break their lances against it without tumbling into the water. In summer there was wrestling, archery and athletics, while the girls—not, presumably, the most respectable citizens' daughters—danced by moonlight. In winter the marshy ground beyond the north-eastern gate, where the Walbrook rose, was frozen over. Here skaters pulled their friends along on blocks of ice, or clashed together with poles, often falling only to be carried farther by their own speed, so that 'whatever part of their heads comes in contact with the ice is laid bare to the very skull'. Richer Londoners could also go hawking on the nearby downs or hunting in the forests, for they had the right to do so in Middlesex, Hertfordshire, the Chilterns and Kent, as far as the river Cray. Wolves, boars and wild cattle were among the animals hunted.

Leaving the citizens at play, Fitz Stephen ends his *Description* by listing some famous Londoners, ending with St Thomas Becket. He has nothing bad to say, apart from the passing reference to drunkards and fires; nor is he concerned with the appearance or health of people, unremarkable to him but strange to us today.

Londoners must always have been of a more mixed stock than other Englishmen. In 1180 the fair, Germanic type was commoner than today, at any rate among the wealthy; links with Scandinavia were still closer than with the Mediterranean, and the Norman conquerors, although French speaking, were of Viking origin. Courtly poets celebrated a similar beauty in both sexes—blonde curly hair, straight features and clear skin—although hardly anyone can have approached this imported ideal. Effigies on tombs, like later suits of armour, show that men might be heavily built but were relatively short; in England they averaged 5 feet 6 inches in the twelfth century.

Everyone lacked vitamin C, since fresh fruit could only be eaten in season and raw vegetables, although nibbled casually, were not served at table. Scurvy was therefore rife, leading to emaciation, dysentery, blotches, and teeth falling from bad gums. The habit of stoking up with meat and alcohol, particularly in the winter, brought further risks from circulatory diseases, although Fitz Stephen's emphasis on sports helps to explain how many people escaped an early death from apoplexy or heart attack. Germs were another danger, accounting for many mysterious 'agues', although familiarity brought some immunity. As it was, a small minority survived childhood. A man, if he reached his thirties, could perhaps look forward to another twenty years of life; for women, who survived only the smoothest childbirths, the average expectancy was still lower. The shadow of death, adding urgency to the present, distinguishes the lives of all earlier generations from ours today.

A modern visitor to Fitz Stephen's London would be repelled chiefly by the smells and dirt. Slops were thrown from windows, muckheaps piled up outside doorways. A hundred years later people—not all of them drunks—were often accused of relieving themselves in the streets; these offences usually took place at night and must, like other nuisances, have become serious long before they led to regulation. Henry I's queen, Matilda, built a 'necessary house' at Queenhithe, and there were probably several public latrines by 1180, as well as private ones draining into the Thames or its tributaries. Not until about 1350, however, do we hear that privies or sieges lined the Walbrook and that the stream had to be cleared of sewage.

Domestic animals, alive and dead, added to the stench. The waste products of butchers, poulterers and other tradesmen were a growing problem. Pigs, which most people kept, were particularly apt to stray, fouling the streets and causing obstruction and damage; they were later to be confined to the owners' premises, lest they should be slain on sight, and only the pigs of St Anthony's Hospital in Threadneedle Street were to be allowed to rootle anywhere, with bells around their necks. Indoors, in dark, low rooms with the wooden shutters often closed, the atmosphere must have been worse.

Only the rich could afford wax candles, with their pure flames, and most households made do with home-made tallow lights, lumps of kitchen fat with rushes for wicks, or with torches soaked in pitch, tallow or oil. The resulting smell and smoke might explain the popularity of outdoor pursuits.

Occasionally, by a mighty effort, the main streets were tidied up for one of the ceremonials which appealed so strongly to all medieval people. In 1184 London gave a resplendent reception to the archbishop of Cologne and the count of Flanders; although this is a hundred years before we first hear of official scavengers, the streets must have been specially cleaned, since it was the king himself who insisted that his guests should visit the city. In fact there was much less apathy about dirt and smells than is often imagined. Washing was more popular than after the Reformation, when nudity became shameful, and economical steam-baths could be enjoyed by pouring cold water onto heated stones. Men and women were segregated in the bath-houses of Southwark, where the evil name later won by the 'stews' masks the perfectly respectable origin of many of these places. London stank, not because its people were insensitive, but because they could not solve the problems of drainage and of refuse disposal, and of accommodating so many humans and animals.

The city, although more impersonal, is no more congested and noisy today than it was eight hundred years ago. To the clatter of wheels, hooves and poor men's wooden shoes were added the cries of street-vendors and the noises of craftsmen working in open-fronted shops. Bells sounded everywhere, tinkling from the necks of animals and the hands of beggars, chiming from scores of churches to mark the services, pealing in thanksgiving and tolling for the dead. Men listened for bells when they would now look at a clock. Curfew was rung from St Martin-le-Grand and sometimes repeated from other churches (in 1370 it was rung from St Mary-le-Bow, All Hallows by-the-Tower, St Bride's and St Giles Cripplegate) and bells heralded the dispersal of the watch and the start and finish of all organized business. Most historic of all was the great bell of St Paul's, which still summoned citizens to the folkmoot.

Business often began at dawn, although it varied from craft to craft, and crowds were thickest in the middle of the morning. Sundays, when everyone had to attend Mass, were much quieter, although regulations against Sunday trading were not issued until the later Middle Ages. After dark there was little to be seen in the streets, for the gates were closed from sunset to sunrise; two hundred years later men had to stay indoors after curfew unless they had a good reason and in 1180, whether or not he was so restricted, a wise man would not have loitered.

Complaints about the seamy side of modern London are based on comparisons with the very recent past. Life was cheaper and property far less secure in the Middle Ages. Fitz Stephen's understandable silence is more than redressed by Richard of Devizes, whose *Chronicle* begins with the accession of Henry II's son Richard the Lionheart in 1189. An old French Jew, advising a boy who is leaving for England, urges him at all costs to avoid London, where 'every race brings its own vices', where 'every quarter abounds in grave obscenities' and which teams with prostitutes of either sex, perverts, quacks, magicians, beggars and extortioners. The city fathers might have replied, with some justice, that the true sink of iniquity was Southwark, over which they had no control. Brothels there were so well entrenched that Henry II is said to have contented himself with ensuring a fair deal to all parties. The houses were to be inspected, no women were to be detained against their will or charged too much for their rooms; they were to be expelled on holidays or if they were infected; men could not be enticed, but if they paid money they were to stay for the night.

Richard of Devizes, a monk at St Swithin's, Winchester, was a jaundiced provincial. His list of parasites comes straight from Horace and he has no use for London, or indeed for any city other than his own. Like most clerics he was roused more easily by sin than by crime, although the first often led to the second. Later records show that 'the immoderate drinking of fools' ended in countless murderous quarrels, as well as in fatal accidents.

Many people were forced into crime by sheer poverty, which is no longer known. Even so, more offences sprang from greed than from desperation. The protection of consumers was a major headache, and later records abound with charges of adulteration, false weighing and measuring, and the sale of harmful goods. Tampering with the coinage was also common. Attempts to hurt one's enemies by witchcraft persisted and were often taken seriously. As was inevitable when authority relied more on respect than on physical resources, insults to civic dignitaries were severely punished.

Crime could also be highly organized. In 1177, perhaps the very year when Fitz Stephen wrote, the king vowed vengeance after a nobleman had been killed at night in his lodging and his body flung out of doors. This murder seems to have been one of a series of assaults and robberies in private homes, carried out by a gang which inspired such terror that it had the run of the streets after dark. Some of the culprits, themselves young men of good standing, were at last surprised when breaking through the stone wall of a wealthy victim's house; confessions led to wholesale arrests and to the execution, among others, of one of London's most respected citizens. Gangsterism on this scale eventually led to rather stricter policing in the later Middle Ages.

The law, to maintain respect, had to make public examples. Trading offences usually led to the pillory or to being dragged on a sledge-like hurdle through the filthy streets; there might also be several months' imprisonment. The culprit's business and misdeeds were identified, to make the sentence as apt as possible; a sample of his goods might be slung around his neck (*Fig. 10*), and a vendor might have his stinking food burned under his nose or be drenched in his own sour wine. Scolding women were jeered (not ducked, as in later days) and prostitutes, clad in hoods of coarse cloth and holding penitential wands, were paraded in carts. Such sights, which were thought funny rather than pathetic, must have been common to Fitz Stephen, although most known sentences come from later years, when they were passed by the mayor and aldermen at the Guildhall.

The mayor's court could order capital punishment, which once

Fig. 10 *A baker drawn to the pillory, from a 14th-century sketch in the* Liber de Assisa Panis, *about 1293* (By courtesy of the Corporation of London)

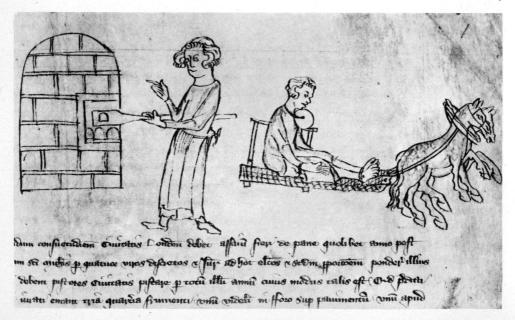

had included stoning or burning, but which by the end of the twelfth century was usually hanging; this in itself could be a painful end, since the victim did not have his neck broken but was throttled as he swung on the end of the rope. Frequent as were the executions of petty criminals, Londoners often saw more distinguished sufferers. Heretics, rare until the appearance of the Lollards around 1400, were always burned. Nobles were usually beheaded. For high treason, the victim was drawn through the streets to a gallows, where he was strung up but cut down again while still alive; his body was then carefully marked out for dismemberment and his entrails ripped out and burned, before he was beheaded and quartered.

From the first, political prisoners must have been killed within the Tower, although there are no references to this practice until the later Middle Ages. Sometimes victims were led right through the city to the common gallows by the Tyburn, a name now linked with executions rather than with the stream. The spot was also called the Elms—more aptly, if it was chosen because of the trees which conveniently grew by the water's edge. It was an important road junction where Watling Street, now Edgware Road, comes in from the north to meet the long western highway out of Newgate, which continued west along what is now Bayswater Road. The first recorded death took place here in 1196 when an agitator, William Longbeard, was dragged from the Tower to be hanged in chains, with nine accomplices. (*See p. 165.*) By 1220 there were no more suitable trees, for the king ordered two permanent gibbets to be set up. These and their successors remained a popular attraction until 1783. Where the early ones stood is uncertain; probably it was close to Marble Arch, as in Shakespeare's time. Special reasons might lead to the choice of a different site, and burnings normally took place on the open ground at West Smithfield, where Stow says that there was another place called the Elms. Plaques in the wall of the nineteenth-century hospital building, facing the circular recreation ground still known as West Smithfield, recall several executions. No one could afford to be squeamish in the Middle Ages. If a Londoner shrank from watching other people die, he could not escape from the spectacle of traitor's heads and limbs rotting over the gateways.

Nothing makes town life seem uglier than the treatment of Jews. Denied any part in public affairs, they worked hard, prospered and turned suspicion into hatred. Money-lending was useful but unchristian, so there was always an excuse to attack them, and rumours

45

of sinister rites multiplied with the number of creditors. Wherever the Jews settled they were haunted by bullies and fanatics. London, with the first and largest colony, set the pace.

Gilbert Crispin, the scholarly Norman who became abbot of Westminster about 1085, was one of the few churchmen who opposed anti-Semitism. He tells of a foreign Jew who asks why his fellows in London are beaten and chased like dogs. Under the mercenary Henry II, the first king to allow them burial elsewhere than outside Cripplegate, they reached their height. Jews were barred from the coronation of Richard I on 3 September 1189, but some of them hopefully brought gifts and one man tried to enter the abbey. Rioting started and while the king feasted in Westminster Hall, Londoners turned on the infidels' houses; entire families were burned to death or cut to pieces as they ran out. Richard, who wanted Jewish money for his crusade, watched helplessly as the hysteria spread to the provinces. The Jews struggled on for another hundred years but they never recovered from the savagery of the citizens of Fitz Stephen's time.

A writer who ignores crime can hardly be expected to mention prisons. The Tower always held political victims, but in 1156 London had its own prison, which had probably been founded by 1130 when a hereditary gaolkeeper was paid 5d. a day. This was a stone building, later moated, called in Fitz Stephen's day 'the gaol of London' but in 1196–7 the Fleet, from its situation beside the stream which it was later to contaminate. It became so crowded with people awaiting trial in the king's courts that in the 1180s work began on a second gaol at Newgate, perhaps an actual enlargement of the gatehouse. Newgate, although meant to cater for London and Middlesex, was inevitably to go the same way as the Fleet, receiving prisoners from all parts of the country.

Fitz Stephen says nothing of hospitals, perhaps because disease too has no place in an earthly paradise. Before and after the Conquest men were fascinated by medicines, and quacks did a roaring trade. Leechdoms, methods of bleeding with leeches, and examples of 'wort-cunning', knowledge of the medicinal properties of plants, abounded: diet itself was partly dictated by the powers ascribed to various herbs and by a suspicion of fresh foods. There was much faith but little knowledge: surgery was unknown, save for wounds, and few serious illnesses lasted long. The normal practice was therefore to dose oneself in one's own home. Hospitals, from the Latin *hospes*, a guest, started simply as shelters for wayfarers. In the twelfth century pilgrimages and crusades joined with growing trade to raise the demand for accommodation. They also helped to spread disease, and the care of sick pilgrims became a charitable duty. Beds were available at the hospital of St Bartholomew, Smithfield, founded in 1123, and at Southwark, for pilgrims to the shrine of Thomas Becket, soon after 1170. These, two of many known to Fitz Stephen, are now the senior teaching hospitals of London.

Leprosy, which was brought from the east, was a special case. This relentless and disfiguring disease, more dreaded than any save the plague, reached its height in western Europe between 1100 and 1300. A suspected leper, who may in fact have contracted lupus, syphilis or eczema, became an outcast; the burial service was read over him, he forfeited his common legal rights and was driven from his home and all assembly places; he might talk only in the open, away from the road, and must eat with his own kind; if he walked abroad he must be covered from head to foot, with a handbell or clappers to warn others to keep out of his way. Medieval travellers cannot have met a more heart-rending sight or sound. Lazar-houses, so called from a belief that Lazarus, the beggar with sores, had been a leper, were founded outside Canterbury and Rochester before 1100. These were in fact little colonies, with a chapel and separate buildings; since leprosy killed by inches, sufferers could look after themselves for years. London itself learned charity from the Queen Matilda who gave her title to Queenhithe; she founded the hospital of St Giles-in-the-Fields, and even washed the lepers' feet and kissed their sores. There were ten lazar-houses around London by the end of the Middle Ages, when leprosy was on the wane; most of these were municipal centres which failed in their purpose. Although the menace hung over everyone, repeated bans on lepers living in the city itself shows how people shrank from formally consigning those whom they loved to a living death.

Fitz Stephen describes Londoners at play, not Londoners at work. The danger in filling out his picture is that so many records begin later. The detailed regulations which governed his successors did not necessarily apply in his own day; they were the result of growth. Yet the more that we learn of man's outlook at any time in the Middle Ages, the more it seems to differ from that of today. The medieval citizen was used to violent contrasts, between riches and poverty which no one tried to hide, between health and sickness, piety and savagery, abandoned relaxations and back-breaking toil. The life of the busiest Londoner today is, by comparison, restful, predictable, almost insipid. Only in his spirit did the medieval citizen enjoy greater security. Whatever his own failings, he knew what ought and ought not to be done, and that in the next world the good would be happy and the bad unhappy.

To Fitz Stephen and his contemporaries, the most striking contrast was between the rare urban scene and the countryside. The concentration of so much human activity in a small space, and the wealth and power which it generated, explain both the raptures of Fitz Stephen and the rancour of Richard of Devizes. By our standards London was still very much a country town. It drew strangers from far afield and had grown by trade, but its basic needs were met locally, from fresh water and timber, fish, crops and livestock. The problems of overcrowding—costly and inadequate housing, traffic congestion, pollution, disease and vice—if known, were not yet acute. Apart from churchyards and monastic precincts, oases which were to outlive the Middle Ages, there were still private gardens: on a September evening in 1276, a man was to be killed when trying to climb a pear-tree belonging to one Lawrence in the parish of St Michael, Paternoster Royal, which lay in the busiest quarter, close to the wharves and almost midway between the eastern and western walls.

Those aspects of the twelfth-century city which would most repel us today—the dirt, the stench, the noise, the hectic indulgence, the violence and the suffering—were to get worse during the Middle Ages, in spite of heroic efforts by officialdom. It was the compensations which were to dwindle—the pure air and water, the open spaces and nearby rural walks. It may be better to live in a rickety cottage, at the mercy of the weather, than to be lost in a fetid slum. In 1180 London was a greener, cleaner and therefore probably a pleasanter place than it was to be three hundred years later.

If Fitz Stephen were alive today, he would recognize the ninety-foot high White Tower, with its four turrets, in spite of the classical windows inserted by Wren. As an intimate of the archbishop of Canterbury, he may have visited the royal fortress and have seen the chapel of St John or its crypt, which were already nearly a hundred years old; the structures of both are unchanged, although their present starkness was once softened by costly fittings. Fitz Stephen would also feel at home standing by the massive Norman piers in the choir of the church of St Bartholomew-the-Great, Smithfield, although here too he would wonder at the lack of decoration. Perhaps he passed through the ornate western doorway of the Temple Church, which was consecrated for the Knights Templars in 1185, or knelt in the crypts of St Mary-le-Bow, Cheapside, or of the Knights Hospitallers' church at Clerkenwell. He must have known of St James's hermitage, adjoining the city wall near Cripplegate, whose tiny crypt is now in the former churchyard of All Hallows Staining, Mark Lane. The undercroft of the monks' dormitory at Westminster, now the Chapel of the Pyx and the Abbey Museum, are also of his time.

In a twentieth-century gazetteer, Fitz Stephen would recognize very much more. Some three dozen churches, although rebuilt, retain their old dedications and occupy their original sites. There would be fewer familiar street-names, although more than would be known to an Anglo-Saxon. West of the Walbrook the present Wood Street, Milk Street, Lawrence Lane and Friday Street had been named by 1189; to the east there were Cornhill, Bishopsgate Street and Cannon (then Candlewick) Street. A detailed map would be more reassuring, for a score of roads and alleyways have not changed their course; probably few in fact have changed their names, but of this there is no proof. Streets of 1189 which can be traced today are: Gutter Lane, Honey Lane (now almost a tunnel), Ironmonger Lane, Bread Street and Bow Lane, all off Cheapside; Staining Lane, Aldermanbury and Lothbury, to the north; Distaff Lane, to the south; St Mary Axe, Birchin Lane, Gracechurch Street, Lime Street, Fenchurch Street, Botolph Lane and Mincing Lane, to the east. Before the last war there were also Monkwell Street and Philip Lane in the north-west, near Cripplegate. The northern part of Queen Street, which was extended to the Thames after the Great Fire, was also known to Fitz Stephen, as Soper's Lane.

CHAPTER THREE

The Expansion of London

Fitz Stephen's talk of populous suburbs means that we must now see how London spread out beyond the Roman wall. To make this clear, we have to look back to the earliest settlements and forward to the scene at the end of the Middle Ages. Part of the story is the swallowing-up of land next to the wall, as far as the Bars of London, which have long been the traditional limits of the city. Part is the growth of new centres at Westminster and across the river at Southwark, opposite the city, and at Lambeth, opposite the new royal palace.

The line of the wall itself changed very little. Throughout the period it ran from the south-eastern corner north and west to Aldgate, Bishopsgate and Cripplegate, then through a right angle near Aldersgate and down through Newgate and Ludgate to the river. (*See p. 151.*) In the extreme south-east, however, the wall was replaced by the White Tower and its surrounding defences, which have always formed a royal precinct. Tower Hill, an adjoining plot within the wall, also remained outside London's jurisdiction, as did all the land to the east as far as the River Lea; this area, with Stepney as the main village, was governed by the Constable of the Tower and known from about 1200 as the Tower Hamlets, a name revived for the Greater London Borough created in 1965. In the south-west another stretch of the wall was pulled down soon after Baynard's Castle passed to the black friars in 1279. The defences had to be rebuilt farther west, nearer the Fleet, so as to encompass the new monastery. The Roman plan thus lost a piece in one corner and afterwards gained a rather smaller piece in another (*Fig. 11*).

The loss of the land within the wall was nothing compared to the

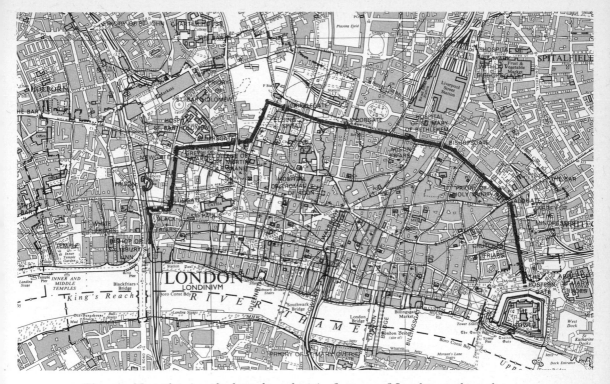

Fig. 11 *Map showing the bounds and main features of London at the end of the Middle Ages; the medieval boundary ran along the south side of Finsbury Circus (Moorfields) (Crown Copyright Reserved)*

encroachments which were soon made outside. On all the main roads, at some distance beyond the gates, there were Bars by the early thirteenth century. These consisted of posts, perhaps linked with a chain, and may first have been set up in the west in order to thwart the abbot of Westminster, who claimed all the land up to the Fleet. Apart from the far side of the Tower (Tower Hamlets) and for a short distance along the middle of the northern stretch of wall, outside the later Moorgate (where lay the undrained marsh of Moorfields), the bounds were everywhere pushed out. London's jurisdiction was legally recognized in 1222. The area of the city had almost doubled, to the square mile which it is today.

These areas between the wall and the Bars were known at first as the Liberties. Later the name Portsoken, the private jurisdiction or soke outside the gates, described only London's eastern extension, beyond Houndsditch. All the other outlying districts, to the north and west, were then usually called 'The Suburb', although in the later Middle Ages this might mean simply the Strand and its neighbourhood. A reminder that the city comprises an old centre, within the wall, and an outer ring of early medieval additions, survives in the ward-names Farringdon Within and Farringdon Without.

The Bars of London are now marked by various boundary stones. Along the eastern road out of Aldgate the city stretches along Aldgate High Street to where Mansell Street joins it from the right and Middlesex Street on the left; Middlesex Street, more popularly called Petticoat Lane, is itself a reminder that here, until the nineteenth century, the city ended and the shire began. The boundary stone is topped by a winged silver dragon, holding a shield with the arms of the Corporation of London. These arms can be seen on all sorts of objects, from lamp-posts to dustcarts, in the city. Heralds describe them as *Argent, the cross of St George, and in the canton the sword of St Paul, gules* (a white shield with a red cross, and a red sword in the upper left corner). They were in use by the mid-fourteenth century and, as one would expect with London, are a very early example of civic heraldry, which is derived from seals, although noblemen had borne arms for some two hundred years (*Fig. 12*). The dragon on the boundary stone has more dubious origins. London's full armorial bearings comprise a shield, surmounted by a crest and flanked by supporters, with the

Fig. 12 *The second mayoralty seal of London, showing the city's arms beneath St Thomas Becket and St Paul, 1381* (Guildhall Museum)

52

motto *Domine dirige nos* (Lord, direct us) underneath. The crest, a dragon's wing with a cross, resting on a wreath which is placed on a helm, and the supporters, each a dragon with a cross on its wing, arise from the misinterpretation of a Tudor seal; the fan-shaped top of a helmet was mistaken for a dragon's wing, so that from the seventeenth century dragons have been included in the arms.

Along the north-eastern road out of Bishopsgate, the bounds reached still farther. Today, we must walk past Liverpool Street Station into a rather dilapidated area, just beyond the entrance to Spital Square on the left and Primrose Street on the right. Here, in the middle of the road, with a garage on either side, the dragon of London on a metal pedestal faces outwards, holding the civic shield. This is nearly the northernmost point of the city, since the boundary was soon forced sharply inwards by Moorfields. Houses along the northern route out of Cripplegate and the north-westerly one from Aldersgate, however, pushed it out again, so that the northern limit is in fact in Aldersgate High Street, beyond the junction with Charterhouse Street. From here the bounds irregularly run south-west, embracing West Smithfield, with the hospital and former priory of St Bartholomew.

At Holborn the bounds stretched along the road from Newgate, London's main artery to the west. This route survives today in Newgate Street, Holborn Viaduct (crossing the stream now beneath Farringdon Street), Holborn, High Holborn, New Oxford Street and its relentless westerly extensions. It was older and at first commercially more important than London's other western outlet, the riverside road to Westminster. Moreover the land was drier than farther south, encouraging settlement long before the lawyers came. Under Stephen the Knights Templars lived in the district later generally known as Holborn, where they had settled by 1128; there on the south side of the main road they had a round church, a churchyard, houses, stables and gardens. In 1161 they sold this land to the bishop of Lincoln and moved south to the increasingly fashionable road out of Ludgate. They still contributed to Holborn's growth, however, since they were so active as bankers that the Treasury and the Exchequer were sited in the New Temple. Lawyers, who needed to be close at hand, flocked to sites to the north: a royal order of 1234, closing all law-schools within the city itself, finally entrenched the legal profession in Holborn.

The Bars of Holborn, first recorded in 1183, originally left within the city everything east of the northern end of Chancery

Lane. In the mid-thirteenth century however they were shifted east, when the king created liberties for his house for converted Jews (*see p. 228*) and for lands held by the bishop of Chichester on both sides of Chancery Lane. Lawyers secured further small adjustments, so that the Bars were eventually fixed where Gray's Inn Road enters Holborn from the north-west. Today they are marked by a stone monument at each kerbside. As elsewhere, the familiar winged dragon faces outward, holding his shield. The southerly one can hardly be missed, since it is next to the former Staple Inn, a site unique in London; although this is an Elizabethan façade, repeatedly restored, it gives some idea of what many town houses looked like at the end of the Middle Ages.

The most famous of the Bars, and the one farthest from the wall, is Temple Bar, on the road out of Ludgate. This is the way by which the sovereign normally rides from Westminster to the city. Even in the Middle Ages there was probably an imposing entrance here, the predecessor of an early Stuart gateway and of Wren's triumphal arch, which is now in Theobalds Park near Cheshunt in Hertfordshire. In 1880 Wren's arch was replaced by a squared, pillar-like monument in the middle of the road, a few feet west of Bell Yard. Queen Victoria looks south from her niche across the stream of traffic to Glyn Mills Bank (No. 1, Fleet Street), while the Prince Consort gazes north across another stream to the eastern end of the Law Courts. On top a winged dragon or griffin in black metal faces westward along the Strand, as once did the heads of traitors.

On the river side of the point where Fleet Street joins the Strand, the boundary bulges westward almost to Essex Street, enclosing the precinct of the Templars. It then retreats to reach the Embankment nearly due south of Temple Bar; silver coloured dragons mark this spot, one on each side of the road, east of Temple Place and opposite the moored sloop *Wellington*. The city's southern boundary runs along the middle of the river, bisecting London Bridge and turning in just short of the Tower.

'The city' means the whole area within the Bars, but building in some places extended even farther. The longest and grandest development was on the westerly route out of Ludgate and across the Fleet, well beyond Temple Bar. Ludgate's Roman origin shows that this was a very old route. It followed the present Strand, under the Anglo-Saxon name of Akeman Street, until it came to the *cierring* or turning in the river, which by Fitz Stephen's time had supplied a name for the hamlet of Charing. Here Akeman Street itself turned inland, up the present Haymarket and along the line of Piccadilly and Knightsbridge, where it crossed the Westbourne, and so to the village of Kensington and the west. Early settlements at Westminster, however, led to a branch road from Charing southwards, where Whitehall runs today; this was, in Latin, *strata regia* (a 'royal street') in 1222 and had become King Street by 1376, an obvious reference to the palace at its southern end.

Ludgate, although Roman, was an afterthought. It was built later than Newgate and for nearly a thousand years there was no comparison between the riverside track and the busy highway to the north. The bank here was not of firm, well-drained gravel, like the two hills in the city, but alluvium, mixed deposits left by the water. It sloped more steeply than today, since soil was continually swept down from higher ground to the north; settlement would make sewage a problem, particularly at the river-bend where there was more space along the road than along the foreshore. These drawbacks had to be balanced against the pleasant outlook of a riverside house and, in calm weather, easy access by barge. Long after Fitz Stephen's time there were open spaces and bushes along the route from Temple Bar to Westminster, which in 1315 was a dangerous and muddy track. It was the rise of Westminster which produced lordly buildings along the unpromising Strand.

By 1300 we know who owned the sites along the Thames side of the road from London to Westminster. Instead of the uniform ribbon development that we would expect today, there were yet more of the contrasts which were so familiar in the Middle Ages. Waste patches, hovels and shops alternated with high walls and imposing gateways; behind the walls lay mansions, even palaces, which were almost self-supporting, with their orchards and gardens, quaysides and stables, brewhouses and bakeries, guardrooms and chapels. Town houses were often called Inns, since the Old English *inn* meant simply a dwelling-place, as it still does in the case of the four Inns of Court. Most of the Inns along the river bank were held by bishops until the Reformation, when they passed into lay hands.

A fourteenth-century traveller to Westminster would leave by Ludgate and descend the hill to the Fleet bridge. On his left, the wall bulged out to enclose the house of the black friars; on his right, close to the bank of the Fleet, lay the prison, surrounded by its moat. Riding along what since Fitz Stephen's time has been called Fleet Street, he would pass the church of St Bride, on its Saxon foundations; the wedding-cake spire of Wren's church can best be seen from Ludgate Hill itself. Around St Bride's, from the road to the Thames, lay a large plot, where King John had a castle or tower which afterwards fell into ruin. The eastern half of the site up to the mouth of the Fleet lay desolate until Henry VIII built his riverside palace of Bridewell, which is commemorated by a plaque behind the area railings of No. 14, New Bridge Street. The western half was granted to the bishops of Salisbury, who were licensed to add battlements to their house there in 1337; opposite Shoe Lane, Salisbury Court leads to Salisbury Square, which was once the bishops' courtyard.

The next important site on the left belonged to the Carmelites or white friars, who had land here from 1241. Two gateways gave onto Fleet Street itself, where Bouverie Street and Pleydell Court emerge today. Behind the friars' wall lay their cemetery and, in the fourteenth century, some property of Hugh de Courtenay, earl of Devon. Courtenay helped to rebuild the church, which lay south of the cemetery and whose site crossed that of *Punch*'s dignified office in Bouverie Street; there were more monastic buildings farther south, beyond which gardens stretched to the waterfront. Immediately before the walled enclosure a lane led from Fleet Street to the Thames along the present line of Whitefriars Street and Carmelite Street. A quick diversion down here reveals, in a brick wall on the left, the entrance to Britton's Court. Beneath one corner of this unlikely site is the only relic of the monastery, a simple vaulted room built about 1420; it was once part of the prior's house and was afterwards used as a coal-hole before its purchase and restoration by the *News of the World*, which will allow anyone to visit it at twenty-four hours' notice. Whitefriars Street is now a dingy slope, often lined with delivery vans and filled with the rumble of printing presses. Probably this was the lane where the clamour of men visiting bawdy houses so disturbed divine service that in 1345 the king, at the friars' request, ordered all the prostitutes to be expelled.

Along the river, the white friars' land was joined to the still larger estate of the Knights Templars, which reached to the city limits. The New Temple was set back from Fleet Street, however, until just before the Bar, where Inner Temple Lane is today. Part of the roadside gap was filled by an Inn of the Dean and Chapter of York, which in the fifteenth century they leased to some serjeants-at-law, who were eventually to make it their headquarters as

Serjeants' Inn. Serjeants were superior lawyers, summoned to their degrees by the Crown, and by the end of the Middle Ages they were tending to live apart, with judges, rather than with their fellow barristers. The reconstructed courtyard of their Inn, which was abandoned for another site in Chancery Lane in the eighteenth century, can be reached through an archway in the Norwich Union's offices or by the narrow road which turns in a little farther on, Mitre Court.

Behind and to the west lay the New Temple, the main English centre of the Knights Templars for 150 years after they sold their site in Holborn in 1161. Almost the whole of this lay within the city, although one shop faced the road on the far side of the Bar. The Temple itself housed four classes: the knights, who had taken monastic vows, their gently-born esquires, the indoor and outdoor menials, and the priests and chaplains. Each group had its own living quarters. The knights themselves probably dwelt around a cloister south of the church, in the consecrated part of their precinct, and their hall probably occupied the site of the present Inner Temple Hall. This church and the hall beyond it are still reached from Fleet Street down the narrow Inner Temple Lane. Newspapers and magazines are sold by the arched entrance, beneath an unobtrusive sign pointing to the church. Middle Temple Lane, a scarcely wider opening farther west, was separated from Temple Bar in the Middle Ages by seven shops which the order owned; this lane was a public right of way, cutting through the estate to a wharf or quay by the Thames.

The templars grew so rich as European bankers that the king of France, alleging every conceivable vice, incited the pope to condemn them. In 1308 Edward II commanded the mayor of London to seize the knights' property and allowed the inquisitor to treat their bodies as he pleased. With hindsight, the sudden fall of one of the two great Christian orders of knighthood seems to foreshadow the Reformation; a gigantic, overblown corporation, having long forgotten its original duty to protect the holy places of Palestine, was swept away with little danger to its destroyers. Yet if this brutal episode sounded the knell of other religious bodies, the end was a long way off. Rome decreed that the Templars' lands should go to their rivals, the Hospitallers. In the 1330s the king reluctantly gave up the site of the Temple, which did not finally pass to the lawyers who leased it from the Hospitallers until this order in turn fell victim to Henry VIII.

It is ironical that, of all the proud landowners along the royal way to Westminster, only the persecuted Templars have left anything substantial. During the 1950s their church was restored, after a fire in 1941 had undone most of the loving but drastic repairs of the Victorians. In spite of these sufferings, the building is full of fascination. The two-tiered stone drum behind the plane trees is in fact the nave of one of England's five medieval round churches and of the only one in London; its startling and unfamiliar plan, copied from the Holy Sepulchre at Jerusalem, was always used by the Templars. The roundness is relieved by a sharply projecting late twelfth-century porch. This shelters a late Norman or Romanesque doorway, London's one, battered survivor from an age of exceptionally rich stone-carving. The church, a private chapel of the knights and now of the members of the Inner and Middle Temples, ranks as a royal peculiar; like Westminster Abbey and the Savoy Chapel, it is subject directly to the sovereign and not to the bishop.

The nave, intriguingly, was built at a time when round-headed Romanesque was giving way to the severe, pointed Gothic known as Early English. Its window heads are rounded, as are the interlaced arches inside the drum against the middle section of the wall, the *triforium*. Yet the builders were quick to learn, for the arcade of the aisle itself is entirely Gothic and its six columns are the earliest known examples of marble from the Isle of Purbeck; this beautiful material, formed from the crushed shells of millions of pond snails, was quickly to become popular. The circular nave, fifty-nine feet across with its surrounding aisle, was consecrated by Heraclius, Patriarch of Jerusalem, in 1185—he performed a similar service at Clerkenwell, where the Hospitallers too had a circular church, now destroyed above ground, whose diameter was six feet wider. To the east a short choir was soon replaced by a longer one, consecrated in the presence of Henry III in 1240; this extension too is unusual, since the centre and aisles are equal in size. Excavations have shown that the work put an end to what was perhaps a small chapel and probably also a treasure-house. The chapel was rebuilt outside the south wall of the nave, as the chapel of St Anne, and has now vanished. The 'treasure-house' can still be reached by a curving stairway underneath the south porch. Low stone shelves, perhaps for chests, run the length of the room and emphasize its narrowness. A capital of about 1170, carved as were many others with acanthus leaves, is almost hidden in the dark corner to the left of the doorway. At the far end there are still four iron hinges in the wall, which once held the doors of a double locker. In what safer place could the Templars have kept their own and their clients' treasure than here, in the heart of their precinct and beneath the choir of their church?

If we are tempted to stroke the smooth blocks of creamy stone or the slim shafts of dark grey marble, we will not feel the actual surfaces cut for the Templars. Paring and recarving in 1841 and the splitting of the marble after the collapse of the burning roof one hundred years later have led to overall restoration. The reredos is Wren's design, the glass and practically all the other fittings, save the tombs, are modern. Yet the core of the building is medieval and Fitz Stephen may have watched the first material being landed from barges at the foot of Middle Temple Lane. The church is all that we would expect from its builders and its age—up-to-date in materials, design and execution, costly but austere, confidently proportioned, light but not flimsy.

Even more arresting are the medieval effigies on the floor of the nave. This is one of the few places where we can lean right over such sculptures, since they are normally to be seen only in profile on the tops of tomb-chests. All have been damaged, save that of a

Fig. 13 *Marble and stone effigies of William Marshal the elder (d. 1219), and William Marshal the younger (d. 1231), earls of Pembroke, in the Temple Church* (A. F. Kersting)

fourteenth-century member of the de Ros family, but the very names of those which are identified show the enormous prestige of the Temple in its heyday. One of the figures is said to commemorate Geoffrey de Mandeville, earl of Essex, scourge of the Londoners and a byword for baronial lawlessness, whose outcast body was taken to the Templars when they were still at Holborn (*see p. 103*). Two other effigies, animated knights in chain mail, are those of William and Gilbert Marshal, earls of Pembroke; a third, more sedate, is that of their father William, the first earl, who as regent for King John's infant son Henry III held the destiny of England in his hands (*Fig. 13*). Away from all these, in the south-east corner of the choir, gleams the black marble tomb of a mitred prelate, the most perfect if not the most eloquent of all the figures. Some think that this is Sylvester, bishop of Carlisle, who was fatally thrown from his horse in 1254, others that it is the Patriarch Heraclius himself.

The north side of the main road, away from the water, was less fashionable. Expansion along Holborn and the riverside, however, made it inevitable that settlers would fill up the intervening land. By 1300 there were three main links between Holborn and Fleet Street, as there are today. In the east Shoe Lane came out opposite Salisbury Inn; its name recalls, not the work of cobblers but perhaps a piece of land shaped like a shoe. Near the western end, opposite Serjeants' Inn, lay Fetter Lane, once perhaps the haunt of *faitors*, impostors or cheats. At the very end of Fleet Street, just within the Bar, came what in 1185 was called New Street and later the Converts' Street, the Chancellor's Lane and, by the mid-fifteenth century, Chancery Lane. Tradition says that it was made by the Templars when they moved south from Holborn to the Thames. Its many names are explained by the foundation in 1231 of a home for converted Jews, which afterwards housed the rolls of the court of Chancery. This site now forms part of the Public Record Office, whose entrance can be seen from Fleet Street. (*See pp. 229, 234.*)

Another sign of life along the north of Fleet Street is a mention of the church of 'St Dunstan over against the New Temple' in 1237. The road was then narrower so that the medieval church, between Fetter Lane and Chancery Lane, was slightly farther south than the present St Dunstan-in-the-West. This is the church whose nineteenth-century tower, topped by an octagonal lantern, draws the attention of anyone looking down Fleet Street from the foot of Ludgate Hill. Next door was a plot granted by the king in

1310 to Robert Clifford and leased from his heirs by legal apprentices. The Cliffords were northern barons, who played a leading part in the Wars of the Roses and later became earls of Cumberland. Except during their spells of disgrace they kept lodgings in Clifford's Inn until Stuart times, long after it had become an Inn of Chancery. Their arms form the chequered shield over the modern gateway down Clifford's Inn Passage, although the main building was replaced in the eighteenth century and the society itself was dissolved in 1902. Both sides of Fleet Street thus attracted lawyers, thanks to the royal courts and, in the first place, to the banking activities of the Templars.

After passing Salisbury Inn, Whitefriars and the Temple, the traveller at last left London. Today he would at once enter the city of Westminster, but this did not exist until 1604; moreover the jurisdiction of the abbots of Westminster, in spite of their large claims, was pushed back halfway along the Strand in 1222 to a point near the present Shell-Mex House, some fifty yards east of where Ivy Bridge carried the road over a small tributary of the Thames. In the Middle Ages the intervening area, like the Westminster estates themselves, was part of Middlesex. Between the Strand and the river, however, the land acquired a special status from the mid-thirteenth century. This rectangular buffer-state still belongs to the Crown, as part of its duchy of Lancaster, and is called the Liberty of the Savoy.

Like most large estates, the original manor of the Savoy was extended by buying nearby plots, so that many other notable buildings along this stretch of riverside later fell within its bounds. The string of ecclesiastical mansions continued beyond Temple Bar with those of the bishops of Exeter, Bath and Wells, and Llandaff. Exeter Inn was built on a site acquired from the Hospitallers by Bishop Walter Stapledon, who was slaughtered in 1326 (*see p. 112*). Its fate after the Reformation, when it passed through the Pagets and Dudleys to the Devereux earls of Essex, is recalled by Devereux Court and Essex Street, the first two openings on the left after passing Temple Bar. Bath Inn, which the bishop probably held by the 1230s, was set back towards the river, with a row of meaner houses screening it from the Strand. Again nothing survives, but its Tudor owners included Thomas Howard, duke of Norfolk, whose heir was earl of Surrey, and later the earls of Arundel; hence the names of the next three streets on the left. Llandaff Inn, granted to

61

the bishop in 1280, is unmarked; it was swallowed up by the duke of Somerset, Protector of England and uncle to the boy king Edward VI, for the palace which he started on the site of Somerset House. Another of the duke's victims was the church of St Mary-le-Strand, first mentioned in 1274; this was moved to the north side of the road, where Gibbs built the present church; like St Clement Danes, it has formed an island only since the beginning of the present century.

Opposite these Inns were the church of St Clement Danes and, a little farther on, an old *wic* or dairy farm, mentioned in 1199. St Clement Danes was probably founded because of the nearby well, which attracted Danish troops or settlers who were not wanted in Saxon London. Whether they were first allowed to live here under Alfred or whether they formed a garrison for the victorious Cnut is uncertain. One chronicle says that the corpse of Cnut's usurping bastard Harold Harefoot, which had been exhumed by his brother, was rescued from the marshes by the monks of Westminster and reinterred in the Danish burial ground here. The church, recorded between 1100 and 1135, stood north of the Strand throughout the Middle Ages but became an island on the construction of the semi-circular road early in the twentieth century, when the name Aldwych was revived. Wren's church, restored since the Second World War, had medieval, Norman and, presumably, pre-Conquest forerunners, of which nothing survives save some masonry from the thirteenth-century tower. To the north lawyers had settled before 1479 on a site known as Clement's Inn; many of their buildings had been replaced by the Law Courts before the society was finally disestablished in 1885.

The next stretch of riverside, from Llandaff Inn to Ivy Bridge Lane, boasted the most palatial private home in England, the Savoy. Pagan Saxons had settled here (*see p. 19*) and houses and gardens were scattered along the slope in 1233. Henry III, an unhappy ruler like most patrons of the arts, notoriously favoured the relatives of his wife, Eleanor of Provence, who was once pelted with mud as her barge tried to make its way from the Tower to Westminster. Her uncle Peter, count of Savoy, received land by the Thames in 1246 and soon afterwards added pieces to the east and west. He died abroad in 1268 but two years later his manor was bought back by Queen Eleanor, from whom it passed to the line of her younger son, Edmund, earl of Lancaster. The Savoy first became an English place-name in 1293, when Edmund was permitted to fortify his mansion with a stone wall. His younger son Henry had a paved way laid down along the Strand frontage in 1330.

It was Earl Henry who built the palace, at what was then the staggering cost of at least £35,000, which he had gained as booty in the Hundred Years' War. The captive King John of France died here in 1364, as the honoured guest of Henry's son John of Gaunt, later duke of Lancaster. Chaucer and, for a time, Wyclif were both in Gaunt's service and must have known the Savoy in the days when London's poor loathed it as a symbol of luxury and pride. Threatened during Wyclif's trial for heresy in 1377, the palace which many thought unequalled in the land was burned down in the Peasants' Revolt four years later. There was no plunder, even the plate being hurled into the flames, which were fed with barrels of gunpowder, although some of the mob were carousing in the duke's wine-cellar when it caved in. Gaunt, luckily for himself, was in the north. Neither he nor his heirs, the Lancastrian kings, had the heart to rebuild, so the site lay semi-derelict for over a century. A wall was kept in repair and, by the 1440s, there was a prison. Royal interest revived only at the end of the Middle Ages when Henry VII, the first of the Tudors, left money for a hospital, whose chapel was finished in 1517. Nothing remains of the hospital itself, a cruciform building planned like a church, which had a faltering and unhappy history after the Reformation until its final suppression in 1702.

We do not know the layout of Gaunt's estate, which stretched from the present Somerset House as far as the Savoy Hotel. Behind a wall, with gates onto the Strand and onto the river, there were state apartments, a chapel, a cloister, and many humbler buildings, some of them thatched, as well as gardens, stables and a fishpond. The present Queen's Chapel of the Savoy is not the building known to Chaucer, which was sacked, nor even the one erected under Henry VII's will, which was burned in 1864. The early Tudor chapel, however, was rebuilt as it had been, and so gives an idea of what was greatly admired in 1520, when it was one of London's sights. It is unusual in not facing east and is yet another royal peculiar, now used by the Royal Victorian Order. The chapel is approached from the Strand down Savoy Street and, cowering as it does beneath the lavatorial back walls of the hotel, it deserves a visit, if only to show how history crops up in unexpected places.

If it were not for the Savoy, the credit for fashionable development between London and Westminster would go almost entirely to the Church. Between the west wall of the Lancastrian estate and

Ivy Bridge was land which the prior of Carlisle granted to his bishop in 1402–3. No trace remains of Carlisle Inn, whose site is partly covered by the Savoy Hotel, although seventeenth-century prints show the mansion of the marquesses of Worcester, who eventually bought the Inn. Next door, to the west, the bishops of Durham had land by 1237. Theirs was one of the largest mansions, for the bishops were powerful guardians of the marches, enjoying vice-regal powers in their exposed northern see. Post-Reformation plans show a gatehouse near the middle of the Strand wall, court-yards, a chapel, and the great hall by the river, with gardens to the east. Henry III, forced by a storm to leave his barge, was given shelter here by the baron whom he professed to fear more than thunder or lightning, Simon de Montfort; other guests included Prince Henry, later Henry V, and the young Katherine of Aragon as a bride-to-be. Cardinal Wolsey, who held the bishopric among his many appointments, often stayed here while building was carried out for him at Whitehall. Durham House Street, reached down steps from the Strand, recalls this estate, which was sur-rendered to the Crown in 1536. To the west the bishops of Norwich probably possessed an Inn by 1237, which they too held until the Reformation. Its other boundary was where Villiers Street runs down to the Thames, by the side of Charing Cross station. The names of half a dozen office-blocks and streets recall the later owners of Norwich Inn, the archbishops of York and the Villiers dukes of Buckingham.

The medieval traveller now reached the hamlet of Charing. Any map will show how the beginning of the river-bend forced the old Akeman Street and its successor, the Strand, to head not due west but south-west. At Charing the point was reached where the Thames no longer ran from west to east, as opposite the city, but from south to north. Akeman Street, essentially a westerly route, turned inland, while King Street, from Charing to Westminster, kept parallel to the river and therefore headed south.

Near the end of the Strand, a rural scene is still conjured up by the name St Martin-in-the-Fields, found in 1254 and attached ever since to the churches here. Even the riverbank was not particularly sought after, since the curve made more space along the road than along the Thames; by Tudor times there was serious trouble from debris piled up alongside the ditches which drained the higher ground. Significantly, there were no bishops at Charing. Such importance as it had came from the fork in the road. At the meeting of King Street with Akeman Street, where Whitehall now enters Trafalgar Square, a cross was set up by the iron-willed Edward I, stricken with grief at the loss of his wife, Eleanor of Castile. Twelve such Eleanor Crosses marked the resting places of her body as it was borne from Lincoln to Westminster Abbey. Only three remain, the one nearest to London being at Waltham Cross in Hertfordshire, although pieces of the cross in Cheapside are now in the Guildhall Museum. Charing was the last halt, where the most expensive cross of all, in Caen stone and Purbeck marble, was consecrated between 1291 and 1294 (*Fig. 14*). Roundheads pulled it down and royalists set up a statue of Charles I after the Restoration.

Long, narrow strips of land ran from the road to the river. Next door to the bishops of Norwich was a private Inn, called the Bell in 1480; then came the Lion Inn, belonging to Westminster Abbey, and then the mansion owned by the Hungerford family, when they were not in disgrace, at least from 1422. Charing Cross station, faced by what purports to be a replica of the old cross, now covers all three sites. The Hungerfords were colourful but unlucky,

Charing Cross.
Erected for Queen Eleanor.

Fig. 14 *Drawing of Old Charing Cross* (British Museum)

65

suffering as Lancastrians in the Wars of the Roses; despite their recovery under the Tudors, a dowager Lady Hungerford was hanged at Tyburn in 1523 for poisoning her husband, and her step-son finally lost the barony in 1540 on his conviction for treason and sodomy. They were commemorated in a late seventeenth-century market, which replaced their Inn, and afterwards in the iron railway bridge between Charing Cross and Waterloo. This bridge has a footway, which gives a good view to the north-east of the bend in the river.

Next to Hungerford Inn was some land held in the fifteenth century by the Hospitallers, including a beerhouse and, by the road, eleven cottages. Then came another private Inn, the Christopher in 1514, with its own right of way down to a wharf. Beyond this there were six more cottages and an Inn owned by Westminster Abbey in 1540, when it was called the Rose. This adjoined the earliest known property in Charing, the hospital of St Mary Rouncevall, founded in 1231 by William Marshal the younger, earl of Pembroke, who lies near his father in the Temple Church. William gave all his houses here to the priory of Roncesvaux in Navarre, so that they might help sick travellers and pilgrims to the Confessor's shrine at Westminster. The hospital, which had a chapel near the roadside and a wharf, passed into English hands and eventually fell victim to Henry VIII. South of its main entrance, which almost faced the Eleanor Cross, another group of houses belonging to Westminster bordered the road at the beginning of King Street. Next to them, roughly where Craig's Court faces the Whitehall Theatre, was St Katharine's Hermitage, a cell for a holy man which had been founded by 1253. To the south, between King Street and the river, stretched a large plot called Scotland; in 1436 it was said to have been given to the Scottish kings, but the story that they stayed there when fitfully acknowledging English overlord-ship may be no more than propaganda. After the Reformation the Rose Inn and much of St Mary Rouncevall were replaced by a succession of noble houses of which the last, Northumberland House, was destroyed in the 1870s for Northumberland Avenue. Great Scotland Yard, Whitehall Place, the War Office and, nearer the river, the clubs along Whitehall Court, cover the south-western half of the hospital and most of Scotland.

Anyone standing near Scotland and looking down King Street would see the abbey church of Westminster at the far end, towering above its walled precinct. Between this and the Thames lay the king's palace. Its closeness made the intervening riverside stretch along King Street extremely desirable, in spite of the flat, marshy ground. It was sold in 1223 by Westminster Abbey and acquired in 1240 by the archbishop of York, who turned it into an official residence for his successors. After an uneventful history York Place passed to England's last great statesman-prelate, Cardinal Wolsey, who bought Scotland on the north and more land on the south, to make an orchard, and started a new palace to vie with its royal neighbour. Henry VIII may well have coveted this more than that other tactless showpiece, Hampton Court, since the abbey, the marshes and the river left him room to expand only to the north. In 1529, a year after Wolsey had finished the seventy-foot-long great hall, the king took over what was soon renamed Whitehall, perhaps after Wolsey's new stonework. The cardinal's fall was the prelude to the break with Rome and the disappearance of the monastic properties which had dominated medieval London. Although the royal palace of Whitehall, except for Inigo Jones's Banqueting House, was completely burned down in 1698, its seizure by the Crown explains how the site eventually became available for government offices.

While Whitehall was being made ready, a smaller palace was built farther inland, to the west. A hospital for fourteen leper women had been founded here, traditionally before the Conquest and certainly by Fitz Stephen's time. This poor house was later given to Eton, which exchanged it with the king in 1532. It can be seen well behind the riverside buildings in part of a view of London and Westminster sketched by Anthony van den Wyngaerde about 1550, the first panorama of its kind (*Fig. 15*). The hospital's dedication of St James the Less explains the name St James's Park and of the Palace, whose brick Tudor gatehouse still stands.

The cause of all this travelling and building was the foundation of Westminster Abbey. Its museum displays a charter, written nearly 1200 years ago or perhaps copied a little later, from which we first learn of the abbey's existence and name: Offa, king of Mercia, for a hundred gold pieces, gives land in Hertfordshire to 'St Peter and to the people of God who live in Thorney [that is, the Isle of Thorns], in the dreadful place which is called *aet West-munster*'. The life of this community, presumably cut off by the Vikings, had been resumed by the 960s. Probably it was again destroyed in the second wave of invasions, before Edward the

Fig. 15 *Late medieval Westminster, showing St James's hospital in the background, from a panorama of London and Westminster sketched by Anthony van den Wyngaerde about 1550* (British Museum)

Confessor lavishly endowed the abbey and built a new church of St Peter, slightly to the west of an older one.

When Offa said that Thorney was dreadful he meant that it was awe-inspiring, already in some way sanctified. The island, however, was set in a peculiarly unattractive neighbourhood, whose natural features are now even harder to find than those of the city of London. The low ridge which bore the Strand turned inland at Charing and continued westward along Akeman Street, following the present line of Piccadilly and Knightsbridge. South-west of the Strand, where the river changed course, there opened a flat plain, always open to floods. The downward slope is still visible from the Piccadilly ends of St James's Street, Lower Regent Street and streets parallel to them. In the Middle Ages, if no mist hung over the marshes, one saw a wide green level cut by the Tyburn and, further off, by the Westbourne; in the middle distance a small mound, the Toot Hill, occupied the present site of St James's Park underground station at the end of Tothill Street. The Tyburn, now flowing under Green Park and Buckingham Palace, turned east around this mound and, near the present foot of Tothill Street, forked north-east and south-east. The northern branch entered the Thames near the present New Scotland Yard, the southern ran by Great College Street to enter beneath the northern end of Victoria Tower Gardens. The streams and the Thames formed a rough triangle, the Island of Thorney.

The vital thing about Thorney is that part of it had gravel, so that building was possible. The Romans had forded the Thames here and made a small settlement on the island, to which stone could be brought by water. Naturally the firmest ground was chosen for the Confessor's church and the surrounding abbey buildings; elsewhere, piles had to be sunk into the alluvium to support the weight of masonry. In the later Middle Ages the abbey precinct had its own wall, while the royal palace lay between this and the Thames. Apart from their link with London along King Street and some humble houses in Tothill Street, both groups of buildings were hemmed in by the river and the marshes. Abbot and king, monks and courtiers, were thrown together, so that the abbey church became intimately linked with royalty, as St Paul's was with the city. Money was lavished on the abbey as on the palace, to form an architectural group all the grander by contrast with the emptiness around.

The name Westminster Abbey is confusing: it should really be the Collegiate Church of St Peter, since the present building is only the church which served the monastery. The medieval abbey comprised many domestic ranges, courtyards and gardens, at first not clearly separated from the palace on the eastern part of Thorney. About 1370 Edward III extorted some ground, where he built the Jewel Tower which now almost faces the Victoria Tower of the Houses of Parliament across Abingdon Street. The resentful monks at once ringed their property with a wall; it had to bulge inwards to exclude the Jewel Tower but it nicely blocked the royal view. Southern and eastern stretches of this wall enclose the garden of Westminster School, allowing only the top of the Jewel Tower to be seen in a corner.

The abbey's precinct was sometimes called the Sanctuary, since Edward the Confessor had granted rights which were unique in southern England until William the Conqueror also gave them to St Martin-le-Grand. (*See p. 219.*) For over 500 years fugitives of every rank could seek safety here for life. In a sudden twist of fate during the Wars of the Roses, Elizabeth, Edward IV's queen,

69

arrived to give birth to an heir in 1470. Thirteen years later she fled again in the hope of saving her younger son from his uncle, Richard of Gloucester, although she was soon persuaded to let the prince join his brother, with whom he died in the Tower. The abbey's protection, which could so thwart the highest interests of state, also threatened local peace. Part of the precinct north of the church became a scandalous haunt of criminals, who at times broke out and terrorized the neighbourhood. Sanctuary for treason was abolished in 1534 and sanctuary for debt on the creation of Westminster City by James I.

We do not know the plan of the Norman abbey, but can picture the scene in the late Middle Ages. At the end of King Street, where Parliament Square now opens, the traveller was faced with a gateway in the north wall of the monks' precinct. On the left another gateway led to the palace by the river. The only open way was to turn and skirt the sanctuary wall along Thieving Lane which ran west, where Great George Street does today, and then curved around to the foot of Tothill Street. Here stood a double gatehouse slightly to the west of the nineteenth-century pink granite column in the present square before the west door of the abbey church. Southwards the wall ran parallel with part of the northern branch of the Tyburn, which by the late fifteenth century had here been straightened into the 'Long Ditch'.

Behind the righthand (southern) gate lay a prison and then the abbot's lodgings, parts of which still cling to the south-west corner of the church. If, instead of walking ahead into the church, one turned right and passed between the gateway and the prison, one reached an open space, the Elms. This ground, rather soft for building, was the south-west corner of the precinct and is now Dean's Yard. It was used for storing farm produce, with an almonry to the west and guesthouses, an entrance to the kitchen and the house of the cellarer, who had charge of the farm, to the east. Although the yard is ringed by later houses, in the corner closest to the church there is still a way to the medieval abbot's rooms and to the cloisters, where none but the monks might go. The infirmary and other monastic buildings, whose site is covered by Westminster School, lay east of the Elms, with a garden to the south. Below these flowed the south-eastern branch of the Tyburn, diverted a few yards north of its original course so as to work a mill at its juncture with the Thames, on the south-eastern tip of Thorney; this stream marked the southernmost limit of both the abbey and the palace grounds. Beyond, marshes and water-meadows stretched to the village of Chelsea.

Although the rights of sanctuary applied to the whole precinct, the monks' use of the land south of the church meant that fugitives had to settle to the north. 'The Sanctuary' therefore became the name of the space which was reached through the left-hand gate at the foot of Tothill Street and which now stretches from the north wall of the abbey church as far as Great George Street. Like the Elms (Dean's Yard) on the other side, this was marshy ground, so that the only large building in the north-western corner of the abbey precinct was a thirteenth-century belfry, for which huge wooden piles had to be sunk into the alluvium beneath what is now the Middlesex Guildhall. At some unknown date individual houses were built here and profitably leased to 'sanctuary men'.

East of these houses, but still inside the precinct, was the church of St Margaret. This had been founded, according to tradition, by the Confessor himself. Certainly it stood there within a hundred years of his death, although it was rebuilt in the fourteenth century and again at the end of the Middle Ages. It seems odd to find a church so close to Westminster Abbey, particularly if we can ignore the contrast in size and see that St Margaret's, so far from being a toy building, is itself large. The abbey's history supplies the answer. The monks and their attendants, anxious to worship on their own, had to provide somewhere for the local laity, whose number rose as Westminster became a seat of government. St Margaret's was always in effect the parish church of Westminster, although in the Middle Ages it was under the abbot and not, as now, under the bishop of London.

What we see today is essentially the church consecrated in 1523, although refaced and partly rebuilt. Later additions include the triple porch to the west and the small south-east porch opposite the Houses of Parliament. The tower, an eighteenth-century reconstruction, is unusual in standing against the north wall instead of to the west. Inside, the church seems spacious and cool, in spite of its wooden roof. The careful proportions are those of Robert Stowell, master-mason to the monks of Westminster. John Islip, a keen builder and the last of their abbots to die before the Reformation, himself paid for the church.

Few churches are so bound up with British history, for St Margaret's has been used by the House of Commons since Stuart times, when Members refused to join the Lords at the 'Romish' services next door. Medieval associations, of course, are few and late. William Caxton, who printed England's first book within the abbey precinct in 1476, is commemorated by a tablet in the dark south-east corner, and John Skelton, the laureate who satirized Wolsey, was also buried in the church or its graveyard. The glory of St Margaret's is the east window of Flemish glass, Renaissance rather than medieval but one which could not have been brought here after the triumph of Protestant austerity. It was in fact overtaken by the chill winds of the Reformation, having formed part of the dowry of Katherine of Aragon on her marriage to the short-lived Arthur, Prince of Wales. Probably it was meant for Henry VII's Chapel in the abbey but had not yet been installed when Henry VIII broke with Rome in order to divorce Katherine, his brother's widow. After wandering in disgrace from home to home, the window was bought by the churchwardens in 1758 and reset when the east end was extended in 1905. Katherine, whose failure to bear a son was to unleash so much destruction, kneels in the bottom right-hand corner, beneath a saint, with Prince Arthur opposite her. Like everything else in sight, these figures pale beside the brilliant cobalt blue sky behind the central Crucifixion. For 400 guineas the churchwardens, who were venomously attacked for desecrating what had become a Puritan shrine, have given us London's finest example of pre-Reformation glass.

Everything at Westminster, including the royal palace, was dominated by the abbey church itself, as we can see from Wyngaerde's panorama. Today there is competition, in spite of the fact that the church is taller, since its two western towers were continued above the level of the nave roof in the eighteenth century. This belated addition reminds us of the very slow growth of the present church, and also that it had its forerunners; the Saxon saw something quite different from the Norman, who in turn would have wondered at the work which began a few generations later. Firstly there was the Anglo-Saxon abbey or series of abbeys, of whose appearance we know nothing. Then came Edward the Confessor's great church whose chancel was consecrated only eight days before his death; the nave, towers and monastic buildings to the south were added over the next decades. Finally the present church was started in 1245 by Henry III, who pulled down the Norman east end; Edward was splendidly reburied in 1269, by which time the new chancel and transepts were finished, as were five bays of the nave, which served as a choir. The Chapter House and part of the existing cloister are also Henry's work. Another spurt of building began when the destruction of the Norman nave was started in 1375, and led to the completion of the west end, as well as to the rebuilding of the infirmary and the abbot's house to the south. Another hundred years separate these from Henry VII's Chapel, now the easternmost projection; it was not begun until 1503 and represents a late flowering of Perpendicular, the last and most elaborate of medieval styles. John Islip, who supervised work on the new east end, also built himself a chantry chapel, where he was laid in 1532, and added to the abbot's lodgings, which survive in part but are not open to the public.

Westminster Abbey often disappoints, because it offers too much. Nowhere else is it so important to know what we are looking for. If it is the Middle Ages we should concentrate on the structure itself, essentially medieval in spite of its repairs, and try to forget most of the monuments, which are later. To trace its life over the centuries we must also separate the church itself from the other monastic buildings, since the earliest remains (the only Norman ones) are the former treasury, the Chapel of the Pyx, and what was once a common-room beneath the monks' dormitory, now the Abbey Museum. A vividly carved late Norman capital, perhaps from the cloister, is now kept in the Muniment Room.

Both the Chapel of the Pyx and the Undercroft, reached from the east range of the cloister, are some nine hundred years old. The first of these was evidently built as a chapel and has a stone altar of about 1240. By then it may already have been a royal treasury, with pyxes or boxes holding trial plates and samples of the coinage, which were to be tested for weight and purity (the plates are now kept at the Royal Mint and the trial takes place at the Goldsmiths' Hall). The Undercroft next door is more than twice as large, with fat circular piers supporting groined vaults. Whitewash makes it seem more modern and the architecture is easily forgotten because of the exhibits. Here there is a plan of the Confessor's church which it once served, showing that the nave more or less corresponded to the present one but that the east end stretched no farther than the high altar in the sanctuary. Among the medieval relics none holds such human interest as the royal funeral effigies; Edward III's, carved in wood from a death-mask and betraying the effects of his final stroke, is the earliest in Europe. A visit to the Museum can also be helpful before starting on a thorough tour. The story of Westminster is summarized in pictures and captions, the colouring

73

of the medieval church can be seen in a plaster-cast of one of the stone angels which are high up in the south transept (overlooking Poets' Corner) (*Fig. 16*), and there is a view showing the layout of all the buildings on Thorney as they must have been just before the Reformation.

Westminster Abbey has so many guidebooks that there is no need to do more than point out how it was set apart from its rivals. Edward's church was the earliest Norman work in England, built for a half-Norman king, to a Norman pattern, by masons from the duchy and with stone from Caen. It set the fashion for a wave of rebuilding after the Conquest, when English riches combined with foreign skills to produce a nave longer than that of any Norman church of its day. If this was a marvel to all who saw it, the same was true of its successor. Henry III employed native architects and used stone from Reigate in Surrey and marble from Purbeck in Dorset, but in all else he followed the latest models of northern France. This is obvious in the layout, with a many-sided east end or apse, from which small chapels radiate like jewels from a pendant; although Gothic architecture was of French inspiration, the English much preferred square east ends, as almost any cathedral can show. The curving plan was repeated when the tip of the thirteenth-century apse was replaced by Henry VII's Chapel, even though this is Perpendicular, the most English of medieval styles. The pointed, aspiring nave is also strange; nowhere else in England does one rise to 103 feet, although Westminster's model at Rheims is still taller. The walls are so high that they can only be held up by a huge double tier of flying buttresses, the most striking external feature. No church in the island is more French than Westminster Abbey, the shrine of English royalty.

As for the monuments, they range from some superb medieval effigies through an extravagant display of marble to plain modern plaques whose only interest is that they bear famous names. The church could be visited solely for its unique collection of funeral sculptures, but these are not neatly arranged as in a gallery, so that it is easier to contrast the taste of different generations than to compare works of the same age. Luckily we can make straight for the Plantagenets' tombs around the shrine of Edward the Confessor. Here in spite of many additions, including the mid-Tudor wooden covering which has replaced the Confessor's golden coffer, royal figures have largely survived the Reformers and the Roundheads, who had to be content with pilfering. Ironically the beautiful if

Fig. 16 *Censing angel in the south transept of Westminster Abbey, about 1254–8* (Photograph by Kerry Dundas, Copyright Gordon Fraser Gallery Ltd)

Fig. 17 *Alabaster weeper from the tomb of John of Eltham in St Edmund's Chapel, Westminster Abbey, about 1340* (A. F. Kersting)

idealized gilded bronze effigy of Henry III, to whom we owe the present church, lies on so high and grand a tomb that it can hardly be seen. On the other hand his daughter-in-law Eleanor of Castile, laid here after resting at Charing Cross, can be studied quite closely. Even more ironic, amid so much rich artistry, is the dominance of the stark grey-brown marble slab which covers her husband Edward I (although this was once painted and had its canopy). Later, and more life-like, are the effigies of Edward III, Richard II and their queens. Later still but in the same tradition, are the early memorials in Henry VII's Chapel. The first Tudor and his wife, Elizabeth of

75

Fig. 18 *Gilt copper weeper from the tomb of Edward III in Edward the Confessor's Chapel, Westminster Abbey, about 1377–80* (A. F. Kersting)

Fig. 19 *Brass of Eleanor de Bohun, duchess of Gloucester, in St Edmund's Chapel, Westminster Abbey, about 1399*

York, lie inside a bronze screen east of the chapel's main altar, while the king's mother Lady Margaret Beaufort rests beyond later, more overpowering monuments, in its south aisle. Other outstanding medieval tombs are in the sanctuary before the Confessor's shrine, notably Edmund Crouchback's, and in St Edmund's Chapel off the south ambulatory, where William de Valence and Edward III's brother John of Eltham lie.

Often, in eagerness to gaze upon the faces of the great, other details are overlooked: the niches in the base of the Confessor's shrine, where sick people might kneel all night; Italian porphyry, set in the sides of the shrine and of Henry III's tomb (Cosmati work, of which the most elaborate example anywhere is the pavement in front of the high altar, now always kept covered); the little mourning figures which still line some of the tomb-chests, especially Edmund Crouchback's, John of Eltham's and Edward III's (those on the last two showing how taste could change in forty years) (*Figs. 17 and 18*); the pieces of Limoges enamel beside William de Valence; the iron grille protecting Eleanor of Castile; the delicate sculpture of Henry V's chantry chapel, beneath which we must pass to reach the Confessor's shrine; the engravings all over the gilded robes of Richard II, whose cape is bordered with pods of broom, the *planta genesta* of his family. Henry VII's Chapel is encrusted with emblems and deserves a book to itself, with its exquisitely carved wooden choir stalls, its wrought metal, and the figures which line the walls up to the fan-vaulting and its pendants (*Fig. 23*). A complete list is impossible, but to see how brilliant these tombs must have been we can visit St Paul's Chapel in the north ambulatory, where the fifteenth-century monument to Lord Bourchier has been freshly painted.

The carved effigies can be compared with the brasses, which were a cheaper form of memorial. Westminster has many which would be famous were they not overshadowed by so much sculpture, the finest being those of Eleanor de Bohun (*Fig. 19*) and Robert Waldeby in St Edmund's Chapel. Opposite the adjoining St Nicholas's Chapel is the most magnificent thirteenth-century painting on this side of the Alps, a retable which may once have stood behind the high altar (*Fig. 20*). There are also wall-paintings in the south transept, St Faith's Chapel and the Chapter House.

The church's place in the history of London and the kingdom is even higher than its place in architecture. It was the traditional graveyard of royalty until George III was laid in St George's

Fig. 20 *Disciples' head, from a painted retable perhaps once behind the high altar of Westminster abbey church, late 13th century* (University of London, the Warburg Institute)

Chapel, Windsor, and coronations and royal marriages are still celebrated there. Westminster's fame came indirectly from London, since the very name indicates a large church or minster west of the city. It was due more directly to Edward himself, whose obsession with his abbey church made it the grandest sight in England. His burial there was the greatest boon of all, since kings and monks, Normans and English, alike revered him and fostered legends of his miraculous powers. The conquerors, keen to justify their rule, did everything possible to associate themselves with the last monarch of Alfred's direct line. The monks knew that a famous shrine would bring prestige and money, in the form of bequests and pilgrims' offerings. Edward was canonized in 1161 and it was in his honour that the replacement of his cherished building was started by Henry III.

Thorney was so cramped that the abbey even shared the palace's role as a seat of government. A low doorway in the middle of the east cloister leads through two vestibules and up some steps to the

Fig. 21 *Interior of the Chapter House, Westminster Abbey, about 1253* (National Monuments Record)

octagonal Chapter House, where visitors must wear soft overshoes to protect the tiled floor. Looking back at the inner entrance, we can see graceful thirteenth-century figures on either side of the Victorian Christ in Majesty. Here the monks met after early mass to debate and to be given their daily duties; penances were allotted and senior monks were often flagellated against the central marble pillar (*Fig. 21*). Here too the king's council met in 1257, three years after the Chapter House's completion, and here the Commons of England sat in 1295, when Edward I sought their advice and so inaugurated the first Parliament. Although Parliaments might be held anywhere, they usually met at Westminster, where the Chapter House remained the meeting place of the lower house until the death of Henry VIII. In one of England's loveliest medieval buildings the Commons approved the destruction of the monasteries and the pillaging of their treasures; the abbey church of Westminster, however, became for ten years a bishop's cathedral, and its shrines were spared until the next reign brought vandalism a stage further.

Westminster seen from the Thames looked very different. Impressive as were even the outhouses of the abbey, they were obscured by the buildings which made up the royal palace. These, with their grounds, were a motley group, unlike the Victorian palace which now houses Parliament. Something of its higgledy-piggledy development can be gathered today by walking south across Parliament Square and along St Margaret Street, between the churches on the right and the Parliament buildings on the left. First, on the river side of the Square, is the railed enclosure of New Palace Yard; then a garden runs beside Westminster Hall; then the building falls back from the road, which broadens into Old Palace Yard, once the main courtyard of the Confessor's residence. In one corner, covering the site of Richard I's equestrian statue, was the White Hall (quite different from the later royal palace to the north); farther south lay the Painted Chamber, the Princes' Chamber and the apartments of the medieval kings. Still farther south, at the end of the island, lay their private garden (all this is shown on a plan in the Jewel Tower, where there are many relics of early Westminster). Here, as in the city, the medieval river-line was farther back than the modern one—so that Big Ben would have stood right by the water's edge. Later building could only take place to the north and naturally centred around Rufus's Westminster Hall, between which and the river Edward III founded the priests' college of St Stephen. Government servants clustered around and the courtyard north of the Hall became New Palace Yard, so that the palace fell into two halves, an official one to the north and a private one to the south.

In 1512 fire swept away all the private palace except for the Jewel Tower. This presumably escaped because it was situated so far west, on ground which, as we have seen, had been taken from the abbey. A three-storied, L-shaped building in the angle of a moat, it stands today a few yards back from the road, opposite the Victoria Tower at the southern end of the Houses of Parliament. It was so shaped to encase a corner of the royal garden and moated to guard against fire and burglary. Much to the delight of the monks, the palace keeper who was responsible for encroaching on their land choked to death while eating pike which had come from this moat. Inside were stored the king's own valuables, as opposed to the ceremonial regalia, which was divided between Westminster Abbey and the Tower, and the funds of the Exchequer, which were in the abbey's Chapel of the Pyx. Probably the keeper of the Privy Wardrobe occupied the bottom floor, while his clerk worked above and the treasure filled the top rooms. The walls are of Kentish ragstone, which made up most of London's medieval masonry; the doors, windows and battlements were finished with Reigate stone such as Henry III had used for his abbey church. The windows, which always had glass, were refashioned in the eighteenth century—originally there was none on the ground floor facing outwards—and the old foundation of vertical elm piles and horizontal oak beams had to be replaced with concrete in 1954. The walls however are original; if only they could be cleaned, so as to contrast with the tawny, soot-blackened buildings around, we should have some idea of how white and fresh the riverside palace must have looked in the Middle Ages.

Public portions of the palace survive in Westminster Hall and the crypt and cloister of St Stephen's Chapel, of which the first two can be included in a tour of the Houses of Parliament. Fire in 1834 destroyed most of their surroundings and damaged the crypt and cloister, whose restored remnants were incorporated in the present Parliament buildings. The crypt is really misnamed, since it lies above ground and was simply a lower chapel, built to give the king's private circle exclusive use of the one above. St Stephen's itself, sumptuously modelled on St Louis's Sainte-Chapelle in Paris, was begun in 1292, finished about seventy years later and drastically changed by Wren. Some of its fourteenth-century wall-paintings, showing the life of Job, are now in the British Museum. The college was dissolved at the Reformation and its chapel was regularly used by the Commons from 1547, when they abandoned the abbey's Chapter House. Because of the blaze in 1834 we cannot see where they debated for nearly 300 years and rose to become the first power in the land. While England's fate was being decided overhead, the crypt was used partly as a coal-cellar and partly as a dining-room for the Speaker. When it was rescued from this degradation all the stonework except the vaulting was restored and boldly painted in what was thought, from earlier traces, to have been its medieval style. The bright colours of the Middle Ages are so often forgotten that the crypt deserves a visit for these alone. It is now a non-denominational chapel for M.P.s, known as St Mary's or St Mary Undercroft. The nearby St Stephen's Cloister was finished only in 1529, the very year when the Reformation Parliament met. Although pierced by modern doors and windows, with walls that have obviously been resurfaced and with a rebuilt oratory projecting

Fig. 22 *Hammerbeam roof of Westminster Hall, looking south, 1394–1402* (A. F. Kersting)

into the courtyard, its vaulting illustrates courtly taste at the end of the Middle Ages. The cloisters and the crypt, like so much medieval work, can only be fully appreciated by straining the eyes and cricking the neck, for their glories are the intricately carved bosses where the stone vaulting-ribs meet.

The fire of 1834 freed Westminster Hall from a clutter of ale-houses, shops and other small structures. It is not from the outside, however, that the hall impresses. The walls have been refaced, the windows too have been renewed, and the lantern on the roof is modern. Surrounded by taller buildings, the Hall could not in any way prepare us for the awe-inspiring cavern within. The floorspace, nearly 240 feet by 68 feet in area, was measured for William Rufus; some of his stonework has been uncovered at the southern end of the long east wall, close to our right if we stand on the stone dais, and some Norman capitals are now in the Jewel Tower. The great archway behind and the dais itself are modern, but the hall was always lit by two long rows of a dozen windows; much of the carving, including the regal statues in their niches, is late fourteenth-century. This Norman hall, the longest known, seemed less spacious than its successor, as there were two lines of stone pillars or possibly wooden posts to hold up the roof. It was in 1394 that another lover of the arts, Richard II, began to rebuild the walls and to crown them with the present roof of oak. This roof is of hammerbeams—so called from the horizontal baulks, nearly two feet by three feet thick and ending in carved angels. An enormous area can be spanned by this device of making arches spring from brackets fixed to the wall (*Fig. 22*). No other supports are needed, although the walls have to be strongly buttressed outside, as we can see from Parliament Square. Similar roofs cover many fifteenth-century churches and the halls of Oxford and Cambridge colleges. None is so grand as Westminster's, the earliest that can be dated. Nor is there a European rival, for the hammerbeam was an English triumph. It makes up for the foreign style of the abbey and the palace chapel, built for Richard's French-speaking forbears.

Westminster Hall is unique in history as well as in architecture, for no other place has seen so much drama. This began with the ceremonial deposition of Richard himself in 1399, immortalized by Shakespeare, and the coronation banquet of his usurping cousin Henry IV. Later monarchs also feasted here, until George IV's extravagance made it prudent to end the custom. For four hundred years the hall's size also made it an ideal arena for state trials, where

Fig. 23 *Detail of the vaulting of Henry VII's Chapel in Westminster Abbey, showing the Tudor rose and the Beauforts' portcullis, c. 1503–1512* (National Monuments Record)

sovereigns, consorts and statesmen were brought to judgment, if not to justice. Today they are still brought here, to lie in state.

Westminster Abbey often flies its own flag with the arms ascribed by later heralds to Edward the Confessor: *Azure, a cross patonce between 5 martlets or* (a blue shield bearing a golden cross with ends like fleurs-de-lis and five golden doves). These are also on Westminster City's arms, with Tudor roses and the Beauforts' portcullis to honour Henry VII (*Fig. 23*). Edward, at least, deserves his place. He preferred to build to the glory of God, leaving a pleasure-loving Norman to squander money on a splendid hall, yet it was the fame of his abbey which led to the rise of the palace; while Cnut had probably stayed on Thorney, there had been nothing then to distinguish Westminster from other places near the city but away from its dirt and violence. When the palace became royalty's favourite seat, Westminster inevitably became the centre of government, leaving London as the centre of finance. Although this in turn attracted yet more people to the whole area and forced London quickly to spread westward, the division is as clear as ever today.

The main buildings of Westminster Palace faced courtyards and gardens, rather than the river. There was however a long Thames-side frontage, with a wall, water-stairs and, at least in later times, a quay (*see Fig. 15*). Here the boy king Henry III, stepping into his barge, could look across to the low, straight line of the marshes which formed the far bank. To his right, not opposite the palace but a few hundred yards to the south, lay some fishermen's huts. This was Lambeth, known from Anglo-Saxon times as the hithe or landing-place where lambs were shipped.

Officially Lambeth had nothing to do with the city or Westminster, being in the hundred of Brixton and the county of Surrey, as was the whole of what is now London's south bank. Its marshes were rich in game and lampreys, as well as in pasture for sheep. Before the Conquest there may even have been a large house or two, since King Harthacnut had died there at a wedding feast. Yet until the eighteenth century the hinterland was as bleak as the flats behind Thorney, and the widely flowing Thames permitted only a narrow path, often flooded, where the road now separates the archbishop's walls from the river. Throughout the Middle Ages Lambeth would have been no more than a fishing village, if the building of Westminster Palace had not led the archbishops of Canterbury to settle near at hand.

The primate of England was always at the centre of government. Seeing that this was going to be Westminster, Fitz Stephen's contemporary, Archbishop Baldwin, acquired lands at Lambeth by exchange with the bishop and prior of Rochester. He began to transfer there a college of secular canons and in 1197 his successor, Hubert, became lord of the manor. The monks of Canterbury, fearing that the archbishop would desert them altogether, appealed to Rome and had the project condemned. A new chapel was pulled down and all that was left to the archbishop was a dwelling, either the old manor or the house intended for his priests. This included a private chapel, finished about 1245 for the queen's uncle, Archbishop Boniface, brother of Count Peter who gave his name to the Savoy. While King Henry's work at Westminster was in full swing, Boniface obtained papal leave to start on his own palace at Lambeth. He would not have needed one here if the head of the English church had had his seat in London, as St Augustine had intended, rather than in the east of Kent.

Alone of the medieval mansions along the Thames between London and Westminster, Lambeth Palace enjoys its old site. Moreover, it still houses the prelates for whom it was built. To us it hardly looks palatial, for there is no grandiose and monotonous

85

façade. After more than seven hundred years, it is still a mixed collection of buildings, walled about. This explains its interest and its charm, since princely seats in the Middle Ages looked more like miniature towns than single residences.

Although lack of guides means that people can hardly ever go around these unique quarters, except on a fête day, we ought to know of the treasures that exist there. The oldest part is the chapel's well-proportioned crypt, with low rounded piers of Purbeck marble and pale chalk vaultings. This was finished early in the thirteenth century, before the chapel itself, which was gutted in the Second World War but rededicated in 1955. The chapel still boasts a double doorway of about 1230 and some inlaid floor-tiles, as well as typical Early English lancet windows, grouped in threes and with slender marble shafts. Nearby the rebuilt Guard Room, where the archbishops' soldiers used to rest, has fourteenth-century timbers in its roof. Between the chapel and the river the Water Tower or the Lollards' Tower, finished in 1435, stands on the site of an older building; its fourth floor was a prison, although probably not for Lollards, and the wall-planks are carved with the names of inmates down to Stuart times. South of the Water Tower is the seventeenth-century Great Hall, on the site of the medieval one, which now houses the famous library. Further south is Morton's Tower, a gatehouse built in the 1490s by Henry VII's chancellor, Cardinal Morton, whose own splendour was soon surpassed by Wolsey. Its middle section has two storeys, the wings have five; it is now used mainly to store some of the contents of the library, but original panelling exists in an upper room, as do the names of yet more prisoners.

Morton's successor, Archbishop Warham, is notable chiefly for having lived so long that Wolsey was kept out of the see of Canterbury. If Wolsey had realized this ambition, his itch to build would have transformed Lambeth Palace, as it did York Place across the river. Lambeth would then have excited the cupidity of Henry VIII and probably have been lost to the archbishops for all time. Government offices might later have spread there and Lambeth, not Whitehall, would have become the symbol of bureaucracy. This would have been just, since the civil service was run by clerics in the Middle Ages and was no more popular then than now. In 1381 Wat Tyler's men, fearing documents as instruments of slavery, burned the contents of the palace library before wreaking vengeance on the owner himself.

There is a fine view across the Thames from Victoria Tower Gardens, in particular from a mock-Gothic drinking fountain which stands almost opposite Lambeth Palace. Seen from here the palace is dwarfed on the left by St Thomas's Hospital (now being rebuilt) and on the right by Lambeth Bridge House, a grey slab occupied, curiously, by the Ministry of Public Buildings and Works. In the later Middle Ages, when its walls were reflected in the water, the palace must have dominated an otherwise uneventful scene. On the left rises the Water Tower, with the smaller seventeenth-century Laud's Tower tacked on at one end; both are of pale grey Kentish ragstone. To the right a brick wall runs parallel to the river in front of the present library, which is easily recognizable by the lantern on its roof. At the southern end, near Lambeth Bridge, rise the mellow bricks of Morton's Tower; alongside, so close that it seems to belong to the palace and taller than any part of it, is the tower of St Mary's parish church.

Even if this view were not partly hidden in summer by leaves, it would be worth while taking a closer look. We can cross by Westminster Bridge, north of the Houses of Parliament, or by Lambeth Bridge, from the southern end of Victoria Tower Gardens. The northerly walk gives a superb view of the Houses of Parliament but is otherwise less attractive; the palace seems to shrink even more, when seen sideways from the bridge, and we are led inland behind St Thomas's Hospital before turning right into Lambeth Palace Road. Near this end of the road, however, is an entrance to Archbishop's Park, a public space once covered by the palace orchard. This is a utilitarian park, fringed with fine trees but with no sign of the moat which surrounded three sides under the Tudors. It is separated from the road and the river by a leafy enclosure, still the archbishop's private grounds, and from its southern end we can glimpse over the fence the battlemented nineteenth-century wing where he now lives. His forerunners, like the other magnates who lived along London's riverside, always had a garden; seeds of cabbage, spinach, cucumber and other herbs and vegetables were bought for sowing here in 1321.

The southern approach is much more impressive, in spite of a dangerous roundabout at the far end of Lambeth Bridge. On the left looms Cardinal Morton's magnificent gatehouse. The bricks, all the lovelier for being darkened by nearly five hundred years, are decorated with diamond patterns in black, known as diapering, and are dressed with stone. This is the main entrance to the palace,

87

Fig. 24 *The main gatehouse of Lambeth Palace (Morton's Tower), about 1495, and the tower of St Mary's Church, late 14th century*
(A. F. Kersting)

with an iron bell-pull still in use; it was here, until Victorian times, that bread and meat were doled out to the poor. Immediately to the right, outside the walls, is St Mary's, with its four-stage ragstone tower (*Fig. 24*). The top stage looks clean and, like the body of the church, is a Victorian copy, but the rest of the tower is grimier and dates from the late fourteenth century. Many prelates lie here, where the last phase of medieval sculpture can be seen in canopied tombs on each side of the altar. Lambeth has nothing else from the Middle Ages, but the palace in itself is unique: 'a complex of domestic buildings largely medieval and wholly picturesque, which is of such interest and merit that they [Londoners] would flock to see it, if only it were not so near their homes' (Pevsner).

While fashion headed west, industry moved south. Nothing equalled the chain of mansions stretching for a mile and a half along the river bank, but all these sprang from the endowment of an abbey on the Isle of Thorney. It was more natural for London, a bridge-head enclosure, to spread straight across the river, where busy roads met south of the bridge. Westminster, for all its growing brilliance as a centre of government and the arts, was a royal creation. Southwark, despised and increasingly disreputable, was much older. Its inhabitants, in contrast to those of Westminster, were drawn ever more tightly into the city's net. This was only right, since Southwark was a true offshoot of London.

Southwark's patch of firm ground, which allowed successive bridges to be built, is not obvious. Nothing compares with the twin hills of London and most of the area seems as flat as Westminster or Lambeth. Only as we cross London Bridge and make straight ahead for Borough High Street can we see that we are on a spur of high ground; Duke Street Hill, coming from Tooley Street on the left, is a definite slope which does not entirely owe its origin to the artificial raising of the present road. We know that the famous medieval London Bridge was built some 150 feet east of its successor and that an earlier one may have lain another 100 feet beyond this, but the land was probably unsuitable farther east or west. On one side stretched the marshes of Bermondsey, on the other those of Lambeth—good for grazing but easily flooded and difficult to cross, let alone to build upon. Not until late Tudor times was progress made in draining the levels west of Southwark; previously, the grand houses south of Fleet Street and the Strand looked across the Thames to green fields watered by countless tiny streams, planted here and there with willow-trees and with a few mills along the riverbank.

The Romans had settled a few acres around the southern end of their bridge, although they had not bothered with fortifications. In Anglo-Saxon times, after the rebirth of London, this spot assumed great military importance. The bridge, Southwark's *raison d'être* in days of peace, helped to defend London in wartime by blocking invaders who rowed up the Thames. Since the southern end had to be held against a landing party, it is not surprising that Southwark first emerges as London's southern defensive work or *sud werk*, in the Viking wars. There must have been a very strong defence for Cnut to have resorted to dragging his ships overland, and it was left to William the Conqueror, with no naval problems, to storm Southwark as part of his encirclement of London. The settlement never again played so heroic a part, although by 1086 Domesday Book noted that it had a strand, where ships could tie up, a street, a herring fishery and a minster. Stow recites a tradition that this church had been endowed by one Mary and refounded as a college of priests by Swithin, 'a noble lady', who may in fact have been St Swithin, bishop of Winchester in 852.

The medieval street-plan was simple. Passing under the southern gateway of London Bridge, the traveller could look ahead down the northern stretch of Borough High Street (this part curves rather less obviously today, since the bridge from which it starts lies farther west). Close at hand on his right St Mary Overie's Priory masked Winchester House and Bankside. Unlike the roads along the northern shore, which have been left high and dry by reclamation, Bankside has always clung to the Thames; quick crossings by boat from the city explain why this part became the home of the stews. A few yards inland, on the left, St Olave's Street branched east and ran parallel with the Thames towards Rotherhithe and Greenwich; now corrupted to Tooley Street, this route owes its name to the successive churches, which until 1926 stood near its junction with the High Street. These honoured Olaf Haroldson, who helped Æthelred to drive the Danes from Southwark; as king, Olaf established Christianity in Norway, where he was patriotically revered after his murder by Cnut. By 1379 Bermondsey Street, which now leaves Tooley Street just east of London Bridge Station, led to Bermondsey Abbey. All these were mere tracks beside Borough High Street itself, the backbone of Southwark, which ran south to St George's Church, before forking south-west and south-east. The western branch led to the Elephant and Castle, a later coaching inn, and so to Croydon. The easterly one was called Kent or Kentish Street and, from 1877, Tabard Street, after the inn from which Chaucer's pilgrims set out for Canterbury; leading as it did into Kent, it was also London's highway to the Channel ports.

Southwark's history is complicated by its many lords. The king had always held land there but, in the twelfth and thirteenth centuries, he shared the profits with the Warenne family, as earls of Surrey; king and earl each appointed a bailiff until this right was given to the Londoners in 1327. So began London's takeover, a necessary step if defiant criminals were not to seek refuge across the river. More financial and judicial rights were transferred over the next two hundred years, until in 1550 Edward VI granted the city full control of Southwark, which became Bridge Ward Without. Edward's charter was particularly important since it covered the whole of Southwark, whereas earlier grants had dealt only with the royal estate around the bridge. This in medieval times was called the Gildable Manor, probably because it could be taxed for the geld, and it stretched no farther than today's Borough Market, where Stoney Street joins the High Street.

The biggest landowner was the Church. East of the High Street, as far as the Old Kent Road, lay the Great Liberty Manor of the archbishops of Canterbury, which they held from the twelfth century until Cranmer was forced to yield it to Henry VIII. To the west lay an estate granted to Bermondsey Abbey by Henry I and later confusingly called the King's Manor. By 1189 the monks had leased part of this, in northern Southwark, to the bishops of Winchester, who built their town house here, instead of in London, and also had a gaol, from which their liberty became known as the Clink. Farther west, along the riverbank and reaching to the present boundary with Lambeth, beyond Blackfriars Bridge, another Bermondsey estate was leased in turn to the Templars and the Hospitallers; this covered one hundred acres, which had to be protected by embankments, and was known by the fifteenth century as Paris Garden. It was the Reformation which gathered all these lands under the Crown and so enabled them to be handed over to London.

Southwark's varied ownership matched its character. As a waterfront town, a travellers' terminus and an overflow for those who could not or dared not settle in the capital, it had an exceptionally wild and rootless population. Lime burners, essential for making plaster and mortar, were there in the 1280s; soon they caused such air pollution that the king, on complaints from residents and visitors, insisted that only charcoal or wood, not sea-coal, should be burned in the kilns. Foreigners unable to carry on their business in London naturally chose Southwark: weavers and brewers, mainly from the Low Countries, and leather sellers abounded in the fifteenth century. Inns were everywhere and went on increasing until the palmy coaching days which preceded the first railways.

Prisons multiplied, although neither these nor the Londoners' acquisition of police powers kept down the number of criminals. Eventually the Clink, whose damp, low-lying site added to its evil name, passed into English slang, as a synonym for any prison. There were also the gaols of the Counter or the Compter, which was controlled by the city, and the marshalseas of the royal household and the King's Bench. The last two were for people in the custody of the marshals of England, sentenced or awaiting sentence by the central courts. Other marshalseas had been superseded by the Fleet by 1350 and both survivors had settled side by side in Southwark twenty-five years later, where they became known simply as the Marshalsea and the King's Bench prisons. All these gaols were hated and the marshalseas were sacked in the Peasants' Revolt. Freedom from arrest in the bishop of Winchester's liberty, where the stews lay, and later also in Paris Garden, made the riverside area west of the bridge a byword for sinister pleasures. The stews formed a row, with stairs down to the Thames and signs like those of any tavern—the Bell, the Cross Keys, the Cardinal's Hat. The bishops themselves should not be blamed for them, since most of their property beyond the palace was soon leased out. In Elizabethan times it was natural that London's permanent theatres (apart from the very first, beyond the eastern wall at Shoreditch) should cluster around Bankside.

Sleazy docks, inns, prisons, gaming houses and brothels do not make up the whole picture. After baulking the Danes and defying the Normans, Southwark no longer had to bear the brunt of foreign invasions but for 500 years it was a buffer between London and rebels from Kent. Wat Tyler in 1381 and Jack Cade in 1450 both entered London across the bridge, but only with inside help, and as late as 1554 Sir Thomas Wyatt was thrown back from Southwark and forced to cross upstream. The south bank also had many buildings to match those across the river: the priory of St Mary Overie (over the water), the parish churches of St Margaret, St Mary Magdalene, St Olave and St George, two famous hospitals and a cluster of stately houses. As in all medieval towns, squalor crouched next to grandeur.

St Mary Overie was a house of Augustinian canons, founded in 1106, with help from the Warenne family and the bishop of Winchester. Probably it occupied the site of the mysterious 'minster' mentioned in Domesday Book. Out of the infirmary arose a hospital which they dedicated to St Thomas Becket soon after his canonization in 1173. When fire destroyed the priory about 1212 this hospital was shifted across Borough High Street and developed separately. It narrowly survived the Reformation, when St Thomas Becket was discarded in favour of St Thomas the Apostle, and moved to Lambeth only in 1862. In Kent Street, just beyond the Bar which probably marked the limit of the medieval town, stood the Lock, the only medieval leper hospital in the London area south of the Thames. The Lock, whose origins are obscure, was in the city's charge before 1300 and passed to St Bartholomew's at the Reformation; it outlived leprosy by 200 years and was not closed until 1760. Thanks to the bridge and water transport, northern Southwark was as convenient as the Strand for anyone who wanted to be near the capital and the court. The princely bishops of Winchester, eight of whom became chancellor before the Reformation, were followed by the abbots of St Augustine's, Canterbury, the prior of Lewes, the abbot of Battle and other prelates. Finally Charles Brandon, duke of Suffolk, built Suffolk Place almost opposite St George's Church; he exchanged this mansion with his brother-in-law, Henry VIII, in 1536, and a mint was afterwards set up there. Such variety was typical of the Middle Ages, before towns could be neatly divided into fashionable and unfashionable quarters.

Time has been harsher with Southwark than with Westminster or the city. The early street-plan has suffered from the shifting of the bridge and from the knot of railways. The Reformation destroyed the patronage of churchmen, the Puritans and factory builders drove out the pleasure-seekers, the railways put an end to the inns. There was left a down-at-heels industrial suburb which could show little of its past even before the bombs fell in 1940. There are no inns older than a fragment of the late seventeenth-century George and no relics of the prisons or haunts of vice. St Thomas's, which ranks after St Bartholomew's as London's oldest hospital, has only a street and a former chapel, built in 1703, to mark its 650 years in Southwark. Ironically St Thomas's Street now accommodates a third great teaching hospital, Guy's, which was founded there in 1721. Nothing remains of the Lock, the last of whose buildings was pulled down to make way for Great Dover Street in 1809. All the churchmen's mansions, save one, have entirely disappeared.

Modern Southwark, devoted to everyday business and almost completely lacking in frills, still teems with reminders of the Church's heyday. These are particularly obvious if we turn left after crossing London Bridge and walk along Tooley Street (this can be made a circular tour by continuing for nearly a mile as far as the junction with Tower Bridge Road, where we can turn left to recross the Thames by Tower Bridge and so enjoy the best riverside view of the Tower of London). St Olaf himself lives on not only in the corrupted name of Tooley: in the giant new St Olaf's House near the site of his church, in St Olaf's Bonding Co., farther along opposite the entrance to Battle Bridge Lane, in St Olave's Wharf, reached yet farther along down Abbot's Lane, and in the old St Olave's and St Saviour's Grammar School at the junction with Tower Bridge Road. Battle Bridge Lane and, just beyond, a grey office block are named after the property of Battle Abbey; the lane, now a dingy cul-de-sac, once went to the abbot's private water-stairs. Many similar alleys lead off from what is now a long working street, but none offers a glimpse of the river.

Borough High Street, by contrast, is lined with openings which led to the courtyards of inns (a walk from the railway bridge as far south as St George's Church takes us past, on the left, King's Head Yard, White Hart Yard, Talbot Yard, Three Tuns Passage, Mermaid Court and Angel Place). The names, if not the buildings, are sometimes medieval. Before the Reformation the King's Head was called the Pope's Head and Shakespeare mentions that the White Hart was the headquarters of Jack Cade's rebels; the Tabard, most famous of all, stood on the site of Talbot Yard by 1306, when the abbot of Hyde lodged nearby, but the inn from which Chaucer's pilgrims set out was probably pulled down in 1629 and is now recalled only by a plaque. Almost opposite, where Counter Court joins Borough High Street, a plaque in the wall of the Westminster Bank, facing down the street, records St Margaret's church and the Counter. Farther along the high street a plaque in the wall of the Tile Centre commemorates the Marshalsea burned by Wat Tyler's mob. Close by another plaque, in the wall of the Metropolitan Police Recruiting Centre, records the King's Bench gaol, and yet another one against the fence outside St George's reminds us of the medieval church and the fair held here, where the highways from Kent and Surrey met.

The only mansion of which anything remains is Winchester House to the west of London Bridge. This was used by the bishops until Stuart times, for the scholarly Lancelot Andrewes, who lies in the cathedral, died here in 1626. It became a prison for royalists in the Civil War and was never completely pulled down, since it was afterwards split up among several tenants. Piecemeal rebuildings preserved the old layout and explain the survival of part of the great hall, which, like that of the archbishops at Lambeth, overlooked the Thames. Fitz Stephen says that Becket was entertained here on his last journey from London to Canterbury. The hall itself, enlarged in about 1340, took up most of the first floor, with some private rooms under the same long roof at the east end. Its gabled western wall and part of its southern wall still stand. The first boasts three small doorways and, high up, a fine rose-window measuring about twelve feet across. All are now blocked up, as are two more doorways in the southern wall.

The site of Winchester House is now hemmed in by the river to the north, by the cathedral to the east and by the railway as it curves to cross the Thames into Cannon Street station. Just before the trains rumble onto the bridge they pass over Clink Street, behind which lie Winchester Square, outlining exactly the courtyard of the bishops' palace, and Winchester Walk. Since Southwark's only medieval monument is often thought to be the cathedral, it is rewarding to cross the road outside its great west door and plunge into this Dickensian maze of narrow lanes between tall warehouses. Clink Street leads first to Winchester Square, now filled with lorries and crates, where a plaque in the wall of Pickford's warehouse on the northern side recalls the palace. A further twist takes us to the section closest to the river, with the railway bridge at the end. On the left a piece of rough medieval wall some three feet six inches thick is sandwiched between two warehouses; this is the end of the great hall, where the bishops' rose-window can just be seen by squinting sideways from across the street. The doorways below are not visible and neither is the southern wall, which now forms part of Pickfords' building. Farther on, where Clink Street narrows into a dark passage before reaching the railway bridge, the prison itself once brooded by the river.

Another relic of the Middle Ages awaits us at the far end of the High Street. A few yards beyond Borough underground station a turning on the left, Trinity Street, leads to the beautiful early Victorian Trinity Church Square. A lawn, ringed with plane trees and a wire fence, lies before the imposing north entrance of a neglected church. In the middle, larger than life, stands a fourteenth-century king, in a high crown and long robes (*Fig. 25*). The statue resembles those carved for Richard II in Westminster Hall and may have come from there. Although weatherbeaten, the figure is so unexpected that it is seen to much better advantage than if it were ranged with its peers.

The disappearance of the rest of old Southwark has enhanced what was always its chief glory. Apart from Westminster Abbey—unique, because it became a royal shrine—St Bartholomew-the-Great and St Helen Bishopsgate, Southwark Cathedral is the only survivor of London's monastic churches. These were far richer and grander than the parish churches which mostly survived the

Fig. 25 (left) *Statue of a king in Trinity Church Square, Southwark,*
14th century (National Monuments Record)
Fig. 26 (right) *Timber bosses from the roof of Southwark Cathedral,*
15th century (National Monuments Record)

Reformation. The cathedral's full title, the Collegiate and Cathedral
Church of St Saviour and St Mary Overie, helps to explain its
chequered history. It started as the church of the priory of St Mary
Overie, the rest of whose buildings lay farther north near the river
(their position, with Winchester House to the west, is shown on a
wooden model in the cathedral's retrochoir). The chapter house,
refectory, dormitories and other quarters fell into lay hands and
eventually into ruin after the suppression of the priory in 1539,
but the church itself was saved by the creation of a new parish,
St Saviour's. It was the old parish churches of St Margaret and
St Mary Magdalene which vanished and the priory church which
remained, presumably because of its grandeur and the prestige of
the bishops of Winchester. After many adventures, it became a
cathedral when the first bishop of Southwark was enthroned in 1905.

Accidents, too, have changed and menaced the priory church of

St Mary Overie (to use its medieval name). The blaze which swept through Southwark in July 1212 or 1213 made necessary a new church. Ambitious plans, slow in fulfilment, were again thwarted by a fire during the reign of Richard II and the collapse in 1469 of the nave's stone roof, which was replaced by one in wood. The most romantic external feature, the four slender pinnacles on the tower, was not added until late Stuart times. By the early nineteenth century much of the fabric was so rotten that there were calls for its complete demolition; it was damp, too big and, above all, it obstructed the way to the new London Bridge. Drastic restoration eventually won the day, so that visitors who now use the main entrance step into the south-west corner of a nave which dates only from the 1890s; it is in fact the second nave to have been built under Victoria. In spite of everything, Southwark Cathedral is inferior only to Lambeth Palace among the medieval remains of London's south bank. The nave, for all its dullness, at least resembles the thirteenth-century original. This was the earliest Gothic building of its size in the area, tall, severe and betraying the French up-bringing of its creator, Bishop Peter des Roches. It probably influenced the nave at Westminster, begun some thirty years later.

Inside, left of the south-west entrance, are three of Peter des Roches's arcades. Opposite, the north wall holds part of a doorway and recess from the still earlier Norman church. Farther along this wall, near John Gower's brightly painted tomb, a modern door leads to the vestry; on the other side we can see the jambs of another twelfth-century arch, the only sizeable piece of Norman work. The eastern parts of the church have fared better. The walls and arches of the north transept and choir date from the thirteenth century. Those of the south transept are fourteenth century, with repairs carried out in the fifteenth century by Cardinal Beaufort, bishop of Winchester. The outlines of two Norman arches, completely renewed, lead from the north transept to the site of an early chapel which was later used as a vestry before its reconstruction by members of Harvard University in honour of John Harvard, who was christened at Southwark in 1607. The high altar is backed by a stone screen given by another bishop, Richard Fox, in 1520; the figures are modern but the screen itself is one more example of how churches were lovingly embellished up to the eve of the Reformation. The screen masks an unusual thirteenth-century plan for the east end, where a large retrochoir faces four chapels. This area was put to many secular uses and thoroughly but faithfully restored in the

97

nineteenth century; when the church became a cathedral, it was set aside for local parishioners.

Most fascinating of all is the collection of thirty-six bosses in the north-western corner of the nave. These vividly grotesque pieces are from the roof which was put up in 1469 and removed in the nineteenth century. Others survive in the tower but only here can such a collection be studied at leisure, without binoculars. More than any beautiful and pious work of art, these simple carvings bring us close to the medieval craftsmen. Grim or comic subjects were often slipped in among the more usual designs of flowers and foliage. Here, they include Gluttony, with his bloated face, Lying, with his snake-like tongue, a long-nosed King and the Devil gleefully making a meal of Judas Iscariot (*Fig. 26*).

Most of the other monuments are post-medieval. There is however the restored tomb-figure of a knight from about 1280, like those in the Temple Church but unusual in being not of stone or marble but of oak; this lies against the north wall of the choir aisle, left of the high altar. Against the north wall of the nave are the canopied tomb and effigy of John Gower, who shared with his contemporary Chaucer in the revival of English poetry after centuries of rule by a French-speaking court; the red, green, black and gold of his renovated monument remind us of the brilliance of medieval churches. Farther west along the same wall, in front of the much repaired Norman recess, has been placed the worn stone effigy of a corpse mouldering under a shroud—a fifteenth-century reminder, comforting to the poor, of the fate of all flesh. In the south transept the middle shaft of the east wall displays the carved, repainted arms of its builder, Beaufort, under his cardinal's hat; the lilies of France and leopards of England proclaim the royal blood of the cardinal-bishop, who was notoriously rich and active in politics for over forty years. After his death, frighteningly depicted by Shakespeare in *Henry VI—Part Two*, Beaufort was buried in his own cathedral at Winchester.

Everyone who goes by train to Cannon Street station passes within a few yards of Southwark Cathedral, now all the more striking for the cleaning of its stone. Considering the demands of industry and transport its survival seems a miracle, for no comparable building is so placed. Its threatening surroundings at first appear shameful but on second thoughts it seems right that a church which has always looked down on bustle and dirt should not now be bypassed in some quiet close. There is nothing like this contrast to advertise the persistence of the faith of the men who founded St Mary Overie, and of their predecessors who had a church at this end of the wooden bridge before the Conquest.

Southwark grew because of London, which itself grew up around the bridge. We know very little of the structures which must have served the Romans, the Saxons and the Normans, but obviously traffic increased with the volume of trade. Mindful of their dependence on the bridge, Londoners left lands and money for its upkeep and costs are first mentioned as early as 1130. After the fire of 1136 a new bridge had to be built, perhaps the one of elm mentioned in 1163. Its architect was Peter of Colechurch, chaplain of the now vanished church of St Mary Colechurch, on the north side of Poultry, where Thomas Becket had been christened. Peter, as a learned clerk, may have headed some brotherhood which administered the funds of the bridge. His fame rests not on the new wooden structure but on a unique work of stone, begun in 1176 and crucial to London's history for over six hundred years—what is now remembered as Old London Bridge.

The challenge can hardly be exaggerated. Londoners set great store by tradition—wisely, since it formed the basis of so many of their privileges. Such a stone bridge was unheard of, nothing of any size having been attempted in Western Europe after the fall of the Roman Empire. It would be expensive, since there were no quarries near at hand. The work would be difficult, dangerous and slow, since the foundations would have to rest on the soft bed of a tidal river. In spite of all this, Peter took charge of a project which was finished only in 1209, four years after his death. Henry II put a special tax on wool and the archbishop of Canterbury headed a crowd of donors, but the plan would never have been accepted if there had not been citizens of extraordinary wealth, boldness and vision.

Old London Bridge had nineteen pointed arches, springing from twenty massive piers. The piers themselves rested on starlings, lozenge-shaped enclosures of elm piles driven into the Thames mud, filled with rubble and capped with flat beams of oak. Tide must repeatedly have slowed up this grim work—there were forty deaths even during the seven-year building of the nineteenth-century bridge. Picturesque Tudor and Stuart drawings are not entirely accurate, but these and later architects' notes show that the arches were unequally spaced, either because of rebuilding or because of

99

faults in the river bed. The average width planned for the openings seems to have been 28 feet and that for the piers 20 feet. The total length was almost 906 feet, the road on top being 20 feet wide and probably rising in mid-stream, where it ran about 13 feet above high-water at spring tides.

The bridge looked so picturesque from the river because it was lined with buildings. The earliest houses, of wood, were quickly put up, probably because their rents helped to meet the costs. Two arches back from the Southwark end stood the main gateway, which was soon built in stone. This was only the first defence, for the seventh archway from the south was crossed by a drawbridge, which could be hauled up against another gateway; this inner gateway existed by 1258 and it, too, was rebuilt in stone in 1426. Beyond, on the eleventh pier from the south, was a two-storey chapel dedicated to St Thomas Becket; its lower chamber or undercroft could be reached at low tide by boatmen who landed on the starling. Peter himself paid for this chapel and was buried beneath its black and white marble floor.

During the fire of 1212 or 1213 a freak of the wind set alight to houses at either end, trapping a crowd which had massed on the bridge to gape at the burning of Southwark. The chapel itself, which would have been of stone, was badly damaged on this occasion, and it was completely rebuilt at the end of the fourteenth century. Throughout the Middle Ages more ambitious buildings were piled on top of Peter's arches, so that the traveller passed between a double line of shops; occasional gaps gave glimpses of the river, but elsewhere the houses almost met overhead. A model in the London Museum shows the bridge as it was in 1600, at its most elaborate. Not until the mid-eighteenth century were the last of the super-structures demolished and the roadway widened to make room for more traffic.

Old London Bridge defied nature. The nineteen piers alone, taking up some 400 feet, acted as a partial dam; reinforcements around the starlings and waterwheels in some of the arches left a total passageway of perhaps as little as 150 feet, one sixth of the river's natural width. Water, held up at the tide's ebb and flow, roared so furiously through the openings that it was always dangerous and at many hours impossible to get through by boat. The freezing of the Thames, so often described in old stories and prints, can also be traced to this creation of a gigantic pool. Pressure from water and blocks of ice against the stones led to yet more buttressing, so that the mill-race grew narrower and fiercer with every century.

No investment has paid off so well. Old London Bridge was never taken by storm and it was without a rival until the opening of Westminster Bridge in 1749. Only in 1831 did Peter's structure give way to the one which was sold to an American oil corporation in 1968, whose five arches allowed freer passage up the river. The much repaired medieval piers were then dismantled, after an amazingly long life for such practical objects. All old cities were built by rivers and needed bridges, but London had a European landmark. It was started one year before the famous crossing of the Rhône at Avignon and can have had no foreign model, although work on Old Elvet Bridge in Durham had begun perhaps two years earlier.

Old London Bridge reached the northern bank immediately west of St Magnus the Martyr, so that the traveller from Southwark could either go left or right along Thames Street, or straight ahead up Fish Street Hill. The bridge thus lay a hundred feet to the east of its successor, whose traffic is carried on an arch over the point where Upper Thames Street now becomes Lower Thames Street and so up the nineteenth-century King William Street to the city centre. Today stone stairs lead to the foot of this archway, from where we can turn east towards the smells of Billingsgate. Adelaide House, which blocks all view of the river, grudgingly gives way to a small, paved yard, flanked on the other side by the grimy walls of St Magnus the Martyr. The church, rebuilt after the Great Fire, has a blue plaque commemorating the roadway to Old London Bridge. Among the uneven paving stones and bedraggled shrubs are two blocks of white stone, which formed part of the northern-most medieval arch. This was discovered intact only in 1920, during preparations for starting Adelaide House, but could not be saved for lack of £7,000. The courtyard also contains two flower-troughs, which are largely made up of smaller pieces of carved masonry. In the church porch are a squared post from a Roman wharf and a shorter rounded piece, its top coated with birds' droppings, as-cribed to Peter's bridge of 1176. Seated in this sunless corner, on a bench provided by the Worshipful Company of Fishmongers, it is hard to believe that here, every week for over six hundred years, thousands passed on their way from London to the south.

CHAPTER FOUR

London and the Kingdom

The men of London were a political force before the Conquest. Their claims and actions, and efforts to subdue them or win them over, show that this influence persisted during the Middle Ages. The picture is clearer if we look at their role in the kingdom before the growth of their own institutions, remembering that the threads were interwoven, since national importance made possible the march to self-government. 'Londoners' or 'citizens' here are simply those who happened to act for the city at a particular time; there were always factions, so there could be no steady drive towards independence.

William the Conqueror, by building the White Tower, made London a vital military prize. Although the Tower was governed separately, England's mightiest castle and biggest arsenal was physically part of London. The fortress might hold out while Londoners changed sides; it never fell to anyone who had not first gained the streets. The strong rule of the first three Normans gave the citizens no chance to assert themselves, although we have seen that Henry I allowed them to pay their own taxes and choose their own officers. When Henry died in Normandy on 1 December 1135 the picture changed. While his daughter Matilda was still with her husband in Anjou, the dead king's nephew Stephen hurried across the Channel to snatch the Crown. He was barred from Dover and Canterbury but an anonymous partisan says that he pressed on to London, 'the queen of the whole kingdom', whose people unanimously approved his claim. They naturally wanted a quick decision—war being bad for trade—and they also struck some sort of bargain to strengthen their privileges. We do not know the terms but can see, after nearly a century, a return to the citizens' Anglo-

Saxon habit of acclaiming a new ruler on their own. Stephen dashed on to secure the treasury at Winchester—he was the last claimant to have to do this, as it was moved to Westminster before 1200—and was back for his coronation within three weeks of his uncle's death.

London stuck to its choice even after Matilda had plunged the kingdom into civil war. At the height of her success in 1141 she was hailed as 'Lady of the English' by the captive Stephen's own brother, Bishop Henry, in his cathedral city of Winchester. Hoping to sway the doubters, Henry sent for a delegation of Londoners who, he flatteringly explained, held the leading place in England. They came, spoke in vain for their king and left without committing themselves. Some two months later Matilda was grudgingly admitted to London, where a 'commune' or sworn association had been formed, presumably to defend the liberties wrung from Stephen. Matilda, who could not change her title to that of queen until she had been crowned at Westminster, was already losing friends by her arrogance. She now insulted the Londoners for refusing a large sum of money, retired outside the gates and, in the words of a partisan of Stephen, 'with too much boldness ... was just bent on reclining at a well-cooked feast', when the citizens stormed out 'like thronging swarms from beehives' (*Gesta Stephani*). Matilda was lucky to escape and her cause never recovered. London quickly followed up its rebuff by sending nearly a thousand men to take part in her rout at Winchester, and in 1145 it helped Stephen to reduce Faringdon Castle in Berkshire, so averting a new attack from the west.

A fascinating thread in this struggle is London's feud with the most notorious of robber barons, Geoffrey de Mandeville, earl of Essex. Geoffrey was one of Stephen's supporters, who joined Matilda only to desert her after her expulsion from London. He had succeeded his father as constable of the Tower and, as a key figure, could extort lands and offices from either side. Not content with being sheriff of Essex and Hertfordshire, he was made sheriff of Middlesex (including London) by both Stephen and Matilda. Although Geoffrey's grandfather had held this office, his own appointment, making him responsible for justice and tax collecting, violated the freedom granted to London by Henry I. Mutual hereditary loathing is clear from a treaty in 1142 which marked the earl's second desertion of the king: Matilda must make no separate peace with the citizens, who are his 'mortal enemies'. Deprived of the Tower by Stephen, Geoffrey soon afterwards seized a Fenland abbey from which he indulged in an orgy of ransom, torture and pillage. He was killed in 1144 and his body, denied consecrated burial, was taken to London; there it dangled from a tree in an orchard belonging to the Templars, before being ignominiously buried. One of the effigies in the Temple Church may be that of Geoffrey; it was carved about a hundred years after his death and needed much restoration after the Second World War.

In 1153 the weary Stephen agreed that Matilda's son Henry should succeed him. It was under Henry II that Fitz Stephen wrote his description. This, for London, was a quiet time. In 1155 the young king confirmed its privileges, although without mentioning the sheriff, and a charter granted to Oxford stated that its customs would be those of London, whose citizens would settle any problems. Looking back, we can see that London needed such spells of calm, but that anarchy, too, had advantages; peace led to prosperity and so to dreams of independence that could only be satisfied when the Crown was weak; Henry II did not allow the Londoners to choose their own sheriffs; he named them himself and raised the lump sum due in taxation from £300 to £500.

An opening came when Henry was succeeded by Richard the Lionheart, who reigned for ten years and spent only six months in England. Thanks to his romantic adventures, this neglectful Crusader is the only medieval monarch commemorated out of doors by a statue, set up in 1860 in Old Palace Yard. 'If I could have found a buyer,' the new king joked, 'I would have sold London itself.' Richard sailed for Palestine, leaving the government to his chancellor William Longchamp. In 1190 Longchamp, in a bid to regain popularity, allowed the Londoners once more to elect their sheriffs and pay their own taxes in a lump sum of £300. This merely restored the rights granted sixty years earlier by Henry I, but next year the chancellor fell foul of the king's brother, Count John. Longchamp's crimes were recited at a folkmoot by St Paul's and the citizens joined John's party in announcing his deposition. For this and for recognizing John's own claims they were rewarded with the right to form a commune, an organized government on northern French lines, under the first mayor. It is only with hindsight that this grant stands out as a landmark on the road to independence. Richard, for whom London was simply a milch cow, returned in 1194; evidently he accepted the old lump payments and also the commune, but he extracted the equivalent of several years' taxes with fine of 1500 marks (£1,000). When John succeeded Richard in 1199, the payments were confirmed for a further fine, twice as heavy; the citizens could not even have a copy of this charter without supplying the new king with wine and a palfrey.

Under John, a strange mixture of sloth and misdirected energy, the Angevin Empire broke up. Normandy was lost in 1204 and the cost of belated attempts to turn back the French tide only stirred up more trouble at home. The Londoners, to whom John had shown himself too fond of a hard bargain, at last had the whip-hand. On 9 May 1215, five weeks before he was forced to sign Magna Carta at Runnymede, the king tried to win them over by confirming all their liberties and allowing them for the first time to elect the mayor every year—a step which gave them much closer control over their governors. In spite of John's wiles, his enemies were soon admitted to London by a faction. Although they failed to insert a clause into Magna Carta which would have prevented the king from levying extraordinary taxes upon them at will, the mayor and two other citizens were among the twenty-five barons appointed to see that John kept his word. He had no intention of doing so, and England slipped back into civil war. As in Stephen's time, London's role became crucial, although now it was the headquarters of the rebels. The barons organized several large tournaments—mock battles or military exercises, not the formal jousts of later days—but decided against one at Stamford, in Lincolnshire, since it was too far from London. This became more and more the centre of resistance, as John regained lost ground, until in despair the throne was offered to Louis, heir to the king of France, who made straight for London to be acclaimed in May 1216. The pope, now John's protector, replied by placing the city under an interdict, which meant that no sacraments could be administered there. John died in November, leaving as heir the five-year-old Henry III, and for a time it seemed that London had backed the winner. Gradually however England turned against Louis, who retired to France after two years. His bid had been a serious one, thanks to the power-base which he had found in London. Five years later, a brief flare-up of discontent led to shouts of 'Louis of France!' in the streets.

The miscalculation concerning Louis did London little harm, whereas the misfortunes of John were of lasting benefit. Although Bordeaux and its neighbourhood had been saved from the wreck, these were such a long way off that the king generally had to stay in England. The Anglo-Norman barons also became more settled, since most gave up their French estates for their English ones. The primitive government machine, shaped in the royal household to administer an empire, was now confined to England. Apart from the financial department it still followed the king, but his circuit was smaller and London and Westminster were visited more often. By John's death the records and main storehouse of the treasury had finally joined the Exchequer there, so completing the first step in the evolution of a capital. Magna Carta took a second step, in answer to popular demand. No one liked chasing after the royal justices, particularly in cases between one subject and another which were of no direct interest to the king. These, like the work of the Exchequer, were now taken 'out of court', and Westminster became the fixed meeting place for the justices of the Common Bench (the later Court of Common Pleas).

The long reign of Henry III repeated the old lesson, that London could wring nothing from a strong king but might take advantage of a weak one. The citizens, fearful for their hard-won rights, were always jealous of royal authority and during Henry's youth they fastened their hatred on his minister Hubert de Burgh, who fell in 1232. Henry himself grew up as the friend of a foreign clique whose greed and ostentation helped to turn London against him. Paradoxically, his expensive tastes proved beneficial, for he spent so much time at Westminster that officials grew used to working there, drawing still more people to London. At last, in 1258, a baronial party led by Simon de Montfort forced the king to accept its guidance under the Provisions of Oxford, which the mayor and leading citizens quickly ratified at the Guildhall. The tension which followed snapped in 1263 when Henry, hoping to break loose, demanded an oath of loyalty from the chief men of the kingdom, including those of London. On a July day, as Queen Eleanor tried to make her way from the Tower to Windsor, her barge was pelted with mud and stones and she was forced to turn back. Henry quickly reaffirmed the provisions, but too late to save the city and the Tower from falling into the hands of De Montfort.

Once again London became the baronial headquarters. Henry and his son Edward moved to Croydon, while Simon watched from Southwark. Any king could buy the support of a few rich citizens, and Henry now plotted with four of these to trap his enemy by closing the bridge and gates behind him, while the royal forces advanced from the south. News leaked out and a crowd, forcing its way through to Southwark, hustled Simon back to safety. Under the mayor, a De Montfort partisan, Londoners prepared to give whatever help they could in the battle which loomed. They fared badly at Lewes on 14 May 1264, when Edward's cavalry rode them down by the hundred, but Simon won and soon led Henry, king now only in name, to lodgings by St Paul's. Next year Simon took a step which earned him a place among the fathers of English liberty. Under various names the king's own circle of advisers had long been enlarged on special occasions into a great council, attended by the lords spiritual and temporal. To these Simon now added members of the third estate, the commons—two knights from every county and two burgesses from certain towns. Since he excluded several royalist magnates who by custom should have been at such meetings, this was not strictly a Parliament, although it was the forerunner of many. It sat in the obvious place, under the eye of Simon's citizen followers at Westminster.

Everything changed a few weeks later with Simon's death at the battle of Evesham. London could give money, arms and shelter to rebels, the mob could run wild, but citizens were becoming less and less like soldiers and were no match for mounted knights. Henry did not have to batter his way into the city which had comforted his enemies and insulted his queen. The clock was put back seventy-five years, for mayor and commune were swept away and power was vested in two royal seneschals whose seat was not the Guildhall but the Tower. Simon's main adherents forfeited their property and were driven out, and everyone had to contribute towards a crushing fine of 20,000 marks which it took thirty-five years to pay. Inevitably the Londoners tried to escape from this burden by rallying to a new rebel, the earl of Gloucester, in 1267. For two months the royal garrison in the Tower was cut off, while the citizens dug a ditch around their wall and fortified Southwark. Negotiation averted a long siege, which might have ended in fearful destruction, and royal favour again had to be won back. Every medieval king, whether warlike, pious or simply pleasure-loving, tried to squeeze what he could out of London. The citizens recognized that they owed something but were determined to pay only what was customary or necessary. At the same time they saw the need of strong government in the kingdom at large, while kings knew better than to kill geese which laid golden eggs. In 1270 municipal rights were fully restored. Two years later Henry III became the first king since the Confessor to die and to be buried at Westminster (*Fig. 27*).

Edward I, who followed his father, ranks with Henry II among

Fig. 27 *Bronze head of Nenry III (idealized) from his tomb in Edward the Confessor's Chapel, Westminster Abbey, 1291–3* (National Monuments Record)

England's greatest kings, feared by all in his day and admired by posterity for a restless interest in every field of government, which led to far-reaching reforms. Edward was adept at bringing his subjects into line and tapping their resources. London, sheltering behind jealously guarded privileges, was for him like a luxuriant, prickly plant; it had to be pruned so that he could grasp the fruit and, indeed, for its own sake, so as to encourage still stronger growth. At first he worked through a reforming mayor, Henry le Waleys, before suspending the commune, when Waleys's successor protested against a special judicial inquiry. For thirteen years London submitted to a warden at the Tower, while Edward used this chance to attract more merchants from abroad by guaranteeing justice and enabling them to become full citizens. His decrees, later confirmed by charter, helped to make London still more of an

international market. They were fiercely resented by native monopo-
lists and his grip on civic power was still more widely unpopular.
Twice he refused to restore the mayor and nothing could be done
until his hand was forced by a baronial revolt. Altogether Edward's
rule was salutary, although it did not allow London to play much
part in the drama of high politics.

Edward I, although intent on bringing the Church to heel, was
orthodox enough to hate the Jews, as well as shrewd enough to cash
in on their unpopularity. Their lot had grown worse since Fitz
Stephen's time. Papal decrees, including one that their clothes
should be marked, were zealously enforced. John, whose loss of
Normandy had cut the Jews off from their nearest continental kin,
had used all his savage ingenuity to extort money, but at least he
had respected the source: 'If I give my peace even unto a dog,' he
warned the mayor, 'it must be kept inviolate.' Henry III, for whose
love of the arts all had to pay, had bled them with no regard for the
future, and had mortgaged the entire community to his relatives.
Worst of all, the Jews, tolerated only to serve the king, became
targets for his enemies. As early as 1215 the baronial party attacked
Jewish houses, which were pulled down to help repair the city wall.
Simon de Montfort, who had set a local precedent by driving all
Jews out of Leicester, let loose a massacre before the burden of
government after the battle of Lewes opened his eyes to their value.
Even a joyous mob was dangerous: at the coronation of Henry III
and again at his marriage, Jews were taken into the Tower for their
own safety. Between a king who squeezed them dry and an opposi-
tion which resented every drop they gave, forced to be harsher than
ever on their Gentile creditors, the Jews were caught in a vicious
downward spiral. Edward forbade them to lend money but, in a
climate so poisoned, he could not secure them openings in any
ordinary business. Secret usury was added to the crimes of which
they had long been suspected, ranging from the ritual murder of
small boys to plotting for the king in the civil wars. Protection
brought dwindling returns, as they were confined to ever fewer
towns, so the king was taking the easiest way out when he gave the
remnants less than four months to leave England, on pain of death.
The last wretches tramped out of London on 10 October 1290; a
party of their richer fellows had already sailed, only to be tempted
by the ship's captain to alight on a sandbank at the Thames estuary,
where they had been left to drown.

London's finest legacy from the medieval Jews is Westminster

Abbey, which could hardly have been built so quickly or so magnificently without their forced contributions. Jewish homes, to judge by surviving examples at Lincoln, were grander than any others in the city, and part of their stonework must still be embedded in stretches of the wall. The shabby story of their treatment lives on in a few names, for covetous Gentiles forced the Jews to spread out from their original area between Cheapside and Coleman Street, which are still linked by the street called Old Jewry. The church of St Lawrence Jewry recalls the large numbers which settled farther west and, more sombrely, Jewry Street off Aldgate probably commemorates those who crept closer to the protecting garrison in the Tower.

Edward I, after seizing the Jews' bonds and immovable property, was gratefully voted extra sums by Church and laity. Yet the gain was soon outweighed by the disappearance of money-lenders, and is one reason why he turned to raising taxes through Parliament. The English were unskilled in finance, since the Church condemned usury as sternly as ever, and the Jews were replaced by Italian merchants, who had come to banking by way of collecting taxes for the Papacy. For fifty years settlers from Italy lent their services to the first three Edwards and by 1318 an important east-west thoroughfare had changed its name from Langbourn Street to Lombard Street. As wars brought the Crown more heavily into debt, these bankers in turn became baronial and popular scape-goats. By the 1340s the unpopularity of the leading houses allowed the king to repudiate his debt, and so to bring them to bankruptcy.

Edward, who proclaimed his own son the first Plantagenet prince of Wales, enlarged the realm which London served. In 1295 he required two knights from every shire and two burgesses from several towns to join the peers in a uniquely diverse assembly, in some ways the first and therefore called the 'Model' Parliament. There was nothing to ensure that this device would last or that Parliament would win control of taxation, the basis of its later power. It met because Edward wanted money and at first it acted mainly as a court of law. Often the lower clergy too were represented and sometimes there were no burgesses, although in the next reign the former faded out, to discuss their own affairs in Convocation, and from 1325 the commons were always included. Kings ceased to bargain with the city over extra taxation but won parliamentary approval for a general level, applicable to London as to other towns. At the same time Parliaments, by bringing men from all over

England to debate in the king's palace and to lodge nearby, helped to weld London and Westminster into a capital.

This rise of a political centre was slow and uncertain. London's economic primacy came early. Municipal independence followed more slowly but, for all its setbacks, inevitably. The distinction of being the main seat of government was quite another thing: royal patronage singled out Westminster, but much of the administration still accompanied the king, and Parliaments could be summoned anywhere. Long after Winchester had been eclipsed there was still time for a new political centre to arise, and under Edward I there was a danger that this would happen. When interfering with London's liberties the king may have decided that it would be chastening to carry on the government from elsewhere, which would anyway have been more convenient. During his Welsh campaigns the Exchequer and the judges of the Common Bench habitually met at Shrewsbury, and from 1298 until 1305 at York, the centre for his less successful operations against Scotland. Minor offices and some treasure stayed behind in the south—the storehouse in Westminster Abbey's Chapel of the Pyx being robbed in 1303— and both Chancery and Exchequer were left there in his last war, but they were again at York in the next two reigns. If Scotland had been overrun, York would have made a more central capital for the united kingdom. As it was, while London continued to flourish as the chief port, Westminster fared very badly during these pre-occupations with the north: eventually its embittered inhabitants, deprived of great men's patronage, were to secure a commission of inquiry which revealed a drastic loss in rents.

Administrative machinery could not stop a king from digging his own grave. Edward I was a success because he had sound judgment, and none of the assets which he left in 1307 could prevent the reign of his son from resembling the troubled years of Henry III, even if they had not been counter-balanced by heavy debts and an un-finished war. Out of sympathy with the baronage, a prey to favourites and, after his defeat by the Scots at Bannockburn in 1314, a despised military failure, Edward II see-sawed between self-assertion and thraldom to his enemies. Fighting, however, took place mainly in the north, so that London did not figure prominently on either side, as it had in earlier wars. The king cannot have been popular, for in 1321 he too temporarily took London into his own hands, when pressed to repay its loans, but it was only after eighteen years that the citizens' hostility became crucial, in the tragedy of his dethronement. After 1322 Edward ruled unchallenged through his favourites, the Hugh Despensers, father and son, Angered at their rise, the queen, Isabel of France, retired to her native land where she became the mistress of her husband's enemy, Roger Mortimer, who had escaped from the Tower. On 24 September 1326 Isabel and her fourteen-year-old elder son, Edward, landed with Mortimer in Suffolk. She at once asked for help from London, where a party may already have been in league with her, and then marched to Dunstable in Bedfordshire, only thirty-three miles from the uneasy capital. Edward strengthened the Tower, put a price on Mortimer's head and, on 30 September, had a papal denunciation of the invaders (originally aimed at the Scots) read out at Paul's Cross. So lukewarm were the people that he at once fled to the west, where his power melted away.

London, which had ignored Isabel's first request, now made it safe for her to continue west in pursuit. Her charges against the Despensers were published and on 15 October a mob forced the mayor to offer her his support. The royal treasurer Walter Stapledon, bishop of Exeter (remembered as co-founder of Exeter College, Oxford), rode to help mediate at Lambeth but was dragged from his horse near St Paul's and hustled through the churchyard to Cheapside, where his head was hacked off with a butcher's knife. Killings spread, the Tower was surrendered and the houses of the Bardi, the Despensers' Florentine bankers, were sacked. Stapledon's corpse, after a night in the cathedral, was brought to St Clement Danes opposite his inn, where it was turned away by the terrified rector, who had been his nominee. A woman onlooker threw a cloak over the body, which was buried without ceremony; the head was already on its way to the queen. London was committed to the revolution by the bishop's murder. Edward, run to earth in South Wales, was lodged in the Midlands while Parliament met on 7 January 1327 at Westminster Hall, with a mob elbowing through the doors. Londoners took part in all that followed. A deputation asked the magnates to replace Edward with his son; inflammatory sermons and speeches were churned out; representatives of all the estates of the realm marched to Guildhall to swear support for whatever Parliament might decide and for the rights of the city; finally, after the archbishop of Canterbury had announced a unanimous verdict of dethronement, another deputation including three citizens demanded acceptance by the king at Kenilworth. Edward, cowed with the threat that his son too might be cast aside, submitted and passed into the darkness of harsher captivity, which ended with his probably agonizing death in Berkeley Castle.

The revolution set an ugly precedent. In over 250 years since the Norman Conquest no king had been deposed and only two had died violently, William Rufus by assassination in the New Forest and Richard the Lionheart from a chance arrow before the walls of Châlus. In the next 160 years three were to be murdered and one was to be killed in battle; even the direct succession, saved in 1327, was to be broken. Why did London help to bring Edward down? Partly because it resented royal power, particularly as wielded by his minions. The Despensers were of good birth but had been raised too high—for town dwellers of all classes, however despised by the aristocracy, always felt extraordinarily bitter about upstarts. Jealous nobles gave a lead, making it easy for others to follow. More important was the attraction of looting for the really poor. The mob got out of hand and the rich were swept along, saving themselves by sacrificing those associated with the fallen king. The riots, which lasted for a month until Isabel authorized the election of a new mayor, show once again how thin was the crust of law and order. To be fair, none of the citizens could see the full consequences of what they were doing. Deposition was not officially discussed until after the meeting of Parliament, which had been summoned in the king's name, and after it had been falsely announced that he refused to attend. He did not die until eight months later, after two plots to rescue him. Moreover Londoners did not start this nor any other movement to overthrow the king. Yet Isabel's party carefully involved them in every step, presumably to share the blame, and they may have tipped the balance—unexpectedly, considering all Edward's precautions. Nothing seems to have been left to him after he abandoned London, and when the city dropped like a ripe plum into the hands of his enemies, the kingdom fell with it.

Londoners were soon rewarded when the young king promised that their rights would never again be taken away simply because individuals had misbehaved. Beneath his knightly trappings, Edward III now seems lifeless, but the trappings are gorgeous enough. After freeing himself from Isabel and her lover, he laid claim by right of his mother to the French Crown and so started the Hundred Years' War. By 1360 victories which included Sluys, Crécy and Poitiers had made the king of England once more lord of the greater part of France, whose own king was brought a captive to London. Edward loved splendour—he founded Europe's oldest surviving order of chivalry, the Order of the Garter—and until his last years he was successful at war. He was not a great lawgiver and does not shine in critical histories today, but by the standards of his age he was held to be a true king.

The Hundred Years' War put an end to the attempted conquest of Scotland, and drew resources to the south. Within months of the challenge to France the Exchequer was brought back from York; this was confirmed as the supreme financial office from 1355 when a younger rival, the king's Chamber, was restricted to his household expenses. Soon afterwards the Common Bench also returned to its thirteenth-century home. More offices followed. Dislike of pursuing the court, which had helped to anchor the Common Bench, now fastened on the more mobile judges of the King's Bench, who heard cases touching the royal prerogative. In 1365 the king promised 'greater ease', and increasingly these judges too sat at Westminster. The Court of Chancery, which set the Great Seal of England on all the most solemn acts, also began to settle down, although the chancellor himself might stay at the king's side. When Edward was abroad, a council also often sat at Westminster, and it continued to do so while he wandered from one nearby residence to another in his old age. Above all, from the beginning of the Hundred Years' War, Parliaments (then of very brief duration) met again and again at the same place. Between 1327 and 1338 ten had been summoned to Westminster, five to York and five to other towns; from 1339 until Edward's death in 1377 all thirty-one Parliaments were held at Westminster. There were to be exceptions until Stuart times— in theory there could be exceptions today—but the pattern was fixed. By 1377 there is no doubt that England had a political capital.

London and Westminster share the honour. The palace of Westminster, the hub of activity, had to be enlarged by Edward III. Formal sessions of Parliament usually took place in the Painted Chamber, although from 1340 lords and commons did most of their work separately, the commons using the abbey's Chapter House. The council met in the new Star Chamber, which the Tudors were to make notorious as a court-room. Westminster Hall was a vast, confused office—a judicial and administrative market-place—as well as a setting for ceremonies; judges of the Common Pleas might sit in one corner, those of the Kings' Bench in another and the clerks of the Chancery in a third, while the chancellor in person might be sealing writs or hearing cases. The little marsh-girt settlement of Westminster, of course, could not possibly hold all the officials, the hangers-on, the litigants and the provincial members of Parliament, who thronged the royal halls. Just as the magnates had city or suburban houses, so the bureaucrats settled nearby, mostly near Fleet Street or the Strand. The Exchequer had many lay officials but the clerks of the Chancery and of the Privy Seal were in holy orders and therefore celibate, leading a corporate life. Sometimes clerks lived in the chancellor's own house but this became too inconvenient and eventually they took over the house for converted Jews in Chancery Lane (*see p. 228*).

Not much government business was done within the city, as this would have led to friction. There was a Customs House slightly east of the present one, perhaps as early as 1275 when the king began to collect export duties on wool and leather, and an Exchange where foreigners received English coin in return for their bullion. The Tower, under royal control, was different. Some treasure was always kept there; it was the main factory for the king's armourers; it housed the keeper of his ships and receivers of special war taxes; it was a mint by 1300, replacing Westminster and soon becoming the king's chief mint. Sometimes it also held his Great Wardrobe—set up by Henry III as a depot of clothing, groceries and other heavy goods bought for him at fairs all over the country—and the Chamber. Military emergencies in the Hundred Years' War gave birth to a specialized deposit for arms, the king's Privy Wardrobe in the Tower; its rise helps to explain the Chamber's final subordination and its removal from the Tower to Westminster. The Great Wardrobe also moved out, to hired lodgings and, in 1361, to a house which had passed to the Crown at Baynard's Castle (where Wardrobe Place and Wardrobe Terrace recall the site). Edward III's queen and eldest son, who brought their own exchequers to Westminster, also set up wardrobes in the city, for easier dealings with the merchants who supplied their finery. By the late fourteenth century the city with its royal storehouses was sandwiched between the active offices farther west or at the Tower. Southwark too played its part, with its two Marshalsea prisons. In one sense, the story of the development of England's political capital was the story of its suburbs. These, however, would have been nothing without London itself, which supported the men who ran the government machine and, being so near, could bring pressure on its workings.

The Londoners also had an economic interest in the struggle with France. Unlike the Wars of the Roses in the next century, the

Hundred Years' War was not just a dynastic squabble, carried on regardless of trade. England's wealth sprang mainly from wool, shipped in enormous quantities to the weavers of Flanders, whose own independent spirit turned them against their ruler, the count, and his overlord, the king of France. An assured Flemish market and a Channel free from French privateers were as vital to London as was English rule in Gascony to Bristol, which controlled most of the wine-trade. The naming of a port as a 'staple', through which all exports had to pass, was also favoured by rich citizens who wanted a concentration of trade, as well as useful to the Crown for tax-collecting and diplomacy. Calais, taken in 1348 and fated to remain English for 210 years, became the staple for lead, tin and cloth, and for wool in 1363, when it was placed under a group of London capitalists, the Merchants of the Staple. Meanwhile water-power was replacing foot-power in driving the mills, where cloth had to be thickened and cleansed. A growing cloth industry soon boosted trade with northern Europe, carried on from the eastern ports led by London, at the expense of the Germans. The capital now had strong ties with the East Midlands and East Anglia (where the Norfolk parish of Worstead gave its name to worsted cloth); as a result of immigration to London modern standard English is descended from the East Midland dialect. By this time the king relied on a standard form of direct taxation voted by Parliament, normally one tenth of the value of all movable goods in the towns and royal domains, and one fifteenth in the country. In 1334 a tenth and fifteenth produced £38,170 from the whole of England: London was assessed to pay £733, while Bristol paid £220, and York £162; this was not much compared with the sums from the richest counties, Norfolk paying £3,485 and four others over £1,500, but ten counties including Middlesex paid less than £500 each. Although urban wealth was still comparatively small, London was way ahead of its rivals.

Displays of royal power also show the importance of London, where far-flung campaigns had gruesome postscripts. Nowhere could prisoners be more effectively paraded than through the city, nowhere could they be more surely lodged than in the Tower. Wales and Scotland sent many unlucky champions. Gruffydd, the bastard son of the Welsh prince Llywelyn the Great, spent four years in the Tower; he tried to escape on St David's Day 1244, but was killed when the rope broke (*Fig. 28*). Nearly forty years later the head of his son Llywelyn ap Gruffydd, the last native prince,

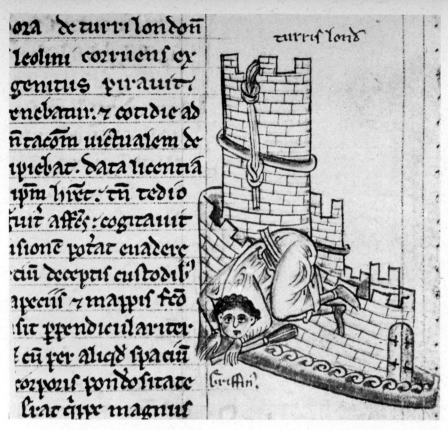

Fig. 28 *Gruffydd's escape from the Tower, from a sketch in the* Chronica Majora *of Matthew Paris, mid 13th century* (By permission of the Master and Fellows of Corpus Christi College, Cambridge)

was sent to be exposed on a lance at the Tower, where his brother David's head was soon set beside it. The Scots hero William Wallace, betrayed near Glasgow, was tried in Westminster Hall in August 1305, and dragged from the Tower to a traitor's end at the Elms, after which his head was stuck on London Bridge (a plaque in the wall of St Bartholomew's Hospital, facing West Smithfield, commemorates his death). Already John Balliol, Edward's own choice for the Scottish throne, had at the end of his short reign been sent to the Tower, and in 1346 Robert the Bruce's son, King David II, conspicuous on a black charger, was taken to the same prison. Soon after David's ransom the richest prize of all, King John of France, was led on a white horse by Edward's heir, the Black Prince, through the awe-stricken crowds. After dearly buying his freedom in 1360 John learned that his hostages had broken their parole; more chivalrous than politic, the king came back to London

117

to die. English victims, too, enlivened the scene. The Templars of the northern province were tried at York, those of the southern province not at Canterbury but at London, where the sensational vices attributed to them could get maximum publicity. After Edward III ordered the arrest of his mother's lover at Nottingham, it was at Tyburn that Mortimer met a traitor's deserts.

In 1348 this thriving city of perhaps sixty thousand people, hardened to the sight of death on the scaffold or in the gutter, was plunged into misery. Western enterprise had brought back an uncontrollable scourge together with the treasures of the east. Along the trade routes to Constantinople and from there with ships' cargoes to Italy sped the Black Death, carried by rats and, more immediately, by fleas. This was a worse form of the ordinary eastern or bubonic plague, which was to sweep London under Charles II; the victims, who could catch it by contagion and rarely lasted more than five days, produced swellings and carbuncles in arm and groin and were also attacked in the lungs—vomiting, spitting blood and giving out a loathsome stench. The Black Death fanned out from Italy over Western Europe, racing to the Channel and, in August, leaping across to what was then the busy port of Melcombe, in Dorset. By October exceptionally wet weather had brought it to London, where it reached its height early in the following spring. Nor was the plague of 1348–9 alone; other epidemics followed in 1361–2 and 1369.

In spite of wide-eyed later stories, there are no figures to show how London suffered. Over England as a whole one person in five probably died during the first outbreak, and further disasters may have halved the population before 1400. Odd instances say much for the ghastly state of the capital, where overcrowding and dirt helped the plague to kill perhaps twenty to thirty thousand people. Parliament, summoned to Westminster for January 1349, dared not meet. Two archbishops died at Westminster within four months, as did the abbot with most of his monks. The nearby hospital of St James was left empty, the keeper and all the brethren having perished. City companies lost all their officers. At least three new cemeteries were opened beyond the wall, at East Smithfield, on the site of the future Charterhouse, and on land belonging to St Bartholomew's Hospital. According to one account two hundred corpses a day were being shovelled into the first of these. In the summer of 1349 a Scandinavian writer recalls that a ship left London, laden with wool, and that the entire crew collapsed at sea; the vessel drifted ashore at Bergen, and this was enough to spread death throughout Norway.

Occasionally, even Edward III got into difficulties. In 1340 when extra money was being scraped together for his wars, discontent erupted. London had already beaten down an exorbitant demand for £20,000 to £5,000, and the king only restored his grip by suddenly crossing from Flanders to order a purge of his own ministers. The popularity of this move was quickly lost by efforts to collect arrears of taxes; street violence broke out and London had to be allowed to buy off a general 'eyre' or judicial session for a modest fine. In 1354 Edward gave further safeguards by laying down that the city must have been fined twice for its offences before it could be seized by the Crown.

At the end of the reign, with the war going badly and Edward sinking into his dotage, London again became a storm centre. In 1371 councillors had to meet at Winchester, for fear of the merchants. Five years later things were worse, for the Black Prince was dying of dysentery and power had slipped into the hands of his brother John of Gaunt, duke of Lancaster, and a clique which included Alice Perrers, the old king's mistress, and Richard Lyons, a grasping and unpopular vintner. At the Good Parliament ministers for the first time were impeached, called by the commons to answer before the lords for crimes against the public good. Gaunt afterwards felt strong enough to annul these acts only because he curried favour with some of the Londoners, encouraging an anti-clerical party around John Wyclif, 'the morning star of the Reformation', and abetting a violent radical, John of Northampton, against the city fathers. Even so London inflicted many humiliations on the duke. After his threat to stop Wyclif's trial for heresy in St Paul's, a mob hounded him from the city, besieged the Savoy and hung up his arms in Cheapside, reversed like those of a traitor. Since Gaunt was bound to be even more powerful during the minority of the Black Prince's heir, the corporation quickly made amends. Edward III died in June 1377 (*Fig. 29*), Gaunt was cheered riding in Richard II's coronation procession from the Tower to Westminster in July, and capitalists lent more money for the war. However, two of Gaunt's toughest opponents among the Londoners, John Philipot and William Walworth, were appointed to look after the funds voted by Parliament. Philipot soon grew so disgusted with the sluggish leadership that at his own expense he fitted out a small fleet which recaptured several prizes seized by the enemy. For teaching them their business, the grocer Philipot was reviled by the nobles, who sneered that young Richard was 'king of London'. After several incidents the second Parliament of the reign was prudently summoned to Gloucester and in 1380 the third met at Nottingham—a clear sign that something was wrong.

The social order began to crumble. With manpower cut down by the Black Death, it was useless to pass laws to peg wages and prices at their old level. London became a magnet for absconding peasants, keener than ever to take advantage of the demand for labour. A primitive communism flared up, aimed particularly at rich church-men and soon expressed by the rabble-rousing priest John Ball: 'when Adam delved and Eve span, who was then the gentleman?' The gentry and merchants in Parliament and the nobles and prelates around the king did not realize that they were sitting on a volcano. Desperate to keep the war going, they brought in a poll-tax, of 4d. per head, which was later graduated with disappointing results and finally in 1380 raised to a flat and therefore extremely unjust rate of 1s. Pious advice to the rich to help the poor could not save England from the biggest convulsion of her history, the Peasants' Revolt. The outbreaks stretched as far north as Yorkshire and Cheshire but most were rural bush-fires, quick to spread and easily stamped out. The worst danger was that rebels from Kent

Fig. 29 *Gilt copper head of Edward III from his tomb in Edward the Confessor's Chapel, Westminster Abbey, about 1377–80* (A. F. Kersting)

and Essex might win the riches, arms and manpower of London. Richard II was at Windsor Castle. His advisers dared not take him farther into the uncertain countryside; hoping perhaps that its defences would make it as safe as the eye of a whirlwind, they headed for the Tower.

The tax collectors had warned that they could not find out details about everyone in London without sparking off trouble. Authority's blindness, followed by panic, may explain the rest. On Thursday 13 June 1381, after storming Southwark, burning the Marshalsea prisons and destroying the legal records stored by the archbishop at Lambeth, Wat Tyler's men of Kent swept unresisted across the bridge and into the city. They moved west along Fleet Street to open the prison and then farther west to burn more records at the New Temple and plunder several houses. The citizens themselves at last evened scores with John of Gaunt by firing the Savoy, the finest jewel in the necklace linking London with Westminster. The palace did not fall victim to simple greed; it symbolized oppressive wealth and a man who was caught thieving silver was thrust into the burning ruins, with his booty.

The Hospitallers' property blazed at Clerkenwell, lawyers' heads rolled in Cheapside, and aliens were lynched. Meanwhile the king tried to harangue the crowd from a turret of the Tower, but failed to get a hearing, as he had previously failed to address the men of Kent from his barge at Greenwich. He then slipped out for a vain parley with the Essex rebels at Mile End. Everywhere was fear and treachery. As soon as Richard had gone the garrison, estimated at 1,200 men, opened the gates of the Tower. Richard's mother was heaped with insults before an escort managed to lead her through the city to the Great Wardrobe. Simon Sudbury, archbishop of Canterbury, who had just resigned as chancellor, was dragged from his knees in the chapel of St John to Tower Hill, where he was beheaded with the treasurer and other ministers. The king, wandering with a tiny retinue among the fickle crowds, at last took shelter with his mother. Next morning at Westminster, the keeper of the King's Bench marshalsea was found clinging to St Edward's shrine and torn away to his death. Never had order in the capital so utterly broken down.

Since London could not hold the thousands of invaders, many encamped north-west of St Bartholomew's Priory at Smithfield. Here Richard rode with the mayor, William Walworth, whose authority had not been formally denied and whose close attendance on the boy had so far helped to protect him. Maddened by a sneer that empty promises were not enough, Walworth struck Wat Tyler down in sight of his supporters. Miraculously, the royal party was saved by Richard, who urged the seething rebels to follow him, their true leader. While the peasants cheered and rallied round, Walworth slipped away to gather a force, part mercenary and part volunteer, which later saw that the confused throng dispersed. Other parts of the country were to rise, but London and the king were saved. That evening, Richard knighted the mayor and two colleagues, John Philipot and Nicholas Brembre, in Clerkenwell Fields. Walworth was not the first mayor to receive this honour, but few have earned it by such crucial services. To this day his company, the Fishmongers', prizes the dagger with which Tyler is said to have been stabbed.

The triumphant gamble at Smithfield must have had a lasting effect on the proud, sensitive boy, who grew up ominously to love the arts, and never to forget a friend or forgive an enemy. His reign resembled Edward II's, although Richard had the stronger and more dangerous character. London's role was prominent and, if understandable, not very creditable. In November 1387 when ill-feeling between the king and his critics, led by his youngest uncle the duke of Gloucester, was coming to a head, Richard was welcomed with unparalleled honour. When the duke began mustering men at Haringey park to the north of the city, however, the Londoners declared that they would fight the king's enemies but never his friends. Richard was forced to greet his enemies, who styled themselves the Lords Appellant, at Westminster Hall and, after the rout of a relieving force, to open the Merciless Parliament on 3 February 1388. Among those sacrificed in the most sweeping legalized slaughter that England had yet seen was the former mayor, Nicholas Brembre, whom a committee of peers refused to condemn but who died after the mayor and aldermen, summoned by the Appellants, had dutifully found against him. Brembre had lent huge sums to the king—in itself an offence to many nobles—and few copied him after his death.

When Richard regained his independence, his attitude to London hardened. Hoping for money but professing to punish a riot, he went back on Edward III's guarantees in 1392. Mayor and sheriffs were imprisoned, a royal warden and new sheriffs were installed, and the law-courts were packed off to York. The city paid up, and a splendid procession advertised the reconciliation. Richard and his queen were given costly ornaments, and some craftsmen who had serenaded the royal barge were even invited to drink at Westminster, but nothing was the same again. Gloucester, soon to be murdered, was popularly credited with persuading his nephew to be content with a 'free gift' of £10,000 rather than a monstrous fine of £100,000. Matters were made worse by peace with France, which exposed the Londoners' shipping to piracy in the Channel, and by royal favours to the fishmongers. In the winter of 1397–8 Richard adjourned his last Parliament from Westminster to Shrewsbury, where it could more easily be overawed, and thereafter circled the country with his guard of four hundred archers, avoiding the capital as much as possible and even taking with him justices of the King's Bench who normally stayed at Westminster. Oaths of loyalty were repeatedly extracted and London, accused with seventeen other counties of having aided the Appellants, was forced to set its seal to blank charters which the king kept for his own use. In the 1390s, however, as in the 1320s, it was up to the barons to make the first move. While Richard struck down his enemies, the citizens sullenly bided their time.

Nemesis came in 1399, when the exiled Henry Bolingbroke landed, ostensibly to claim his confiscated inheritance from his father John of Gaunt. Richard, returning from Ireland to find his forces melted away, surrendered in North Wales. Meanwhile Londoners assured the invader of their support, not just to join the winning side but out of lust for revenge, sharpened by fear: of the twenty-four aldermen in 1399, seventeen had been humiliated in 1392, and Bolingbroke had quickly warned that Richard meant to suspend all municipal liberties. One London writer says that the citizens vainly searched Westminster for the fallen king before asking Henry to have him killed at once, another that Richard begged not to be exhibited as a prisoner there, where the people would gloat. Henry, for his own ends, moved south with Richard, in whose name an assembly of estates was called. At the capital they parted, Henry riding to the palace, his cousin, clothed in black, to the Tower.

Richard II is the first English king of whom we have a painting, although some of his ancestors lie, carved, on their tombs. The stylized full-face coronation portrait in the nave of Westminster Abbey (*Fig. 30*) and the smaller profile in the National Gallery's Wilton Diptych show him as a boy, pale and bejewelled. As a lover of all things French he has been credited with introducing

Fig. 30 *Portrait of Richard II in the nave of Westminster Abbey, 1390–1400* (By courtesy of the Dean and Chapter of Westminster)

many luxuries, as well as with sinister plans to perfect royal power on foreign lines. He was just the man to broadcast his emblem, the white hart, which is recalled by inns all over the country, to order the magnificent tomb in which he now lies with Queen Anne in the Confessor's Chapel, and to rebuild Westminster Hall as it stands today. Few men have been so hated in London as this resplendent, neurotic young autocrat, who in his last years would sit crowned in silence from dinner until vespers, expecting all who met his gaze to kneel. Yet the extravagant setting which he created for himself symbolized the birth of a true political capital. When William Rufus began Westminster Hall, even the treasury had still been at Winchester and government had followed the king. When Richard built higher on the same foundations, the story was over; decisions might be taken anywhere but the work was carried on from Westminster. He never saw the hammerbeam roof in all its glory, for Henry IV held his coronation feast there. A fortnight later Richard, disguised as a forester, was spirited away to Kent and then to a dungeon in the Yorkshire castle of Pontefract.

London's propaganda role was more important in 1399 than in the deposition of Edward II. Henry did not step forward as Richard's cousin, the son of John of Gaunt, since the earl of March, descended from an older cousin, still lived, but as the descendant of a crippled and supposedly elder brother of Edward I (Edmund Crouchback, who lies in the Sanctuary at Westminster). This claim, invalidating every king since 1272, was now declared to have been vindicated by conquest, but everyone knew that it was the conquest which counted. Abdication had quickly to be obtained before the estates could meet, because they would otherwise have formed a Parliament with Richard as king. It was extorted at the Tower on 29 September and read out at Westminster the next day, while the mob clamoured successfully, as was intended, for Henry IV. The city thus supplied the popular reception that Henry did not want from a Parliament, which might take back what it had given. His manoeuvre was not unnoticed and five years later a man was accused of complaining that the king had been elected not by the magnates and 'state' of England, 'but by the London rabble'.

The usurper, paying his debt, reaffirmed that the city should not suffer for the misdeeds of its officials. Never again was medieval London taken 'into the king's hands', although the Stuarts were to try this punishment in a last burst of royal interference. London had nonetheless helped to set England on a dangerous course.

Richard was the last Plantagenet whose claim was undisputed, no matter what efforts were made to twist and obscure the royal genealogy. To hide his weakness, Henry IV was crowned with unusual magnificence and was the first monarch to be anointed with some conveniently discovered holy oil, said to have been given by the Virgin Mary to St Thomas Becket. In everything he had to tread carefully; the great lords were more closely consulted, the Church was won over by fierce persecution of Wyclif's Lollards, the commons were more often summoned to Parliament. London of course had little to fear from such a dynasty, but she needed a king because she needed order. The danger now was that both would disappear.

If it had not been for London, Henry might never have established his line. He was nearly ambushed while celebrating the first Christmas of his reign, escaping from Windsor Castle only twelve hours before it was seized by a band which proclaimed that Richard was now free. Henry, naturally, made straight for London and barricaded himself there until enthusiastic recruits quickly made him strong enough to drive the rebels west, where their leaders were slain. By mid-January 1400 he was back, to display the traitors' heads in the city. Richard's death was announced a month later and his body slowly brought south to lie in St Paul's, where Henry himself attended a service. The king of Scots for years maintained a pseudo-Richard, the subject of northern legends, but Henry could now afford to allow his predecessor quiet burial in the priory church at King's Langley in Hertfordshire. A few years later Richard was brought for the last time to his capital and laid in the tomb which he had prepared for himself.

Henry IV was astute and energetic but, for a man who had won so great a prize, he remains remarkably colourless. Most of his fourteen-year reign was spent in beating down challenges in the north and west, while London backed him with generous loans and was reassured by gruesome trophies. On 20 March 1413, worn out at the age of nearly forty-six, he had a fit while praying before the shrine of Edward the Confessor and was carried into the abbot's Jerusalem Chamber, only to die. He was the first king to die at Westminster since Henry III in 1272, yet he was not buried there but at Canterbury. Fittingly, it was in his reign that the city's present Guildhall was started, in contrast to the royal hall which commemorates his despotic cousin.

The dark clouds which overcast the rest of the Middle Ages

seem briefly to have parted during the nine-year reign of Henry V—a period all the brighter for its shortness. Encouraged by French factions and hoping for popularity at home, Henry renewed the Hundred Years' War and, against all the odds, eclipsed the triumphs of his great-grandfather. Londoners again lent generously and Henry, who pledged them a massive gold collar as security, carefully kept them in touch with his campaign. Very early on 29 October 1415, royal letters told the mayor of the overwhelming victory at Agincourt four days earlier, and on 23 November 1415 London wildly acclaimed its hero as he rode to give thanks at St Paul's. The mayor and aldermen had already escorted him from Blackheath past 15,000 to 20,000 mounted craftsmen, on parade to show the august French prisoners what stout men had stayed behind to guard the land. We can still keep near to Henry's route along Southwark High Street, over the bridge and up Fish Street, through the corn market at Grass Church, west along Cornhill and Cheap to the cathedral, and eventually out through Ludgate. The ground was covered with straw and the houses hung with tapestries, flags, streamers and decorated boughs; the fountains ran with wine and at intervals there were special pantomimes for citizens to show their loyalty. It was not like one of today's decorous processions, with sightseers kept well back from the roadway; Henry and his small escort had almost to push their horses through the crowd, so that it took five hours to get from Blackheath to the palace at Westminster. In a ceremonious age, London's welcome was a pageant to end all pageants.

Even now the crust of order was thin. A few months after his succession, when anxious like his father to champion the faith, Henry sent his old friend Sir John Oldcastle to the Tower on a charge of heresy. London was honeycombed with the influence of Oldcastle, who had been run to earth through some tracts in an illuminator's bookshop in Paternoster Row. He escaped by night with the help of three friends, one of them a Smithfield parchment maker, and plotted to wipe out the house of Lancaster by surprising the king and his brothers during the Christmas of 1413 at Eltham. Warned by spies, Henry moved to Westminster under the cover of a January night and the next evening secretly kept watch at Lincoln's Inn Fields, while small knots of rebels stole towards the city, whose gates they hoped to find open. Band after band was rounded up and the leaders duly hanged, but Oldcastle himself remained free, hidden for over a month by allies in the capital. Although London was not involved in another plot to murder Henry, on the eve of first leaving for France, and although victory made him safer, the unease remained. It is not surprising that he rode with bowed head through the cheering crowds after Agincourt. On Easter Sunday 1417, when the king was again abroad, Lord Strange and his retinue attacked Sir William Trussell in St Dunstan-in-the-East, slaying a scandalized parishioner who tried to intervene. The war was breeding too many armed men who behaved as if they were a law unto themselves.

Henry V pressed home his advantage after Agincourt, until the most glittering prize of all lay within his grasp. In 1420 he was recognized as regent of France and heir to its mad old king, who disowned his son and married the conqueror to his daughter Katherine. Paris and the whole of northern France submitted, and the rest seemed likely to follow. England and France would soon have one ruler but their own, native institutions. London would remain England's capital and would become the twin head of the Lancastrian double monarchy. On 23 February 1421 Henry's bride was led through the decorated streets for her coronation, after which the mayor and senior citizens attended the banquet in Westminster Hall. Henry soon left to resume his conquests, but in August 1422 he succumbed to an attack of dysentery near Paris. Three months later the French king died and the two crowns passed to Henry VI, born at Windsor less than a year before. After resting in Paris, his father's embalmed body was borne slowly to the Channel and from Dover to London, where it arrived on 11 November. So great had been Henry's glory that his tomb at Westminster was unusually magnificent, the oaken effigy being covered with silver gilt and topped with a head of solid silver. So dazzling a work, like Henry's own empire, could not last long; robbers stripped away the precious metal in 1545, leaving the headless wooden trunk which is so arresting among the royal monuments today. The hero's helmet, however, with the shield and saddle paraded at his funeral, still surmount the carvings of his chantry chapel, which include battered portraits of the king at his coronation and on campaign.

Nationalism was being sharpened by the Hundred Years' War, yet two kingdoms now had to be governed in the name of a baby, whose own claim might be disputed. The future could only have been darker if the child had been a girl. It says much for Henry V's brother John, duke of Bedford, that the English impetus continued for seven years, until Joan of Arc put new heart into the French, and that little had been yielded when Bedford died in 1435. In France Bedford was regent but in England power lay with the council, torn between another royal uncle, Humphrey, duke of Gloucester, and the rich and indispensable Cardinal Beaufort. Violence burst out in 1425, when Humphrey controlled the Tower and Beaufort men from Southwark seized London Bridge, hoping to force their way into the city. The Londoners, warned by the duke, closed their shops and flocked to the bridge to thwart the coup, while Humphrey brought the young king from Eltham and Bedford hurried over to mediate. Thanks to London, the crafty cardinal was forced to patch up his differences with Duke Humphrey, and Bedford could return to France. After his coronation at Westminster in 1429, Henry VI crossed the Channel for the only time to be crowned at Paris. His return was hailed by the courtly poet John Lydgate, who was also paid by the corporation to write verses for special occasions. Lydgate was a monk of Bury St Edmunds but he knew London well, presumably from staying at his abbot's house in Bevis (formerly Bury's) Marks. He lovingly describes the seven ingenious pageants which halted the boy along the time-honoured processional route across the bridge, through Cornhill and Cheapside, 'a place of all delights', to St Paul's. A beautiful miniature purports to show the city in Lydgate's time, although it was executed some fifty years later: Charles, duke of Orléans, taken prisoner at Agincourt, is shown three times in the Tower, with the bridge as far as St Thomas's Chapel and the spires of London behind (*Fig. 31*).

As England's strength drained away, it became clear that Henry VI could not save anything from the wreck. He grew up meek, guileless and artistic, more truly a saint than the lavish royal builders of Westminster Abbey. Worse still, his French grandfather had suffered fits of madness (when he imagined that he was made of glass), and in the 1450s it became clear that this taint had passed to Henry, so that at times his feeble hand was removed altogether. Edward, the only child born of Henry's marriage to Margaret of Anjou, became the hope of the dynasty, since the next heir was the duke of York, whose descent from the earl of March passed over in 1399 (*see p. 125*) gave him a strong claim to the Crown itself. In every other respect the marriage was a disaster, producing the classic tragedy of a well-meaning ruler dominated by a foreign wife. Margaret thought that she knew who her friends and enemies

Fig. 31 *Charles, duke of Orléans, a prisoner in the Tower, from an illumination in* The Poems of Charles d'Orléans, *about1500* (British Museum)

were; like many tragic queens, her beauty never overcame a hatred for her supposed foreign attachments, which deepened with each new loss of territory. In 1452 the English were driven from Bordeaux, where they had held on for three hundred years, and only Calais was left. Out of work soldiers returned to a humiliated country, ruled from an extravagant, faction-ridden court. While most people only groaned for peace, warriors began to take sides, often settling private quarrels under the emblem of the White Rose of York, later rivalled by the Red Rose of Lancaster.

London had a foretaste of trouble in 1450, when Kent rebelled against extortionate officials, complaining particularly of the sheriff and his father-in-law, the former treasurer Lord Saye and Sele. This was not, like the Peasants' Revolt, simply a poor men's move against rich landowners; it expressed anger at maladministration that was shared by many gentry and townsmen, if not by the nobility. The king, hurrying from Leicester, took up his stand north of the city, at Clerkenwell, and two days passed in fruitless parleys. The rebels then retired from Blackheath to Sevenoaks, only to turn and rout the pursuing royal army on 18 June. A mutiny at Greenwich induced the government to reopen talks, but these too foundered and the king withdrew to the Midlands. Good order was kept among the rebels by Jack Cade, an Irish-born adventurer who borrowed glamour by pretending to be related to the duke of York. Abandoned by the king, the citizens naturally decided not to resist and clapped a dissenting alderman in prison. On 2 July Cade crossed from his headquarters in Southwark at the White Hart, with many promises not to allow pillage. After cutting the ropes of the drawbridge with his own sword, he rode triumphantly to London Stone, struck it 'like a conqueror' and announced that a Mortimer was now lord of the city. This reality was soon brought home when Lord Saye and Sele was dragged from protective custody at Guildhall to execution in Cheapside; his son-in-law was beheaded before Cade at Mile End, and the two heads were stuck upon poles, carried through the streets and made to kiss each other.

If the government had not panicked, London need not have fallen. As it was, Cade's triumph proved fleeting. He could not keep discipline in the overcrowded capital and soon made solid citizens fear for their property. Meanwhile the Tower held out and on the evening of Sunday 5 July its lieutenant, Lord Scales, in league with the mayor, cut Cade off in his base in Southwark by seizing London Bridge. Cade, breaking open the Southwark prisons to get reinforcements, vainly tried to dislodge the offenders, driving them halfway back and setting fire to the drawbridge in the middle. A conference under the archbishop of Canterbury followed in St Margaret's Church and the rebels, glad of their pardons, disbanded. Cade himself, having been pardoned in the name of Mortimer, remained fair game and was hunted down in Sussex. It was left to the hostess of the White Hart to identify his corpse, which was then taken through London to be beheaded, quartered and paraded through the streets, the head between the breasts; the limbs went to towns in Kent, the head to London Bridge.

Cade's rebellion marked a further twist in England's downward spiral, for it encouraged York to take up arms in the name of good government. Londoners cared for order above everything and so at first naturally favoured the reigning house of Lancaster, to which they had been bound since 1399. When both sides marched from the north-west in 1452, the duke was refused entry and had to cross the Thames at Kingston, while Henry rode straight through the city to face his rival at Blackheath. As the 1450s wore on, however, it seemed that loyalty would settle nothing and the Yorkist alternative became more attractive. In 1460 when Margaret seemed to have the upper hand, London's first instinct was to oppose a Yorkist invasion until one of the leaders, the earl of Warwick, persuaded a deputation to change its mind. York himself soon arrived, fresh from victory and leading the captive Henry. The Tower was then bombarded into surrender and Lord Scales was lynched on his way to sanctuary. London was now a Yorkist base. Yet when the duke entered Westminster Hall at the October Parliament and, a few days later, sat on the throne, he was greeted with a tense silence. Neither the lords present nor the crowds outside were ready to discard the pathetic son of the hero of Agincourt. It was agreed that Henry should remain nominal king for life but should be followed by York and his heirs.

In the next few months London played its most decisive part in the Wars of the Roses. Queen Margaret was still at large and on her victory at the end of December the duke who had so nearly become king was given a paper crown, before his head joined many others on the walls of York. While the Lancastrians plundered their way south Henry was led from London by the Yorkists, only to change hands after another defeat. London would now have to accept Margaret or openly demand a change of dynasty. Submission would have been the obvious course if it had not been for the terror spread by the queen's northerners, who ransacked St Albans and its famous abbey. As it was, while artfully seeking reassurances from Margaret, the city opened its gates to Warwick and York's heir, the twenty-one-year old earl of March. After acclamations from his soldiers and the citizens, March took the royal oath in Westminster Hall, gave thanks at the abbey and received homage as Edward IV. He claimed to be the legitimate king and, since no parliament was sitting, these steps amounted to a recognition of his title in which the Londoners spoke for the people as a whole. The capital had chosen and, with the rest of the more advanced south-east, set itself against the wilder, Lancastrian north. There Margaret retreated and there Edward pursued her, avenging his father's death.

With Edward's coronation at Westminster in June many must

have hoped that the wars were over, but Margaret stubbornly menaced the north for three years. At last she left for France with her son, while her husband wandered in the dales until his capture in 1465. Now that Edward was crowned, there could be no more question of paying Henry even nominal respect; his life was safe only because the boy who would inherit his rights was still free. At his coronation he had been greeted by choirs dressed as angels and at his return from Paris the citizens had worn white to show their sincerity. Lancastrians later reported that their king, with feet bound beneath his horse and wearing a straw hat, was led by Warwick along Cheapside and Cornhill, through hooting crowds. Whatever his treatment there was no sadder spectacle in the Middle Ages than that of Henry VI's passage to the Tower.

Edward was everything that Henry was not—young, strong, genial, pleasure-loving, naturally astute, lazy when things went well but ruthless in a crisis. The pious Henry was a medieval figure; the new king was before his time, a gilded Renaissance prince not yet run to seed. Lured by profit, Edward himself became a merchant. He shipped wool and cloth from several ports but most of all from London, bringing back luxuries which ranged from spices, fruit and rich material to soap, pins, spectacles and writing paper. His exotic tastes led him to patronize foreign merchants, in spite of his own subjects' jealousy, yet he was willing to ban many imports to boost native industry, and courtiers were encouraged to dabble in trade. Glamour helped with the London populace and bonhomie with their betters; Edward knew that an invitation to the mayor and aldermen to make merry with him at Windsor was both rewarding and cheap. No previous king had so closely shared the citizens' interests, nor, so enemies said, their wives. None was so good a businessman.

London might change a campaign and so hoist a man to the throne, but it could not keep him there. Military power was still dispersed among the great landed families. Edward's triumph only made more galling his dependence on the Yorkist barons and especially on the earl of Warwick. Inevitably Edward and Warwick quarrelled. The earl, enraged at the king's marriage to Elizabeth Woodville and jealous of her family, for a time put Edward under restraint and, after a reversal, left for France. Warwick, with his resources, was the only man who could give hope to the Lancastrians; they, with their royal blood, could alone cloak his vengeance in legality. After a reconciliation which must have been searingly bitter to both parties, the earl returned to live up to his nickname, 'the Kingmaker'. His landing in Devon gave the signal to supporters in Kent to make for London, where they robbed the foreign merchants who had settled in Southwark. Edward, deserted in the north, escaped by a hair's breadth to the Low Countries, and on 6 October 1470 London had to open its gates to Warwick. The pro-Lancastrian John Warkworth relates in his *Chronicle* how the dazed Henry VI was found in the Tower, 'not so worshipfully arrayed nor so cleanly kept as should seem such a prince', led back through the city to St Paul's and then to the neighbouring bishop's palace. Four days later his reign was officially resumed and on 21 October the Burgundian Georges Chastellain saw him 'looking like a crowned calf', as he walked in state, his former captor holding the royal train.

Fortunately for the Londoners Queen Margaret stayed in France during this counter-revolution. Warwick could not hope to win them over, as he needed French help and tried to cut off trade with the Low Countries, which were ruled by France's enemy, the duke of Burgundy. Shipping dwindled and exports piled high, for nothing could make up for the old Flemish connexion. England's hereditary enemy was backing a dreaded French-born queen; the duke of Burgundy, on the other hand, gave shelter to Edward IV, whose sister he had married. London was unimpressed with the French goods that were shipped over and was pleased only at the execution of a ruthless Yorkist, the earl of Worcester, who was nearly lynched on his way to Tower Hill.

Late in March Edward reached the bleak Yorkshire coast, where Henry IV had landed to set in train the long dynastic conflict. History was repeating itself, for Henry at first had claimed only the duchy of Lancaster and Edward now demanded only York, throwing aside the mask as support snowballed on his way south. The earl left London with his army but Edward side-stepped him and was outside the capital by 10 April. On that very day Warwick's brother the archbishop of York paraded Henry through the streets, in a last effort to rally the crowds, but the response was so chilly that he was forced to seek terms. Edward entered at noon the next day and Henry was bundled back to the Tower, to be led out for the last time on 13 April when Edward marched to Barnet. If Warwick had won this battle on London's doorstep, the city which had anticipated his defeat would have paid dearly. As it was, the Kingmaker fell and Edward had time to return before setting out to meet Margaret, who at last had landed in the west, and to rout her at Tewkesbury.

It remained only for the Londoners to beat off a Lancastrian privateer, the Bastard of Fauconberg, and Edward IV was settled on his throne more securely than before.

London, once so enthusiastic for the house of Lancaster, now saw its obliteration. Margaret's only child had been stabbed to death after Tewkesbury and she herself was trundled in a barred waggon to the city which, if she had landed sooner, would have had to receive her as queen. There was no longer any point in keeping Henry VI alive. Edward IV reached his capital on 21 May and that night his youngest brother Richard, duke of Gloucester, had Henry murdered in the Tower. The body was exposed at St Paul's, as Richard II's had been, and then at the house of the black friars, before being taken west for burial in Chertsey Abbey. Henry, like other unhappy rulers, had found solace in the arts. His predecessors had spent so much on Westminster that he had concentrated on his own foundations, King's College, Cambridge, and Eton College, whose chapels date from his time. London would have no fitting memorial if Gloucester, as king, had not moved his victim's body to Windsor and if his supplanter, Henry VII, had not intended it for Westminster. Hoping to have the last Lancastrian canonized and to stress his own dubious link with that house, the first Tudor replaced the thirteenth-century lady chapel with the present chapel, which was to house the bones of Henry VI. The abbey, glad to have another royal saint, paid large sums for the body to be brought there, but Rome demanded too high a price and the building work was dragging on when the king himself died. So it happened that Henry VI stayed at Windsor and that the chapel built in his honour was named after Henry VII who, with his queen, there occupies pride of place.

Henry VI, the fourth king to be murdered since the Conquest, was the first so to die in London. In 1478 the Tower claimed another famous victim in Edward IV's brother George, duke of Clarence; although tradition maintains that he was drowned in a butt of Malmsey wine, it is more probable that he died in his bath. No one could see that this death paved the way for the drama which was to shake London five years later, for the king was only in his thirties and was settling down with a surprisingly popular mistress, Jane Shore, the wife of a city mercer. There was no reason to suppose that he would die suddenly, leaving a political vacuum which could be filled either by Gloucester or by the Woodvilles, but not by both. Yet this was what happened at Westminster on 9 April 1483. The mayor and aldermen of London trooped in after the lords to see the body, which was taken first to St Stephen's Chapel in the palace, then to the abbey church, and finally to Windsor.

Edward V, aged twelve, was proclaimed king, but had to be fetched from Ludlow. Half-way to London the Woodvilles among his escort were arrested, whereupon his mother at Westminster fled to sanctuary with her second son. On 4 May Edward arrived with his uncle, Gloucester, and was led in state to the Tower, where kings always stayed before their coronation. The duke retired to Crosby Place (*see p. 190*), a rich merchant's mansion near Bishopsgate, and laid his plans. Pressure was put on the queen to let the younger boy join his brother; at a council in the White Tower on 13 June Gloucester's chief opponent Lord Hastings was accused of witchcraft and led off to instant execution; on 22 June Friar Ralph Sha ominously preached at Paul's Cross that Edward IV had been pre-contracted in marriage when very young, so that his children by Elizabeth Woodville were bastards; well co-ordinated sermons in other parts of the city suggested that Edward too had been one. Three days later the aim of this propaganda became clear when an assembly of lords and commons at Westminster, originally summoned as a Parliament, asked Gloucester to claim the throne. On the next day their petition was publicly read by his confederate the duke of Buckingham to a large crowd at Baynard's Castle; Gloucester, riding to Westminster Hall, sat in the royal chair.

Earlier usurpations had been the fruit of successful campaigns. Richard III, after clearing the ground by arresting the Woodvilles, carried out a coup d'état in the capital. Friar Sha, who first tested Richard's case on the public, was brother of the mayor. Since no one under the Tudors dared show much sympathy for the last Yorkist it is hard to check the Shakespearian story that popular consent amounted to the cheers of a few retainers. The fate of the princes in the Tower, who were seen playing in its grounds at rarer intervals, aroused general pity. Many believed them to be dead before the coronation, for by then they had disappeared from public view, and everyone thought the worst by the autumn. London could at least comfort itself that an able, adult king had many advantages and that Richard had quickly collected so many troops from his northern strongholds that there was nothing to be done. Bones found at the foot of a staircase in the Tower, presumed to be those of Edward V and his brother, were placed in 1674 in Henry VII's Chapel at Westminster.

Richard spent little of his short reign in London, restlessly journeying or keeping watch from Nottingham, the central point of his kingdom. The death of his only child in 1484 left him the last Plantagenet, for the young son of Clarence remained, disqualified, in the Tower. In Brittany lurked Henry Tudor, earl of Richmond; he had a little French royal blood, for his father had been born to Henry V's widow Katherine and her Welsh husband, Owen Tudor, whose presumptuous marriage had landed him in Newgate gaol; he also had an English claim through his mother, a Beaufort descendant of John of Gaunt. This was not much, since the act legitimizing the Beauforts had barred them from the throne, but, if backed by conquest, it would be enough. The manner of Richard's accession and the mystery about his nephews, whose fate was never announced, were a permanent excuse for rebellion. There was good reason to fear Henry, even after a fiasco late in 1483 when he failed to join forces with Richard's ex-crony, Buckingham, who was duly executed. London was spared any fighting, rebels from Kent being baulked at Gravesend, but reprisals included the seizure of all Breton goods in the city.

It was from Nottingham that Richard rode out to die at Bosworth Field. On the evening of 22 August 1485 his naked corpse was taken for burial in Leicester, while England submitted to the returned outlaw who had been denounced a few weeks earlier as 'one Henry Tydder'. Remembering London's Yorkist sympathies and the horror aroused by Queen Margaret, Henry restrained his men from plundering on their way south. While he waited, as she had done, at St Albans, the Londoners prepared a brilliant welcome. On 3 September a procession of 435, representing every guild and with the mayor and aldermen in scarlet, met Henry at Shoreditch and led him to St Paul's. He then lodged in the bishop's palace nearby, while his reign began with an outbreak of sweating sickness which killed the mayor, his successor and six aldermen within a few days.

The coming of the Tudors did not end the Wars of the Roses. Henry VII followed the usurpers' rule: the more doubtful the title, the more splendid the coronation. As soon as possible he married Elizabeth of York, sister of Edward V, so ensuring that true Plantagenet blood would pass to his children. If the princes had still been alive in the Tower, Henry would have had to kill them, as he killed Clarence's son on reaching manhood. Lack of an alternative at last made him safe, but not before impostors had been

Fig. 32 *Wooden head of the funeral effigy of Henry VII, from his death mask, in the Westminster Abbey Museum, 1509* (By courtesy of the Dean and Chapter of Westminster)

routed in battles which might easily have gone the other way. His troubles were those of a medieval king, menaced by over-mighty subjects, and his capital was still a medieval city. Church building and decoration went on until the Reformation, when his son's destruction of the monasteries at last changed the face of London. The ditch had to be kept intact and the wall in good repair. Wat Tyler and Jack Cade were echoed in the 1550s, when Wyatt's Kentish men stormed in from the west, to fall back only in Fleet Street. Even under the Stuarts it seemed that the wall would have to be manned—against the Crown itself.

In spite of appearances, England was slowly slipping away from the Middle Ages. Henry VII, shrewd and painstaking (as we can see from his effigy (*Fig. 32*)), took the path towards centralization which his family was to follow. Increasingly, power was seen to lie not in castles but at court; winning the king's ear became more important than arming retainers in the provinces, and more government business than ever was carried on from the capital. After heresy was stamped out in the early fifteenth century the Church, which had once brought kings to their knees, was glad to jog along with royal protection. Perhaps it was only a noisy minority which loathed clerical privileges but in 1514, when riots followed the death of a merchant tailor, Richard Hunne, in the bishop's gaol near St Paul's, many apprentices were hanged by the young Henry VIII, whose own faith was still intact. London had heaved with the first rumblings of the Reformation.

England's chief port had always been her only city in the European league. By 1500 there were no rivals to Paris but London may have had 75,000 people. It was bigger than anywhere in Germany and was compared by a Venetian to Rome or Florence, dazzling cities but ones which had nothing like the same opportunities ahead. Already Europe had started the voyages which were to turn London into a world-wide trading port. Discoveries by Spain and Portugal were soon to boost France and England, the other Atlantic powers, at the expense of the Italians, Netherlanders and Germans who had dominated medieval trade. In another generation Londoners would form their own companies for far-off enterprises, and some would bring back undreamt-of wealth.

A city so disproportionately large could hardly fail to influence politics. It might have done still more, only there was nothing heroic about the city fathers. Repeated work on the defences was not put sternly to the test, for London never knew a long siege, as did so many continental cities. Time and again the mayor and aldermen waited on events before trooping out in ceremonial scarlet to greet the victor. After they had escorted him amid ringing bells to the usual Te Deum at St Paul's, they gave thanks less for one man's triumph than for a decision which should once more allow them to get on with their own business.

Even cautious Londoners had their preferences, which were often decisive. Before the Conquest and in the early Middle Ages they actually chose kings, although Edgar the Ætheling's failure after Hastings shows that this was not enough without an army. Most artful of all was the bargain struck with John by which the city got its commune. After his day, however, hereditary right struck root and the throne passed to the eldest son or grandson until 1399, depriving London of its claim to elect the best man available. On the other hand the magnates who engineered the depositions in 1327, 1399, and in the Wars of the Roses, were desperately keen to involve the Londoners. The old habit of acclamation persisted (as it still does in the coronation service) and in every usurpation save Richard III's it was exercised gladly. Although the citizens never held out against a conqueror, they often swayed a campaign. They supplied a base for their favourites, for Stephen against Matilda, for the barons and Louis of France against John, for Simon de Montfort against Henry III; they played for time with enemies whom they dared not defy, keeping Margaret at a distance while the Yorkists regrouped. In the Middle Ages, when so much depended upon battle, London had more say in the fate of governments than it has ever had since.

London's grimmest medieval survival is the huge concentric fortress at its old south-eastern corner, the Tower. City and castle did not grow at the same pace. London expanded throughout the Middle Ages, in answer to human needs; the Tower, founded and spasmodically enlarged by royal policy, had more or less assumed its present form by 1300. Military changes would one day leave the king's work high and dry, but they had not done so by 1500. The Tower was still, in the words of William Dunbar, 'the house of Mars victorial, whose artillery with tongue may not be told'.

Details of the Tower are supplied by many good, cheap guidebooks and, for nothing, by the Yeomen Warders. A visit can even be enjoyed without consulting anybody, since the main buildings are clearly named and dated. The dates of course do not take account of changes and repairs, some of them drastic, and the current names are not always those of the Middle Ages, which was inconsistent in such matters. So much has been done to the Tower that it is easy to dismiss it as a bogus tourist-trap, forgetting that the plan itself is old and ambitious enough to make it 'the most important work of military architecture in England'. It is more helpful to realize how closely the Tower's history is bound up with London's and to picture the fortress in its early years, so as to see if much of what was familiar then is there today.

The Tower escaped from the city because it was begun a century before there was either a mayor or a commune. The original site was waste land yet it lay within an angle of the walls, part of which were afterwards knocked down so that the fortress could expand eastward, into a few acres of Middlesex. Londoners, remembering this, sometimes vainly claimed jurisdiction over what became known as the liberty of the Tower. They could never ignore the castle itself and were not intended to, for William's chief aim was to overawe them. His successor 'oppressed' many counties by requiring men to build a wall around the Tower and work on his hall at Westminster. The collapse of part of Henry III's masonry was pointedly said to have been foreseen in a vision, in which St Thomas

Becket threw down the walls as harmful to his fellow Londoners. After the present moat had been dug, the king had to threaten death to anyone bathing in it. As space became more precious, it was also tempting to tip rubbish there or simply to leave it on Tower Hill, which brought more stern warnings. However ungrateful for the Tower's protection, the citizens came to take pride in the royal lair. Fitz Stephen boasted that its mortar had been mixed with the blood of beasts, and many thought that only Julius Caesar could have built such a stronghold.

The Tower, from the city, seems to be a confusing jumble of buildings. Essentially they are no more than a keep inside a double ring of walls, themselves fortified with towers, although from the first other buildings have littered the intervening space. For nearly seven hundred years the normal approach by land has been from the bottom of Tower Hill. After passing the pit of an outer drawbridge and the site of the Lion Tower, most visitors turn left through the outermost surviving fortification, the Middle Tower. This leads to the main bridge across a wide, grassy moat and through another gateway, the Byward Tower. We are then in a narrow precinct, the Outer Ward, between double lines of walls which stretch ahead parallel to the river, forming the south side of the Tower, and leftward, to the north. The precinct, which runs all round, resembles a street, and in fact the stretch leading northward from the main gate was called Mint Street before the Royal Mint moved out to its present site. We must now walk straight ahead until a gateway on the left, the Bloody Tower, brings us through the inner wall to the heart of this stone network, the White Tower itself. A different approach is to go down to the Thames, leaving the Middle Tower on the left, and walk along the tree-lined quayside to cross the moat by the narrower Middle Drawbridge, roughly half-way along the Tower's river-front; we can then cut straight across the Outer Ward and through another opening in the inner wall to face the White Tower. This attractive but less awe-inspiring route is all the better for reaching the centre without too much distraction from later buildings. Since the whole complex spread outwards around the Conqueror's work, its growth can best be traced by forgetting all that we have seen before reaching the middle.

The first stronghold, erected within months of the battle of Hastings, was presumably a wooden structure on a mound, with a bailey or forecourt protected by the Roman masonry and by earthworks (*Fig. 34, Plan 1*). This was one of the many crude castles with which the Normans tightened their grip on the land. Its exact site is uncertain but the White Tower now lies so close to the line of the old city wall presumably because it was squashed into a corner of the same enclosure. We know that the wooden building survived into the 1140s, since Matilda granted to Geoffrey de Mandeville 'the tower of London with the castle which belongs to it', in other words the White Tower with the more primitive fortress nearby.

The White Tower itself, begun perhaps in the late 1070s and almost finished within twenty years, was probably the first English castle to be turned into stone. Materials were shipped from Caen for this gigantic keep, with tapering walls that are fifteen feet thick at the base. Luckily it is still first seen close at hand from the south, although in the Middle Ages there was too much bustle for a neat lawn. The main courtyard lay on this side, where a building that has disappeared carried the stairs up to the keep itself; the old doorway is marked by the large window on the left in the bottom row. Nothing remains of William Rufus's wall, which was perhaps simply a renewal of his father's defences along the north and west, the other two sides still being protected by the city wall. Today from most angles the White Tower peeps over a forest of outer stonework. In 1100, when it was the keep that mattered, there was nothing bigger in England except at Colchester. On the citizens' side, with no Roman masonry in the way, all eyes were drawn to the White Tower, gleaming in the whitewash which has given it its name and with only narrow slits to pierce the ninety-foot high walls that are now relieved by the spacious windows of Wren.

Today, although we have to go round to the north, the entrance to the keep is still on the first floor. Above there are two further floors and below there is a basement, all devoted to a collection of arms and armour. The exhibits, few of them either English or strictly medieval, detract from the strong, simple Norman design by which a stone wall divides every floor into a larger and a smaller room. The glory of the White Tower, and of Norman London, is the Chapel of St John on the second floor, with its crypt below. This is an unspoiled example of the very earliest Norman work, too early for more than the slightest decoration on the stone capitals. Embedded as it is in the walls of the fortress, there has been no room for additions or improvements; devoid of monuments, it remains the chapel in which every medieval king prayed (*Fig. 33*).

Fig. 33 *Interior of St John's Chapel in the White Tower, looking east, late 11th century* (Crown Copyright)

The Norman fortress was a hundred years old when Fitz Stephen saw it. There had been little change, although repairs were carried out to the White Tower itself and to various offices in the bailey—in his own day there was a kitchen, a bakery and a gaol. He may have lived through the next major work, begun in Richard I's absence in 1190. Just as the Conqueror had built his castle because of London's hostility, so Longchamp strengthened it against Count John and his friends among the citizens. This work of course contributed to the chancellor's unpopularity and so to his downfall.

143

Longchamp enclosed a large area, making the original bailey an inner courtyard. Probably he did not go beyond the Roman walls to the east but repaired these and continued around the other three sides, fortifying his circuit with towers. The White Tower stood closest to the vanished eastern wall of this enclosure, which ran south from today's Bowyer Tower, through the Wardrobe Tower on its ancient bastion, to the Lanthorn Tower. The other three sides of Longchamp's enclosure coincided with the present inner line of fortifications west of the Bowyer and Lanthorn Towers; most of this has been rebuilt except for the Bell Tower, at the south-west corner, which is therefore the second oldest tower in the fortress; it is also the only polygonal one, for previous plans had been square and those of a hundred years later were to be rounded. Outside his new walls Longchamp dug a ditch along the north and west, where the Outer Ward now runs from the Bowyer to the Bell Tower. This was not a success, apparently because the water drained away at low tide for lack of sluice gates, but it did provide inspiration for the future. King John thus inherited an old keep encircled by stone fortifications and partly moated. In his reign there was a second chapel, forerunner of the present St Peter-ad-Vincula, but none of John's work survives (*Fig. 34, Plan 2*). A mud wall put up between the Tower and the city in 1214–15 was probably simply to mark the boundary.

Henry III brought the modern plan a step nearer by breaching the Roman wall and taking in another acre to the east. The entire circuit was now reinforced: part of the Bloody Tower, the Wakefield Tower and the ancestor of the existing, Victorian, Lanthorn Tower were added to the old defences on the south, the Devereux and Bowyer Towers on the north; the new, eastern length of wall was given the Martin, Broad Arrow and Salt Towers. The southern walls still rose sheer from the water, so boats could reach the Bloody Tower at its landing stairs. The main entrance was probably in the middle of the western wall, where the Beauchamp Tower now stands; it faced the end of today's Great Tower Street, known as Tower Street by Henry's time and itself an extension of East Cheap. Anyone coming from the city could not make his way straight to the White Tower, whose door still faced south; he had first to reach the inner bailey through the Coldharbour Gate at the White Tower's south-west corner. Henry III rebuilt the bailey's wall, which ran south from this gate to the Wakefield Tower by the Thames, although strong outer defences were to make a cramped

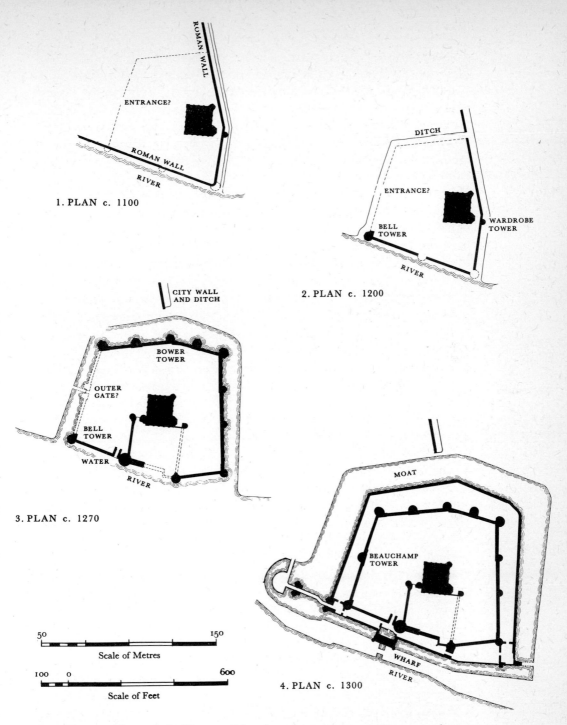

ROMAN WALL

ENTRANCE?

ROMAN WALL

RIVER

1. PLAN c. 1100

DITCH

ENTRANCE?

BELL
TOWER

WARDROBE
TOWER

RIVER

2. PLAN c. 1200

CITY WALL
AND DITCH

BOWER
TOWER

OUTER
GATE?

BELL
TOWER

WATER

RIVER

3. PLAN c. 1270

MOAT

BEAUCHAMP
TOWER

WHARF

RIVER

4. PLAN c. 1300

50   150

Scale of Metres

100   0   600

Scale of Feet

Fig. 34 *Plans of the Tower of London about 1100, 1200, 1270 and 1300*
(Crown Copyright)

inner enclosure unnecessary. The foundations of his Coldharbour Gate can still be seen, with part of the bailey's tall rubble wall revealed after the bombing of later buildings. The inner bailey could only be reached directly by a postern or small back gate which Henry III inserted in the river wall east of the new Wakefield Tower, to lead to his own quarters. His private entrance is commemorated by a plaque in the Outer Ward, immediately east of the rounded bulk of the Wakefield Tower (*Fig. 34, Plan 3*).

These changes sprang from Henry III's unpopularity with the Londoners and from the current military demand for a ring of flanking towers. The White Tower was now less commanding but it enjoyed a more central position. Nearly £10,000 was spent during the reign and in 1241 all the money due from the city was earmarked for work on the Tower. Progress varied with the ups and downs of politics, falling off in the troubled 1250s, rising when Henry reasserted himself, declining in the civil war and rising again after London was finally brought to heel. Henry's love of luxury pushed up the cost. He himself stayed within the inner bailey, where the great hall backed onto the south wall next to the Wakefield Tower (hence the little watergate) and where rooms for the royal couple were painted and panelled. The king wanted a better home, regardless of expense. Domestic offices, including the kitchen and a 'saucery', were improved, as well as the chapels. A house measuring twenty feet by forty feet was built for England's first elephant, sent by the king of France in 1255. Purbeck marble was bought, although none survives, and a coat of whitewash was ordered for the whole collection of buildings, inside and out. Henry was a pernickety spendthrift: he insisted that drainpipes should come within a few feet of the ground, lest water should mark the walls of his fortress-palace.

Under Henry's son the Tower assumed the basic form which it has kept for nearly seven hundred years. The western wall, from the Devereux Tower in the north-west to Longchamp's Bell Tower in the south-west, was finished as had already been planned. In 1275 the present moat was started, much wider than the old one and farther out, surrounding the castle on its three landward sides. This involved taking private ground, chiefly from St Katharine's Hospital to the east, but payments in compensation could be balanced against sales of the freshly dug earth to local tile-makers. Where the moat joined the Thames on either side of the Tower a water-mill was built (perhaps there were two by St Katharine's); a

Flemish expert was hired and the mills may have been tide-mills, worked by sluices. From this time the Tower remained an island until the moat was drained in 1843.

Between the now complete tower-flanked wall and the new moat lay the site of the old moat. This was filled in and a low revetment (retaining) wall built, anything taller or freestanding being impractical on such loose soil. Along the riverside, however, this outer line could not easily be carried, since water still lapped the old fortifications. An embankment was therefore built and the outer circuit finished, only here it was given elaborate fortifications like those all round the inner ring. The Byward Tower, St Thomas's Tower (incorporating Traitors' Gate), the Well Tower and the Develin Tower, with perhaps another one opposite the inner wall's Lanthorn Tower, all faced the river by about 1300, as they do today; only the Cradle Tower had yet to be added. Behind this frowning line the new ground level was so high that the Wakefield and Bloody Towers had to be heightened, as can still be seen where the smooth rectangular blocks of stone known as ashlar give way to rubble. The Wakefield Tower was joined by a bridge to the upper storey of St Thomas's Tower, so named because it held an oratory tactfully dedicated to London's favourite saint. Beneath this tower lay Traitors' Gate, from now the chief riverside entrance and the obvious passage for prisoners who were being sneaked in from Westminster without having to pass through the city itself.

Edward also shifted the main landward entrance to near its present position in the south-west. The Beauchamp Tower was built into the inner wall, blocking the old passage, and the new moat was bridged at the corner. Entrants then passed through an outwork or barbican, later the Lion Tower, over a curved branch of the moat to the Middle Tower and across the main moat to reach the Outer Ward by the Byward Tower. The main differences now are that the Lion Tower is ruined and the water is gone, whereas the outer wall immediately across the moat looks far more fearsome, being solid nineteenth-century work (*Fig. 34, Plan 4*).

Although more Spartan than his father, Edward I redecorated the royal chambers, and he entirely rebuilt St Peter-ad-Vincula. Most of his plans were finished by 1285, when the Mint had been set up in the Tower. Later kings were in general content to tinker with his work, producing its modern aspect by adding crenellations, the battlements and loopholes now popularly associated with all medieval castles. Edward II crenellated the four towers of the

147

eastern wall—the Salt, Broad Arrow, Constable and Martin Towers—and his son heightened and crenellated the south inner wall. Edward III also built the Cradle Tower into the riverside wall and inserted a new postern gate nearby after moving his lodgings farther east. Richard II spent more money on this southern front and was perhaps responsible for carrying it eastward across the moat to the now vanished Iron Gate. Another change was the construction of Tower Wharf, which prevents the southernmost wall from being washed by the Thames. After Edward I's encroachment on the river an embankment was made from the Byward Tower westward to a street called Petty Wales, now part of Tower Hill. This quay, presumably of earth and timber, was lengthened eastward in the 1330s and encased in stone some thirty years later.

The Tower was kept in good repair in the fifteenth century, when domestic buildings were often added or altered. The Londoners, prickly as ever, told Edward IV that a nearby gallows infringed their liberties. Edward denied that he had ordered it to be set up but he afterwards repaired the main defences and is said to have built a brick outwork on Tower Hill called 'the Bulwark'. The castle, brooding over an essentially medieval scene, had never looked grander than when the fall of the monasteries announced the passing of an age. In the 1530s Henry VIII added battlements everywhere, roughcast the walls and carried out further repairs in Caen stone and brick. The two massive rounded bastions known as Brass Mount and Legge's Mount were set at the north-east and north-west angles of the outer wall. More homely building also went on: the picturesque half-timbering on the inner sides of the Byward and St Thomas's Towers dates from Henry's time, like the governor's residence in the south-west corner of Tower Green, once called the Lieutenant's Lodgings and now the Queen's House. When the earliest riverside panoramas were drawn later in the century, the Tower with its ramparts in the east neatly counter-balanced the pinnacles of Westminster at the other end.

Another early Tudor survival is the Chapel Royal of St Peter-ad-Vincula, rebuilt after fire under Henry VIII. St Peter's is as near in time to us as it is to the Normans, yet it is linked to St John's Chapel by history, being one of the last fruits of medieval piety. The Reformation would have made its building impossible a few years later, and it was finished just in time to play its part in the Tower's bloodiest years as a burial place for the most famous victims of Tudor politics. Many of this grim procession, starting with Queen

Anne Boleyn, died within a few yards of the chapel's south wall, on Tower Green, where a plaque records the site of the scaffold. Others were led out to the top of Tower Hill, now Trinity Square, where another plaque to the west of the Merchant Seamen's War Memorials recalls their more public executions. Each spot had been used earlier, the green for Richard III's victim Lord Hastings in 1483, the hill for Richard II's favourite Sir Simon Burley a hundred years before. St Peter's, like its contemporary St Margaret Westminster, is cool and spacious, in spite of many later monuments, but it has none of the unique interest of the chapel in the White Tower. Normally it is closed, save for Sunday services and to guided tours, whose conductors linger on its role as a charnel house. It is worth joining one of these parties simply to see the canopied tomb of John Holland, duke of Exeter, in the north-west corner, some sixty years older than the chapel itself (*Fig. 35*); ironically this,

Fig. 35 *Detail from the tomb of John Holland, duke of Exeter (d. 1447), in St Peter-ad-Vincula, Tower of London* (National Monuments Record)

the loveliest medieval work in the Tower, was previously in St Katharine's Hospital, which was so over-shadowed by its mighty royal neighbour. (*See p. 228.*)

For the king, the Tower's unpopularity was far outweighed by its military value. Although, like the city itself, it often surrendered to the winning side, it was never taken by storm and sometimes it held out with decisive results. Even the Conqueror's stark keep was strong enough for Geoffrey de Mandeville to resist the Londoners, who turned on him after expelling Matilda; not until captured by Stephen did the earl buy his freedom with its surrender. John's more elaborate castle defied the barons who controlled London in 1215, so that Magna Carta had to insist that it should be placed in the neutral hands of the archbishop of Canterbury. Henry III twice asked his barons to meet in council at the Tower instead of at Westminster, which they understandably refused to do, fearing a trap. Although the king lost it in Simon de Montfort's brief hour of triumph, his renewed grip on the fortress which had cost him so much made it easy to crush Gloucester's rising in 1267.

The Tower was at its most formidable under Edward I. The second ring of defences had been added and artillery had not yet begun to reduce the value of castles. They continued for hundreds of years to fend off rioters, if not professional armies, and the Civil War was to show that even by the 1640s they were by no means white elephants. Medieval kings usually took shelter in the Tower if Westminster seemed unsafe. Edward II shut himself up there to denounce his wife and Mortimer before fleeing west, and it was an obvious refuge during the Peasants' Revolt, when treachery for once allowed the mob to rampage through the precincts. The Tower's steadfastness during Cade's rebellion helped to turn the tide and in 1460 its Lancastrian defenders held out against the popular Yorkists until they made terms. Henry VIII was wise to improve it in an age of cannon-power, for the Tudors were rarely free from the threats of invasion and of insurgence in the streets. If the counties which encircled London had had a stormier history there would have been much later glory, as there was for Edinburgh Castle, and if England had become an absolute monarchy the Tower would have been a hated symbol, like the Bastille. Instead it declined into a barracks and a showpiece. Charles II was the last king to stay there, on the eve of his coronation, although the strengthening of defences against the Chartists in 1848 provided one more justification of the Conqueror's vision.

The Tower, being the king's concern, rarely appears in the civic records. Walls, ditches and gates, by contrast, are often mentioned. Anglo-Saxon Londoners used all the landward stretches of the Roman wall, which had been built shortly before AD 200. Their example was followed throughout the Middle Ages, except for breaches in the south-east and south-west, where the wall had met the river. The south-eastern corner, as we have seen, became part of the Conqueror's castle and was pulled down 150 years later to make more room for the Tower. The south-western section lasted little longer, for in 1282 the black friars were allowed to enlarge their church at the expense of the wall, which was set up again farther west. Only along the Thames, where the Romans had built on piles, was their work neglected, but here there had been a different kind of wall. Fitz Stephen's talk of defences which had been undermined by the water led to the belief that nineteenth-century finds along Upper Thames Street belonged to some riverside fortifications. Recently, however, discoveries of parallel walls in Lambeth Hill and Knightrider Street make it most likely that all this stonework retained a series of terraces along the riverbank.

To trace the two miles of the land wall along modern streets is not to suggest walking along their entire length, for there is little to see, but to help connect the isolated fragments which survive. From the site of the postern gate immediately north of the Tower the line runs north-north-west, parallel to Minories, along the west side of America Square and the east side of Jewry Street to Aldgate, and then north-west, parallel to Houndsditch, along Duke's Place and the north side of Bevis Marks and Camomile Street to Bishopsgate. Here it takes a more westerly course along the north side of Wormwood Street and London Wall to Moorgate as far as the entrance to Blomfield Street, where the present road bends and widens so that the line runs beneath the middle of London Wall to Moorgate (this straight stretch, in spite of culverts, for centuries hindered the drainage of Moorfields, the marshy ground to the north where the Walbrook rises). From Moorgate the line continues west-north-west, parallel to Fore Street and diverging north of the new Route 11, which for no good reason has also been named London Wall. The line turns sharply south beyond the south-west corner of St Giles's Church, running across Route 11 and along Noble Street as far as the entrance to Oat Lane. It then heads west-south-west to cross the city end of Aldersgate High Street and skirt the northern

151

side of the Post Office buildings to the middle of their main loading yard. Here it turns south again, running parallel to Old Bailey, across Newgate Street and through Amen Court to the top of Ludgate Hill. The original wall continued from there straight down to the Thames across what are now the western ends of Carter Lane, Queen Victoria Street and Upper Thames Street; after the arrival of the black friars, its course was shifted westward almost to the Fleet, which flows under New Bridge Street.

Most medieval remains can only be seen in conjunction with Roman work. On flint and clay foundations in a trench the Romans had piled Kentish ragstone for the bulk of their wall, fixing it in very hard mortar and achieving a finished appearance by roughly squaring and coursing the inner and outer faces. A sandstone projection or plinth ran along the external base, and the whole structure was bonded (held together) by double or triple lines of thin red bricks, embedded between every fourth or sixth course of stone. At each of these bonding courses the wall was set back some three inches, so tapering it from the seven- to nine-foot thickness at its base. Earth was banked up inside and a ditch dug outside. Later the wall was strengthened by bastions, towers built on a semi-circular or occasionally a horseshoe plan, which survive at irregular intervals.

London's defences in the Middle Ages must have been as impressive as those of Londinium, if not so carefully constructed. The Roman height may have been over twenty feet but this is not certain, for the tallest survivals are topped by medieval work, which brings the section at Cooper's Row to thirty-six feet. This stonework looks coarser than the Roman masonry, although at the end of the Middle Ages there were some elegant repairs with bricks said to have been made of clay dug from Moorfields. Medieval masons, too, used Kentish ragstone and resorted to brick and tile courses; it is now agreed that they even added some of the twenty-one known bastions, all of which were once thought to have been Roman. In the last violent years of John's reign they also surrounded the wall with a ditch—perhaps the successor to many, since ditches could be dug with little skill but easily became filled up. According to Stow, it was the dead dogs thrown with other filth into this medieval work, the City Ditch, which earned it the name Houndsditch.

Roman London, in its later days, had at least six gateways: from east to west Aldgate, Bishopsgate, Cripplegate, Aldersgate, Newgate and Ludgate. The first and last two owed their positions to the roads which radiated outwards before gates or wall were built. Aldersgate was probably later than the wall and Cripplegate at first served not the city but a square fort at its north-western corner (this fort was older than the other defences and its northern and western walls were thickened and incorporated into the city wall). All six gates were maintained in the Middle Ages, as well as a Bridge gate in the middle of Peter of Colechurch's structure, a postern north of the Tower (where there may have been another Roman entrance), and, from about 1400, Moorgate. Only Moorgate, which also began as a postern, is remembered among these additions. Stone causeways had been laid across swampy flats beyond the long northern wall, so that people could walk to the villages of Islington and Hoxton, and in 1415 Moorgate was rebuilt farther west, on a grander scale.

None of the elaborate medieval gateways would have been recognizable to the Romans. Described by Fitz Stephen as double gates, and drawn as such by Matthew Paris, they were frequently repaired and made to serve many purposes. Newgate and Ludgate, being used as gaols, attracted pious bequests which included one from Richard Whittington which led to the rebuilding of Newgate in the 1420s. Aldersgate and Cripplegate were ordered to be roofed with lead and to have small houses built underneath for their keepers in 1337, and these and other gates were soon afterwards leased as desirable homes. Geoffrey Chaucer, when comptroller of the customs in the port of London, found it convenient to live nearby over Aldgate, where he became tenant of a 'mansion' and cellar in 1374.

Archaeology cannot exactly date repairs, but sometimes threats are known to have inspired a frenzy of work, such as the alliance between the citizens and the barons against John. Again, under Henry III, the hostile Londoners built or strengthened several watch-towers, only to be forced to dismantle them after the king's triumph. Outside Aldersgate one of these towers, perhaps part of an extra line of fortifications, was probably rebuilt; known before 1300 as the Barbican, it soon gave its name to Barbican Street, itself later shortened to Barbican, and so to London's most ambitious modern development plan. In 1377, with all the perils of a regency and a French invasion, it was decided to equip the gates with chains, portcullises and outer barbicans. One hundred years later the wall along the north, from Aldgate to Aldersgate, was extensively repaired with brick during the mayoralty of the draper Ralph

Jocelyne. This work, apportioned between the richest companies, was carried out during a long lull in the Wars of the Roses, after London had beaten off the Bastard of Fauconberg's frenzied assault. Ordinances were always in force to make certain wards responsible for guarding the nearest gate or stretch of riverbank, and whenever a gatehouse was let it was always agreed that the city could take it back in a crisis. Moorgate and Bishopsgate were both rebuilt in the 1470s, the latter by the German merchants of the Hanseatic League who for over two hundred years had been charged with its upkeep in return for freedom from toll.

Although repairs were sometimes done in a spirit of defiance, it was more common for the king to have to galvanize the citizens. When there was no danger, enthusiasm gave way to indifference or resentment. Money had to be raised, in London as in other towns, by periodic royal grants of murage, a carefully graded levy on all manner of goods brought in through the gates. The tax was so bad for trade that select groups were exempted even before Edward I excused all foreign merchants from payment in 1303. This only threw a greater burden on the citizens themselves, so that the provisions had to be suspended. In spite of a request to Edward II that no more murage should be collected, since business was being driven elsewhere, it was still levied under his successors, although exemptions multiplied. Often the king showed his concern by granting murage for a special purpose, such as the rebuilding of the wall around the black friars' house or repairs to Newgate gaol. He did more than earmark spending on the defences; he kept an eye on their general state. Edward II, hearing that timber had been stolen from the gates and stones from the wall 'in contempt of ourselves, and to the detriment of our city and the manifest peril of all dwelling therein', ordered the mayor and sheriffs to make an example of the culprits.

Wealthy Londoners, with much to lose, were naturally keener on defence than were the poor. Being also more worried about law and order, they ought to have prized their wall as highly as the king valued his Tower. The wall, allowing control of the passage of people and goods, was indispensable. Without it, for example, the city fathers could hardly have hoped to keep London clean by sponsoring brothels in Southwark. It also helped them to carry out royal commands, which ranged from bans on exports to Scotland to orders for the exclusion of lepers. Even when daytime traffic was thickest, the gates were watched, and rules were repeatedly issued

Fig. 36 *London, from a sketch in an itinerary by Matthew Paris, mid 13th century* (British Museum)

for their safe keeping. In 1321 the main gates were to be closed from sunset until sunrise and the little wicket-gates from the hour when curfew rang from St Martin-le-Grand until the sound of the first bell from the hospital of St Thomas of Acon; each gate was to be guarded by twelve armed men. When the gates were strengthened in 1377 steps were also taken to police the city, involving oaths from every citizen, closing of the gates and taverns by 9 p.m. and a ban on ordinary townsmen carrying any arms save a long dagger or baselard. In the wake of the Peasants' Revolt, with a stormy session of Parliament ahead, the number of guards was raised to eighteen or twenty per gate and the gates themselves were to be shut at 6 p.m. for twelve hours. No such measures would have been of the slightest use if it had not been for the encircling wall.

In the long run, shortage of space, even more than cost, was bound to affect a line of defences which had been laid down by the Romans. Houses were not supposed to be built within sixteen feet of the wall, but the number of orders for the 'abatement' of property, or of fines, shows that this was a losing battle. The City Ditch became a still graver nuisance, overflowing with all kinds of rubbish; time and again it had to be cleaned out, and in 1463 a rich fishmonger was excused from all civic offices on paying 100 marks for its repair. During the Dark Ages and probably until the building of the Confessor's abbey and the Conqueror's keep, the wall, gateways and bastions had been London's dominating feature. The city's common seal shows a stylized cluster of spires and turrets protected by an oversize wall and gateway. So too does the drawing by Matthew Paris, which depicts London from the north, with the

155

Tower to the left, Westminster to the right, St Paul's in the middle and the river beyond (*Fig. 36*). The gates remained familiar medieval landmarks, for everyone had to pass through them, but the wall seemed to shrink as settlement spread outwards, until it formed no more than an inner ring. An awkward consequence of this expansion was that citizens living outside the wall did not feel bound to pay towards its upkeep; in 1432 it was ordered that they should be assessed, on pain of losing their civic rights, towards 'the reparation of the walls and cleansing of the ditches . . . which be in great peril and ruin'. Ralph Jocelyne, implied the Great Chronicle of London, undertook his repairs to give people something to remember him by. A levy on the richer citizens was not enough, so the mayor took a collecting box on his tours of duty and paid for the building materials himself. Although such public spirit won praise, for a city of London's size was clearly thought to deserve an imposing wall, the military benefits were not mentioned. Next year the work was abandoned in favour of cleaning the ditch, but it was only to be expected that a new mayor would ignore unfinished business, 'because he thinketh the honour thereof shall be ascribed unto his predecessor and not unto him'. Militarily the Tower had long given better value than the wall. A castle might hold out under a picked garrison; the long circuit of the city's defences could only be held by a sustained popular will. Usually, as we have seen, self-interest pointed the other way.

The wall, then, increasingly served to buttress authority rather than to keep out the enemy. This does not mean that it lost all military value. If London had been threatened by foreign armies, its old defences would have been desperately needed. As it was, the citizens were safe against surprise attacks, if not against a determined onslaught. They had no heart to defy the hordes of Wat Tyler or Jack Cade, but they beat off the Bastard of Fauconberg in May 1471: barrels were slung across the Thames and Bishopsgate was fiercely defended, while other attackers were admitted through Aldgate only to be cut off by the lowering of the portcullis. Fabyan, the early Tudor chronicler, himself helped to man the ramparts when Henry VII was threatened by the pretender Perkin Warbeck, and in 1536 similar precautions were taken during the Roman Catholic rebellion known as the Pilgrimage of Grace. In the 1550s a rich draper paid for the City Ditch to be arched over between Newgate and Aldersgate, but farther east, right round to the Tower, it remained intact until the end of the century. In 1642 when

London was the headquarters of the Parliamentary forces, all buildings near the wall were again ordered to be pulled down and the citizens prepared, unnecessarily as it turned out, to mount guard against Charles I. It was not until 1660 that General Monk, planning the Restoration, removed all chains across the streets, unhinged the gates and jammed the portcullises, so making the historic defences useless.

The wall, being in the way, could not survive. Its fate is all the sadder because it was nine hundred years older than the Tower; in early days it had been vital to London's growth, of which the Tower was but a symptom. Fittingly it has left its mark not in mere names but in the very pattern of the city. Although the roads which radiate through the gates to the far corners of England are older than the wall, its line is responsible for many of the cross-streets, which link the main ones much as threads link the spokes of a spider's web. The wall, inevitably dictating the course of streets which overlie its foundations, accounts for the bend half-way along Camomile Street. Other roads further out run parallel to the old line or to its accompanying ditch—Minories and Houndsditch in the east, Fore Street in the north, Old Bailey in the west.

Few people realize that fragments of the wall survive on all sides, although much is Roman work which can only be seen in private basements. In a typically English fashion, the old fortifications were never swept away in a grandiose burst of town-planning. The solid foundations were left nearly everywhere, being so far below the later ground levels; often tall stretches of walling, built into new houses, stood forgotten for generations. They won scant notice until the Second World War, as the finest sections were hidden from all but their owners and a few enthusiasts. Since the air-raids, ambitious rebuilding schemes have stirred up interest in these reminders that London was once a walled city, like Chester or York. Much is now well displayed and in time there will be still more.

The wall is best seen in the south-east, around Tower Hill. Foundations survive within the Tower itself, next to the Wardrobe Tower, but these are Roman and interesting chiefly for giving us a chance to see the original construction, with its plinth and brick bonding. The first medieval bit is reached by walking up Tower Hill and turning right towards the former site of Trinity Place, in the south-east corner of Trinity Square. Here the wall was broken off to make way for the enlarged fortress, and the postern gate was built between the two. Instead of continuing farther east along Tower Hill, we can turn into Wakefield Garden, where a plaque records London's earliest inscribed monument, to a Roman procurator (the original finds are the British Museum). Beyond this, the ground has been cut away to its Roman level. A few steps go down to grass at the foot of the wall, its rubble core still partly faced with squared, whitish stone and bonded with tile-like bricks; Roman masonry survives to some fourteen feet, with medieval work above. Near the top is a wall-walk, once paced by sentries whose view commanded the Tower itself. Looking up from the foot of this mass, as tall as the young ash trees in the garden, we can imagine the security which it must have given to Anglo-Saxon, Norman and medieval Londoners.

After skirting Wakefield Garden the wall gives way to modern buildings, only to reappear a few hundred yards farther north. We can reach this stretch by turning back into Trinity Square, following its eastern side past the new Tower Hill underground station and entering Cooper's Row. The stones can be glimpsed on the right, at the back of a covered piazza next to the main entrance to Midland House, another very recent building. This piece, although known, belonged for nearly a hundred years to the back of Messrs Barber's warehouse, which was pulled down only in 1961. Preserved at great cost, it is the longest section now on view, although at first sight it loses something from being so closely hemmed in. The Roman ground level, that of the basement car-park underneath, can be seen by leaning over the wall's protecting railings, and a path leads through an archway round to the outer face with its sandstone plinth. An explanation, diagram and map behind a fountain on the south side of the court state that the Roman masonry rises to thirteen feet but that the total height is thirty-six feet. The upper work, although clearly coarser, shows how elaborate were London's medieval defences. There are traces of four loopholes and a window, the latter between lines which mark diverging flights of stairs up to a wall-walk. Squared slots for timber near the bottom of the loopholes show that they were once reached by this walk, which was made of wood. The loopholes, being round headed, date roughly from 1200 and might be relics of the citizens' plans to resist King John. Their work was thorough for, although the loopholes have been partly filled in, there is no sign here of repairs from the later Middle Ages.

There is a large gap between Trinity Place and Cooper's Row, which can be visited in quick succession, and the next, much smaller, medieval survival. This is part of the long northern stretch of the city's defences and is the only bit left along the street called London Wall (at its eastern end, close to the junction with Old Broad Street). The church of All Hallows London Wall was here built right against the old fortifications, so that Roman remains lie underneath its northern side. They continue west of the church, still hidden by the raised ground level but surmounted by a line of whitish medieval masonry, visible from the street. A curious instance of the wall's effect on later development is the plan of the church itself, a medieval foundation, rebuilt in the eighteenth century and recently restored, after bomb damage, as the City Centre for Church Art. The pulpit can be reached only from the vestry, a semi-circular chamber jutting out to the north; since the church pressed close to the wall, its vestry, most of it now blocked to the view outside, had to be built on top of the rounded bastion.

So far we have met none of the brickwork of the later Middle Ages. The best example is farther west, beyond Moorgate, in a much grander piece of this northern stretch. This, too, bounded a churchyard, that of St Alphage London Wall. Some fourteenth-century ruins of a chapel which afterwards became St Alphage's still face the new highway of London Wall (Route 11), but the churchyard, now called St Alphage Garden, lies behind to the north-west, as did the original parish church. We can reach it by turning into Wood Street, which runs up from Cheapside to cut across Route 11, and passing under a pedestrian way, St Alphage Highwalk. An opening on the right leads into the garden, a cul-de-sac overlooked by office-towers, where seats and grass flank both sides of the wall. On its southern, inner, face a plaque again reminds us of our debt to the air raids, which demolished buildings at both ends and against the northern side, allowing the entire section to be enclosed in its garden in 1954. Being so near the city's north-west corner, the original wall here was the northern wall of the still earlier fort; it was strengthened on inclusion in London's own defences. Apart from its great length, this section is remarkable for the battlements at its eastern end, made of darkened red bricks with a diamond pattern on the inner face (*Fig. 37*). These are part of the repairs set in train by Ralph Jocelyne in 1477–8. Steps on the left lead to the old, much lower, ground level at the back, sunless and dominated by the confusingly patched wall. Along the bottom runs the core of the Roman fort wall, some ten feet high. Above is

Fig. 37 *The south side of the city wall at St Alphage Garden, showing the diamond pattern on the late 15th-century brick battlements* (Francis Forty, O.B.E., B.Sc., F.S.A.)

coursed rubble, probably early medieval. At the top on the right mid-fourteenth-century repairs stretch for fifty feet, with courses of flint and tiles set in the masonry. To the left loom Mayor Jocelyne's battlements; seen from the correct angle at the back of the sunken garden, they are silhouetted against the sky.

After St Alphage Garden there is little to be seen. Foundations along Noble Street, to be preserved in a public garden, show where the west side of the Roman fort, like the northern one at St Alphage's, was incorporated into the city's defences. The wall's course is confirmed by a magnificent Roman bastion and a stretch beneath the main loading yard west of the Post Office's King Edward Building, in Newgate Street, while a modest Roman piece underneath Amen House (demolished 1969) in Warwick Square reveals the line farther west between Newgate and Ludgate. A few yards to the south a narrow medieval fragment carries a modern brick wall along the back of Amen Court, a private courtyard which can be glimpsed from Warwick Lane; this, however, is inside the original Roman line. Further demolitions could uncover enormous lengths of wall. The richest treasure-ground is the north-west corner itself, where the square fort once occupied some eleven acres, now roughly bounded by Aldermanbury in the east and Gresham Street in the south. Most of this area has for years been overrun by builders as part of the Barbican redevelopment scheme. The churchyard of St Giles Cripplegate has been lowered, to reveal more and more of London's earliest wall, that of the fort, with its Roman and medieval additions. Remains have long been known to include more of Mayor Jocelyne's brickwork, along the north, and the medieval sides of two bastions. These are not yet on view, although the imposing walls of the southern bastion can be seen through undergrowth near the entrance to the basement car-park beneath Route 11. It was thought that the bastions must have been reared on Roman foundations, but recent finds of early thirteenth-century pottery in pockets of earth beneath the junctions of the bastions with the wall prove that the stonework is medieval—perhaps one more result of London's fear of King John.

Unlike the wall and its bastions, the gates have completely disappeared. The postern by the Tower collapsed in 1440 and was never properly rebuilt, although remains survived for nearly three hundred years. Pictures of all seven named gateways are common, but they would have been unfamiliar to the men of the Middle Ages. Traffic congestion and the desire for up-to-date ceremonial entrances led to the rebuilding of Ludgate under Elizabeth, of Aldgate and Aldersgate under James I, of Newgate, Moorgate and much of Cripplegate under Charles II, and of Bishopsgate as late as 1731. Their final demolition began with Bishopsgate in 1760 and ended with Newgate in 1777. However we can still see where London began to exceed its walled limits, with settlement spreading along the roads from these gates to the Bars. A plaque on the south-east side of Aldgate High Street, over the Mirella restaurant and just beyond the entrance to Jewry Street, commemorates Aldgate. One on the west side of Bishopsgate, over Horne's, and another opposite, over the Midland Bank on the corner of Camomile Street, recall Bishopsgate. A plaque for Moorgate is set in the modern block on the east side of Moorgate, where it joins London Wall from the north. One on the south wall of Roman House, a new block at the corner of Wood Street and St Alphage Garden, marks the site of Cripplegate. There is a plaque for Aldersgate on the west side of Aldersgate High Street, on the wall of Alder House. One for

161

Newgate looks down on people queueing to visit the Central Criminal Court, facing Newgate Street. Sometimes the road changes its name when passing over these forgotten sites: Aldgate as it heads north-east becomes Aldgate High Street, St Martin's-le-Grand becomes Aldersgate High Street and Newgate Street gives way to Holborn Viaduct.

The names of the gates, now used by all manner of streets and buildings, are Anglo-Saxon or medieval. Aldgate, said by Stow to have been the 'old gate', is not so mentioned until the 1480s; for most of the Middle Ages it had been 'Alegate', having first appeared as *Æstgeat* (Eastgate) a few years before the Norman Conquest. Bishopsgate, recorded in a Latin form in Domesday Book, was traditionally ascribed to Bishop Earconwald, the seventh-century founder of All Hallows by-the-Tower; it may however simply owe its name to the bishops of London, who were supposed to make its hinges in return for one stick from every cart carrying wood through the gate. Moorgate, the late comer, is called after the desolate marsh to its north, known by William the Conqueror's time as the Moor. It is doubtful whether crippled beggars, of whom there were plenty everywhere, or St Giles their patron saint was responsible for the name Cripplegate; the nearby church seems to be later than the gate, which, perhaps because of a *cripele* or burrow (some underground passage or covered way reached through the gate), is *Cripelesgeat* in laws issued by Æthelred II before 1002. Aldersgate is named in the same laws, as the gate of one Ealdred. Further back in Anglo-Saxon history, in 857, a reference to the 'west gates' presumably applies to Newgate, either by itself as a double gate or to Ludgate as well. Newgate, the chief Roman opening to the west, may owe its present misnomer to a rebuilding early in the Middle Ages; it was so called by 1275 but was also known as 'the chamberlain's gate', perhaps after the family of William the Chamberlain, who held a vineyard in Holborn at the time of Domesday. Ludgate, the other western entrance, probably began as a postern, in Old English a *ludgeat*; it appears in the 1160s and was for many generations ascribed to the legendary King Lud.

CHAPTER FIVE

The Londoners

So far we have seen how the Londoners gradually won self-government and that they were a power in the land. Who exactly were they? Except in crises like the Peasants' Revolt, when the mob ran wild, it was the city's rulers who acted in its name. To find out about those men, we must trace the growth of many institutions which are familiar today. The landmarks in the struggle with the king are clear enough, but neither these nor royal promises to respect their independence tell us much about the balance of power inside the city itself.

Throughout the Middle Ages there was a real division between those who were citizens or freemen and those who were not. At first citizenship was most likely to pass from father to son, as it had in Roman times, but new blood was soon added by admitting recommended apprentices, who had usually served a seven-year term, and by purchase; in other words a man could become a citizen by patrimony, by servitude or by redemption (as he still can). Everyone else was a 'foreign', if born in England, or an 'alien', if he came from overseas. A citizen had political rights which allowed him persistently to claim some share in municipal government. Attempts to define and assert these rights explain much of the turbulence of medieval London. Among his economic privileges, most of which lasted until the nineteenth century, was the exclusive right to trade within the city.

London has no charter of incorporation, although some 150 boroughs have modelled their liberties on hers. Proudly, the city claims to be a corporate body by prescriptive right, that is from time immemorial, pointing to early confirmation of still earlier liberties. In theory the London of William Fitz Stephen, like that

163

of Edward the Confessor, was democratic. All the freemen were expected to come three times a year to the folkmoot, while more personal business, including issues between English and foreign traders, was settled weekly in the husting court. The folkmoot was an open-air meeting, held on the high ground north-east of St Paul's; the husting (from the Old Norse *hus-thing*, house assembly), as its name implies, was small enough to meet indoors, in a private home or perhaps a church. By 1066 their city had also been divided into wards, in each of which the males over fifteen annually elected a chief officer, the alderman, to preside at wardmoots. In practice the freemen were only a small, if unknown, percentage of the population. Among them inequalities had quickly appeared, as they were bound to do in a thrusting, mercantile society, and from these of course flowed political inequality. The Anglo-Saxon *frithsgild* and the *cnihtengild* both seem to have been powerful mutual benefit associations. Membership was not the same as municipal office, but it was from such circles that London's rulers in the early Middle Ages were drawn.

The oldest civic office is that of sheriff, which arose from the king's needs before even London had evolved posts of its own. The *scir gerefa* was the reeve or official who collected royal revenues and enforced justice within a shire. If we equate him in London with the Anglo-Saxon portreeve (a *port* being a market-town), he can be traced as far back as the seventh century. By the Norman Conquest the portreeve was in charge of Middlesex as well as London, and this link with the shire that surrounded it on three sides was maintained after Henry I granted the right of election; two sheriffs were afterwards chosen and remained jointly responsible for London and Middlesex until the local government reforms of 1888. Since then, even after the disappearance of Middlesex as a county in 1965, there have been two sheriffs for the city alone.

Although the chief royal agents were always important, the leading citizens were most closely identified with the aldermen. 'Ealdorman' in fact was an older title than that of sheriff, for before Alfred's day it had been held by the king's main representative in a shire. After Cnut's triumph it was more sparingly conferred, on almost vice-regal figures, and changed to the Scandinavian 'eorl', which has passed into our language as earl (it was the aggrandizement of a few earls that made necessary a sheriff in every shire). Aldermen then emerged as London's own officers, members of the leading families who almost inherited their wards with their wealth.

A ward was the area in the guard or keeping (Old English *weard*) of its alderman. Although we do not know whether these officers came before the division into wards, the medieval ward-boundaries which still survive may be those of the private areas of jurisdiction, called sokes, of early citizens. One man's scattered property would explain the odd sizes and some still odder shapes, including a piece of Farringdon Within along Noble Street which is quite separate from the rest of that very large ward. This was clearly so with Portsoken, the only ward which grew up wholly outside the wall; the land here was given in 1125 by the citizens' *cnihtengild* to the new priory of Holy Trinity, whose prior was always *ex officio* an alderman until the Reformation. Early wards, twenty of which are mentioned in 1130, were usually named after people, such as the ward of Godwine or the ward of Osbert. Only in a list of 1285 are most of them given the topographical names which they bear today. Even now Farringdon Within and Farringdon Without recall the Farndon family, one of whom left his rights in what was then a single ward as late as 1334, and Bassishaw refers to the *haw, haga* or enclosed dwelling-place of the still earlier Basings.

These aldermanic families were well-entrenched when Fitz Stephen wrote. Any citizen could still speak at the folkmoot, but only outstanding success would admit him to the small committees which took most vital decisions. London's patriciate was if anything strengthened by the grant of the commune, which freed it from royal interference, but nobody else had much cause to rejoice. Five years later when a disgruntled member of the ruling clique, William Fitz Osbert or William Longbeard, cuttingly attacked pride and corruption, he won thousands of followers. The government, fearing that riots would turn to revolution, came to the rescue and at last managed to smoke him out from St Mary-le-Bow. To one writer Longbeard was a cunning trouble-maker, who blasphemously quoted the scriptures to pose as the saviour of the people. To Matthew Paris in the next generation he was a martyr; the chain in which he was hanged at Smithfield was said to have wrought miracles, and the gibbet and the very earth on which it had stood were carried off as relics. Longbeard, however shady, must have deserved some place in the hearts of the poor. Magna Carta might indeed be a landmark in the history of England's liberties; among its supervisors the mayor of London was as far removed in sympathy from the urban mob as were the barons from their peasants.

Between the commune and Simon de Montfort's rebellion,

London was ruled by sixteen families, linked by business and marriage ties. Henry Fitz Ailwin, the first mayor, came from a clan which produced ten aldermen; from about 1100 the Bukerels provided one in every generation for nearly two hundred years. Who were these capitalists? They were not of course concerned with the crafts which humble people could practise in their homes. They were big wholesalers or men who manufactured luxuries from foreign raw materials. After the Conquest, if they were not English they were more likely to be French or German than Scandinavian; often they had relatives at the far ends of the trade-routes to Flanders or Gascony. They were the few who catered for the few—drapers, mercers (dealing in many costly stuffs, but not yet mainly in silk), goldsmiths, pepperers (forerunners of the grocers) and, above all, vintners (a ship's tonnage, which we talk of today, was originally the space filled by tuns or casks of wine). The very richest might supply the royal household and so obtain lucrative posts, vintners supervising the wine trade and goldsmiths the Exchange.

Varied names show how cosmopolitan were London's early rulers. The Fitz Ailwins sprang from a thegn of Edward the Confessor; the Bukerels came later from Normandy, as did the Blunts and the Viels. Like the French-speaking nobles and prelates, they had more in common with opposite numbers abroad than with the poor on their doorsteps. There was nothing odd about this, although it sharpened the contrast between London and the static countryside around, where most families were tied to the soil. A few Englishmen lived in towns and others escaped there, but the easiest way to the top was that of the stranger with something special to offer. Privileges for foreign groups were never popular, but the really enterprising men—with whom we are dealing here—could always strike roots in London. Becket himself, the citizens' idol for nearly four hundred years, was the London-born son of prosperous French immigrants; the first chronicler of the mayors and Henry III's chief supporter was the alderman Arnold Fitz Thedmar, also born in London but of German parentage; his father was a Bremen merchant, his mother the daughter of a man from Cologne, and he himself was the spokesman of German business interests.

When we speak of London in the first century of its commune, we are really speaking of the ruling few, who could turn its very growth to their advantage. The folkmoot became cumbersome, it was difficult for all freemen to choose municipal officers, and electors dwindled to those summoned by the mayor and aldermen. When John granted annual elections of the mayor, he further helped this suspicious, self-perpetuating group, which was intensely conservative in anything which did not affect its own power. It might of course be split by private feuds but it was united in fear of royal interference, foreign competition, displacement by men in the new crafts, and violence by the poor. Sometimes, variously pleading defence of civic liberties or the duties of good subjects, the patricians called in one force to balance against another. By and large, having won all that they wanted, they leaned to Henry III, while the populace, resenting the king's extortions and the leading citizens as his tools, placed their hope in the barons.

London's own history in the Middle Ages is not that of the advance of democracy. It is of an ever more unwieldy community, where power had passed from the many to the few, and of how the few were constantly pressed to widen their ranks. Although the really poor could be dangerous, they had no resource but their numbers and never won permanent gains. The long term threat came from the craftsmen, mostly small men but some of them very prosperous, who were excluded from the ruling clique. As the population swelled, the trades and crafts which catered for it gathered strength, until fishmongers, skinners, corders (who made anything from ropes to braids), cordwainers (who made leather footwear) and others were challenging the old, select businesses. This led to the organization of the various callings and so the the guilds.

The Old English *gild* or *geld* was a money payment (as in the notorious Danegeld paid to the Vikings), and so came to mean a mutual benefit society to which citizens subscribed. Although guilds were originally religious, social and charitable, and to some extent remained so, they naturally attracted men in the same line of business. Just as naturally, they began to further their own interests, regulating their members' economic activities and putting pressure on others. In London, by chance, we know that the weavers were banded together by 1130 and that there were guilds of bakers and saddlers in the 1150s. In 1180 the goldsmiths, pepperers, cloth-workers, butchers and over a dozen other groups were fined and abolished as 'adulterine' guilds, for having no royal licences. None of these can be linked directly with the later city companies, but nothing could stop the growth of economic organizations. In most towns by the thirteenth century all the chief citizens were combining into a single fraternity, the merchant guild, which became not only an exclusive club but the real seat of power. London was so big that the callings never united into one merchant guild but formed separate brotherhoods. All these could be used as pressure groups, but they could not wrest power from the old charmed circle.

These strains explain London's part in the struggle between Henry III and Simon de Montfort. It was a popular rising which swung the capital behind the earl in 1263, when a revolutionary commune was installed in his name, and it was his defeat which brought back the aldermen (and saved Fitz Thedmar who, with other royalists, was to have been attacked at the next folkmoot). As Henry lay dying at Westminster in 1272, the streets rang with the shouts of craftsmen disputing the mayor's election, a clamour quickly silenced by one of London's toughest rulers, Henry le Waleys. A king's man and something of a professional trouble-shooter, Waleys bubbled with new ideas. He planned a new victuals market at the Stocks, on the site of the present Mansion House, new houses near St Paul's whose rent would help to maintain the bridge, and a new prison, the Tun, in Cornhill; he cleared away the stalls from Cheapside, tried to record particulars of every person in London, and rigorously enforced the law. Like several of the most pushing capitalists he was a newcomer, with interests in the wine trade and a regular customer in the king (who also sent him to spend some years as mayor of Bordeaux). Waleys married into the Basing family and so into the very best circles. He and the goldsmith Gregory de Rokesley monopolized the mayoralty for thirteen years, until the king seized London into his own hands. There is no memorial to Waleys but a plaque outside Lloyds Bank in Lombard Street marks the house of Rokesley, the last representative of the old dynasties which were broken by Edward I.

Edward's real grievance was that London was too hidebound, although he had excuses for setting up the inquiry which provoked Rokesley to resign. Ancient popular rights, now fossilized, would have to go, along with the power of those who stifled competition. Even before the seizure Edward had cleared the way by denouncing the site of the folkmoot as a haunt of thieves and vagabonds; although this historic ground, where Anglo-Saxon Londoners had given a lead to England by acclaiming her kings, was the city's freehold, it became part of St Paul's churchyard without so much as an inquest. After the mayor had been replaced by a royal warden, civic offices were thrown open. In 1291 the aldermen for the first time included a fishmonger; of ten sheriffs appointed between 1285 and 1290, six belonged to crafts previously excluded, and from 1293 to 1298 none of the former rulers was chosen; the mayoralty itself, restored in 1298 in the person of Waleys, was soon to pass to new men. More offices were created in the flush of modernization—a recorder, a prosecutor and a common serjeant—and attorneys were retained to speak for London in the royal courts of Westminster.

Now that others had a taste of power Edward must have hoped that London would become more docile, but he soon found the new rulers as spikily independent as the old. Nor did the city become more peaceful, for it had taken pressure from above, not from below, to make a narrow breach into the ruling circle, and a man's fitness for government depended as much as ever on his substance, his ability to share the common burdens. There was still a gulf between citizens and the rest, while a citizen himself might be anything from a hired workman or street trader to a merchant prince. In the fourteenth century citizen families embraced a third of the population at most; by Tudor times this had sunk to a quarter and of every twenty people in the streets less than one was likely to be a freeman.

No one seems to have cared about the non-citizens. The real struggle centred on efforts by the poorer freemen to make their old liberties effective, to help choose municipal officers and so make them accountable. As the crafts began to press for citizens' rights under Edward II, they also tried to control admission to the freedom. Patrimony now accounted for only a few entries and apprenticeship was already in the hands of the crafts, but the third avenue, purchase or redemption, allowed the rich to bring in whom they liked. At last in 1319 Edward II agreed that no stranger could be admitted without the backing of six men from the mystery which he wished to join or, if he was to have no trade, by the commoners. An extreme provision that all redemptioners must serve a seven-year apprenticeship, won forty-five years later, was soon repealed, but the victory of 1319 proved lasting. Inevitably it has confused our picture of late medieval London, since many citizens claimed to follow crafts which they never practised. As the crafts organized themselves into companies, citizenship became almost entirely confined to their members, as it is today.

As well as the inevitable gulf between rich and poor, there were still élite businesses which almost monopolized power. Their number was no longer limited to suppliers of luxuries, but it remained small and as exclusive as it could. In the fourteenth century the dominant interests were those of the mercers, the grocers, the drapers, the fishmongers, the goldsmiths, the skinners, the tailors, and the vintners; in the next century they were joined by the ironmongers, the salters and the haberdashers. Gradually these and many other interests formed themselves into companies (the early dominant groups, plus the clothworkers, being the ancestors of the twelve senior livery companies of today). 'Merchant', previously a term for anyone engaged in trade, even a street peddler, in London came to imply membership of one of the select associations, so that the citizens' groups in the late Middle Ages can be divided into the powerful merchant companies and the lesser companies.

Unexplained references to guilds, fraternities, crafts, mysteries and companies often make the whole subject hopelessly tangled. It is perhaps simplest to say that a guild was a fraternity, a social and religious brotherhood, remembering that in this sense it existed even before the Conquest. Members of a craft or mystery, on the other hand, practised the same business, but we have seen that they often belonged to the same brotherhood, so that the old charitable association often became indistinguishable from an economic one. By the late fourteenth century we can speak of companies, since several had bought royal charters—the goldsmiths, skinners, tailors and girdlers did so in 1327. The earliest charters recognized a company's powers of self-government and allowed it to enforce standards, perhaps throughout the country; later ones granted the legal status of a perpetual corporation. It is with these charters that the histories of the present city companies begin, although in most cases we know that some sort of body had existed much earlier. Sometimes a monopoly was granted, as to the vintners (of the Gascon wine-trade), the fishmongers and the drapers in the 1360s, but it was incorporation which paid most handsomely in the long run. The pious habit of leaving property to religious houses had been curbed by Edward I, since the Crown was losing the profits which it would have had on inheritance by individuals, but a royal charter could allow land to be held for ever, in mortmain. Companies thus began to accumulate land and to build special halls. Their London property has gained steadily in value and forms the basis of their present wealth.

In 1423 there were 111 separate crafts. Most could not afford to buy charters but those which could, on their own or by amalgamating, followed hard on the heels of the élite—so hard that the four or five halls of Richard II's reign had multiplied to twenty-eight a hundred years later. Once incorporated and able to use their common seals, companies sought grants of arms; the Drapers' Company still possesses letters patent of 1439, England's oldest known patent of arms (*Fig. 38*). At all levels there were changes, before or after incorporation, as some businesses shrank while others prospered. The pursers and glovers, 'sore decayed', were allowed to unite in 1498 but were soon absorbed by the leathersellers, to whom the pouchmakers were added in 1517. Other examples include the hatters and cappers, both swallowed up by the haberdashers, and the pinners, who vainly joined forces with the wiresellers before disappearing into

Fig. 38 *Letters patent (in French) granting arms to the Drapers' Company, 10 March 1439* (By permission of the Drapers' Company)

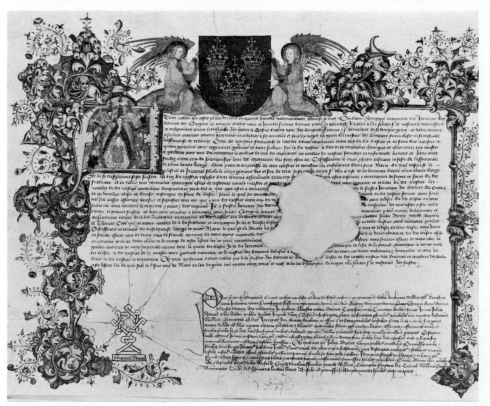

the much richer company of girdlers. Sometimes the name of a modern company, such as the Painter-Stainers and the Barber-Surgeons, reminds us of a union between equals. Even the woollen interests were affected: the fullers and shearmen, separately incorporated, came together in 1528 as the Clothworkers, and so won the last place among the great twelve. The division between the twelve and the rest is therefore no guide to antiquity nor even, sometimes, to wealth, but a reminder that the former once had a near monopoly of office. This invidious order of precedence does not even reflect the historical seniority of the great companies themselves: the Mercers, who now hold first place, were only the fourth to be incorporated, in 1393.

To add to the confusion, within the various companies the rich tried to keep the poor at arm's length. A wholesaler, with his warehouse, did not care to be taken for a retailer who sold over his own shop counter, even if they both dealt in the same goods, and the owner of a workshop must be distinguished from one of his hirelings. Emblems and differences in dress were extremely important in the Middle Ages, when both the tradesman's sign and the nobleman's coat of arms sprang from the need to identify and to advertise. Great men gave their retainers special badges, hoods or clothing, known as liveries (from the French *livrer*, to bestow); the Garter, founded in 1348 as England's first order of chivalry, was itself a royal livery. Inevitably the senior members of merchant companies, and soon those of the lesser companies, devised an official costume which they alone could wear. This, a hood and gown in two colours which changed according to taste, has given rise to the present description 'Livery Companies'. Historically the term is not very helpful, since humbler members never wore their company's livery and, even now, there are guilds which have never been granted one. In their halls the liverymen started to give themselves further privileges, dining apart from the rest, the yeomanry, every quarter. The old religious and social activities went on, but sometimes segregated by class; grand members of the Skinners' Company belonged to the Fraternity of Corpus Christi, which Edward III himself joined, while poorer ones formed the Fraternity of Our Lady's Assumption. An agitator might therefore hope for some support within the richest merchant companies, as well as from the lesser companies, from unrecognized journeymen who were paid by the day (from the French *journée*), and from those who were not citizens at all.

Arguments about trade guilds and craft guilds are full of interest today. The aim was to control wages and prices, conditions of service and standards of workmanship, so that the producers had security and the customers value. Medieval authority was strongly paternalist and in some ways surprisingly modern in assuming its right to interfere with private business: the Church frowned on excessive profits and particularly on usury, money-making not connected with goods or services, while the king wanted the Londoners to be contented by a steady, reasonable food supply. The mayor periodically set prices for different grades of ale, wine, meat, poultry and fish, inspecting markets and shiploads and enacting severe penalties (including loss of citizenship) for anyone who tried to exploit the consumer. The companies were therefore only trying to do for themselves what public authority was already doing, but not all were equally successful. Great merchant companies, dealing mainly in luxuries, were usually left to administer their own by-laws, while lesser companies more often co-operated with the mayor. Luckily most farm produce could be inspected in markets, and baking was a small man's job, so that there were few clashes between public officials and a rich, well-organized company. The chief source of trouble were the fishmongers, fortified by their monopoly, since fish and bread made up the main diet of the poor. The company's efforts to keep out country fishmongers and escape supervision eventually failed, but only after years of resistance.

So detailed were the economic regulations that London, like every medieval city, ought to have been an economic paradise. Yet we have seen that they did not prevent splits within trades, between large wholesalers and small retailers, nor even within the crafts. Men could still grow very rich, particularly through friends at court, and sometimes by very unpopular methods, since monopolies were granted to individuals as well as to companies. Others, foreigners or men with no capital, could be kept out or never allowed to reach their proper level. Some £50 worth of stock was needed to start business in a great company; a man might marry money or the company might lend him some but it is not surprising that so many of the richest citizens, like the famous mercer Richard Whittington, were scions of the gentry who presumably had something to begin with. About the time of Whittington's death an anonymous poem called London Lickpenny told how a poor Kentishman came to seek justice in the capital. Brushed aside by the lawyers in Westminster Hall, where his hood was filched in the crowd, he wandered through the street markets of London, tantalized by the cries of peddlers and shopkeepers. In Cornhill he recognized his stolen hood but, unable to buy it, he trudged in despair down to Billingsgate, where the ferryman refused to take him back across the river. At last he reached Kent, glad to stick to his plough, for everywhere in London it had been the same story: 'for lack of money I might not speed'.

The rules which upheld standards made every craft jealous of its own skills and so encouraged demarcation disputes. Still worse, for those in charge of public order, the more privileges that one group gained, the more cause there was for bitterness. In 1268 over five hundred people were said to have taken part in a fight between goldsmiths and tailors, after other callings had piled in on each side; in 1339 the mayor was seized by the throat while intervening in a bloody battle between fishmongers and skinners; in 1378, when London was simmering over Wyclif, trouble between the pepperers and goldsmiths spread from Cheapside into St Paul's churchyard. In the fifteenth century a royal charter to one group easily provoked outbursts from others. The tailors, furious when the drapers were incorporated, renewed their own charter, with exclusive rights of search (to maintain quality) in the cloth trade; in 1440, when a draper was elected mayor, a gang of tailors was imprisoned for trying to shout down proceedings at the Guildhall.

Many other rules simply proved unworkable. Skilled labour was always short, largely because of the insistence on apprenticeship, which is why so many of the biggest fortunes were made in trade rather than in industry. There were no factories, only small workshops: Thomas Dounton in 1456 employed eleven apprentices and seven hired servants in making pewter, the largest staff recorded in any medieval craft. Fifty years before the Black Death craftsmen were trying to ban the enticement of one another's servants or apprentices, as they continued to do throughout the Middle Ages, and all servants' organizations aimed at higher pay were forbidden by the mayor. Masters, however, were hardly ever punished for paying too much (since it was the masters who sat in judgment), and offending employees were only fitfully imprisoned or fined. In 1380 the cutlers tried to link pay to productivity by devising new tests and allowing increases only on signs of improved skill, yet money wages were rising faster than ever at the end of the century. Consumer protection to some extent worked but the incomes policy, for all its sound and fury, was a dead letter.

In spite of these fissures, the merchant companies kept their grip. A rash king might still have suspended the city's privileges altogether, but in fact he so far abandoned control that by the early fifteenth century the town clerk, John Carpenter, saw the sheriff no longer as the king's right hand but as 'the eyes of the mayor'. Fourteenth-century mayors were always aldermen, as were nearly all the sheriffs themselves and most of London's members of Parliament. Respectable citizens called variously 'the more powerful' (*potentiores*) or 'men of worth' (*probi homines*) sometimes formed large panels to advise or, more often, to consent, but it was the mayor and aldermen who decided whom to summon. Aldermen normally retained office for the rest of their active lives, the average term under Edward III being eleven years. Power lay with them and therefore with the merchant companies, who supplied all but nine of the 260 aldermen known to have been elected in the fourteenth century.

Simmering discontent bubbled over only when the weakness of all authority offered the hope of better things from a new regime. This explains the violence which attended Edward II's deposition, the unrest of the 1370s and 1380s when factions intrigued around a senile king and a child, and the outburst when Richard II was overthrown. The only serious threat to the merchant companies was headed by one of their own members, the draper John of Northampton: in 1376, amid soaring prices and inflammatory tales of extravagance at court, he insisted that the mayor and aldermen should be regularly advised by a council chosen annually from among the crafts. A new charter was granted, with the revolutionary clause that aldermen should retire after one year.

Northampton, with more caution, might have firmly put London's government on a new footing. Thanks to Gaunt's protection and the timidity of his foes, he became sheriff in 1377 and entered Parliament a year later. Like many demagogues he equated riches with debauchery and in 1381, on following Walworth as mayor, he made good his threats. Citizens were told to punish immorality themselves; loose women, their heads shaven, were paraded through the streets and lodged in the Tun. More risky was an attack on the fishmongers, now uniquely hated in the capital. The company's monopoly was abolished and Londoners enjoyed cheaper fish, while elsewhere the price rose. Popularity, however, could not save Northampton from the rich, whose anger grew with their fear. After a second term as mayor, he was replaced by his arch-enemy, the fishmonger Sir

175

Nicholas Brembre. Northampton, by keeping an armed retinue, played into Brembre's hands. He was arrested for sedition, imprisoned in Dorset and then in the Tower, sentenced, reprieved, taken as far away as Cornwall, and finally freed in 1387, only to fade from the public eye.

All reform depended on subjecting the aldermen to popular control. Brembre, quietly ignoring the charter of 1376, allowed them to stand again, and in 1394 Parliament abolished the formality of re-election; aldermen thereafter normally held office for life, as they still do. From 1397, to avoid tumult and 'imprudent elections', citizens no longer filled vacancies themselves but were allowed to nominate two men per ward, from whom the mayor and other aldermen would make the final choice. For the rest of the Middle Ages London was ruled by aldermen drawn from her wealthiest class, whose average term in the fifteenth century lasted twelve years. The great merchant companies were supreme, for every sheriff and alderman now came from their ranks.

Although Brembre himself fell victim to the Merciless Parliament, his conservative regime lived on. There were feuds between the crafts and attacks on foreigners, but civic authority was only once endangered, when Jack Cade broke in, and survived every twist and turn in the Wars of the Roses. One reason was that the rich were not quite so rich and exclusive as in the thirteenth and fourteenth centuries. Fortunes were still made but not on the scale of the early profiteers from the Hundred Years' War; family influence was less blatant among the office-holders, since more men were competing on equal terms and the most successful drifted away to become country landowners, as they have done ever since; contacts at court were still a help, but personal loans to the Crown were seen to be too risky, so that big sums were usually shared among many. The famous capitalists of the 1370s and 1380s—Brembre, Lyons, Walworth, Philipot—were in fact less powerful than some of their more shadowy predecessors, and Brembre's fate warned others against toadying to an unpopular government. Richard Whittington, who died in 1423, was the last medieval mayor to become a national figure, and this was because of the respect earned by some forty years in civic life and by his lavish bequests (*Fig. 39*).

Financial reforms, or rather clarifications, removed one source of trouble. Although the citizens could assess themselves, the mayor and aldermen could not impose direct taxes on their own initiative; when Edward III at last granted this right, he wisely tried to soften

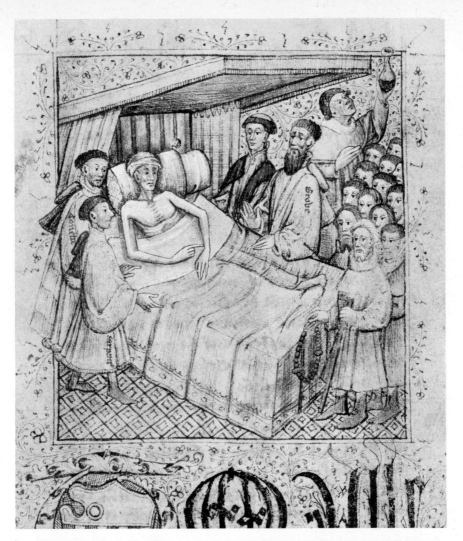

Fig. 39 *The deathbed of Richard Whittington, from the ordinances for his almhouses, 15th century* (By permission of the Mercers' Company)

popular discontent by vesting it in the 'commonalty' as well as in the mayor and aldermen. Common ownership of property was not formally recognized until 1444, by which time even the smallest piece of wasteland had gained hugely in value. The citizens still owed their annual lump sum of £300 to the Crown. The mayor and aldermen drew no salaries but by about 1300 there were regular costs of perhaps £100 a year, from payments to the recorder, the common

177

pleader, the chamberlain, the town clerk, the serjeants, and officers in the wards, and in maintaining the Guildhall, the wall and the water conduits. (*See p.* 248.) Most wages mounted when London had to bid for experts and retain more lawyers in the royal courts. The money came from many sources: fees for enrolments of documents under the mayor's seal at the Guildhall, fines by his court, the customs dues of murage and pontage (to repair the wall and bridge), fixed payments from the farm of the piped water supply and from groups of foreign traders, and rents from the city's property. Occasionally, if money was needed for a new charter, for a special gift or a military emergency, a direct tax might be imposed. Benefactions from individuals or from crafts and companies were very important and helped to build up a special fund for the upkeep of London's life-line, the bridge. Apart from rates, property now supplies the city's main income and the Bridge House Estates is still a separate trust, whose proceeds are spent on the four bridges (Tower, London, Blackfriars and Southwark).

Jealousy also waned because something was saved from the wreck of the democrats' hopes. Under Brembre it was agreed that the advisory council should continue, as Northampton had insisted, to be elective and to meet every quarter. This made more popular and permanent the bodies which had erratically met, at the mayor's summons, for some two hundred years and inaugurated the city's present common council. Members were chosen every year in their wards and from 1430 they had to be resident freemen. Their number, 96 in 1384, had almost doubled by 1549 and was to reach its peak of 240 in the early nineteenth century, before being reduced in 1840 to 206. Today there are 159 members, chosen in the wards by residents or occupiers of rateable premises worth ten pounds a year. With the mayor and aldermen, they make up the court of common council, which acts as the local authority for the city of London.

Although the common council later became the governing body, at the end of the Middle Ages it did not meet as often as it might. The mayor and aldermen alone could influence economic life, by supervising the crafts. Councillors, however, were consulted about London's liberties, when a wide consensus was always wanted, and on public morals; by election and audit, they also had some check on the financial officers, the chamberlain and the two wardens of London Bridge. They met every autumn at the Guildhall to elect the mayor and, on an earlier day, one of the sheriffs (the second being chosen by the mayor) and other officers. The masters and wardens of the liveried companies also attended these elections from 1467, making it harder to pack the meetings, and the liverymen were admitted from 1475; this enlarged assembly became known as the congregation and, later, as common hall. Common councillors thus exercised remote control and could debate and give advice, rather like the commons in the Parliament of England. This elective council put the capital far ahead of most other towns, where the poorer freemen might have economic privileges but hardly ever had the vote. Citizenship in late medieval London gave some kind of political rights to all.

London's aldermen, who are justices of the peace, still meet separately, as a court. They are unusual in being elected in their wards instead of being chosen by the councillors. This is because here they were always key figures, whereas in other boroughs, which copied London, they were merely dignitaries. Their importance gives further meaning to the wards which are labelled on so many modern buildings. Wards did not, even in the Middle Ages, keep pace with London's expansion, but even the most conservative rulers could not entirely ignore the spread of building to the west. In 1394 the vast Farringdon ward, stretching from West Cheap northward around St Paul's as far as Holborn and Temple Bars, was split into Farringdon Within and Farringdon Without (the wall). This only raised the figure to twenty-five and left Farringdon Without as by far the largest ward. The present number, 26, was reached in 1550, when Bridge Without was created after the city had at last bought the Crown's rights in Southwark. This Tudor addition has always been an anomalous ward; its inhabitants have never been allowed to elect common councillors nor even their own alderman, who is always the senior of the aldermen who have held office as lord mayor.

Towards the end of the Middle Ages the city's ceremonial began to take on its modern form. The mayor was for long called 'Dominus maior' and in 1414 he first appears in English as 'Lord Mair'. By 1500 this was general and had been prefixed by 'Full Honourable', which eventually changed into today's 'Right Honourable'. It was unnecessary to confer the lordly title by charter: the mayor was assessed as an earl in 1379, when there was no higher lay rank outside the royal family, and in 1415 he was given precedence in the city over the king's ducal brothers and the archbishop of Canterbury, coming immediately below the sovereign. The honour belonged to

London, not the man, for outside the boundaries he fell away from the peerage to rank below privy councillors. John le Blund is the first mayor known to have been knighted in office, in 1306, but at least four others received this honour at other times before Richard II dubbed Walworth and his fellows. Knighthood became common only under Edward IV and normal under Henry VIII, both genial but calculating kings (the hereditary baronetcy, customary until recently, was invented by the hard-up Stuarts). In 1385 the council stipulated that the mayor must have been a sheriff, 'so that he may be tried as to his governance and bounty', and in 1435 that he must currently be an alderman. Since 1406 he has been elected by the aldermen from one of two names submitted to them by common hall; although chosen in his ward as an alderman and by common hall as sheriff, a controversial character at first might slip through more easily than he would today, only to be passed over by the aldermen. No one could yet sit back in the bland certainty that his turn as mayor would come.

The first mayors took charge straight after their election on 28 October, the feast of SS Simon and Jude. The election date was changed to 13 October in 1346 and to 29 September, Michaelmas Day, under Henry VIII, although lord mayors were still admitted to office on 28 October. They are still chosen on 29 September, although after eleven days had been left out in 1751, when Great Britain discarded the medieval Julian Calendar, they were not admitted until 8 November. John, when conceding annual elections, had tried to retain some hold by requiring the new mayor to be presented to the king or his justices; this has normally been done on the day after the mayor's admission at the Guildhall. Here lies the origin of the grand procession, first noted in 1378, which marks Lord Mayor's Day. There were minstrels by 1401, and a water pageant to Westminster in 1422 set the style for most of the late medieval parades, which grew still more splendid under the Tudors. Modern traffic has forced some changes: since 1952 the lord mayor has ridden from the Guildhall to the Royal Courts of Justice along a fixed route past St Paul's, instead of perhaps going far out of his way to cross his own ward and those of the sheriffs. In 1958 it was agreed that he should always do this on the second Saturday in November, having been admitted on the day before, and that he should hold his banquet on the following Monday.

The pageantry which now gives such pleasure, to the participants perhaps as much as to the onlookers, has always had a more serious purpose: to proclaim the city's hard-won privileges. Two of the three ceremonial officers in the lord mayor's household can be traced to the Middle Ages: the swordbearer at least to 1419 and the common cryer and serjeant-at-arms to 1338 (the third, the city marshal, was first empowered to maintain order in 1595). The city now has five swords but none is pre-Tudor, since each medieval mayor had to provide his own; only in London, Bristol and a very few other towns did Edward III allow a sword to be carried in front of the mayor. Maces have a more curious history: originally, when borne as weapons by the king's serjeants-at-arms, they had lethal heads and the royal arms were on the base. Edward III permitted London's serjeants to carry maces when escorting the mayor and sheriffs. To draw attention to the royal arms the lower end was elaborated until the mace was inverted into its present shape. The city had its great mace by 1338, presumably simpler than the eighteenth-century one used now. The mayor may have had his crystal sceptre for much longer, since the shaft might be Saxon; it was borne at the funeral of Henry VII's queen in 1504 and is still carried before the sovereign.

London in 1500 was organized much as it is today. There were the citizens by patrimony (now once again the commonest path), by servitude and by redemption, although the freedom was not bestowed as an honour until the eighteenth century. There were the livery companies, with their masters, wardens and governing courts of assistants, chosen from the liverymen. There was the lord mayor, an alderman and former sheriff, elected by common hall to preside for a year over his fellow aldermen and the common councillors, and to govern with the help of his sheriffs and other legal and financial officers. In any other city these would have made up the corporation but, while everyone talks of the Corporation of London, the phrase has little meaning. There has been no royal charter to set up a corporate body, any more than there has been one to make a lord out of the mayor, and 'corporation' is a fairly modern word in London. Powers have been granted with many different formulae—most fully on the 'Mayor and Commonalty and Citizens of London'. Even now they are usually given simply to the common council or perhaps to the court of aldermen, and for over seven hundred years the city has confirmed its own acts with the Latin-inscribed seal of 'the barons of London' (*Fig. 9*).

In England, more than anywhere, old institutions outlast their possessions. We have eighty-four livery companies, of which the twelve great merchant companies and many others are directly descended from ones which were there before 1500; several still have their own halls, but the Great Fire, Victorian rebuilding and German bombs have left almost nothing from the Middle Ages. Luckily there is just enough to give us some idea of the grandeur in which the rulers of late medieval London lived. The Guildhall remains the seat of government. The Merchant Taylors' Company still has a hall that is largely medieval. Part of one great business man's house, Crosby Place, survives, although no longer in the city itself. One of the legal societies, Lincoln's Inn, has kept some of its early collegiate buildings.

The cliché that London is an intimate city is daily being falsified by the obliteration of ancient patterns. It remains true in front of the Guildhall, where buildings cluster informally around the seat of government (the whole group of civic offices is sometimes called simply Guildhall, to distinguish it from the hall itself). Towards the end of the Middle Ages Bruges, Ghent, Florence and other foreign rivals were given huge town halls, dominating enormous squares. In London plans were equally grandiose but space was scarce, so that the Guildhall was rebuilt more or less on its old site. It faces only a smallish courtyard and is hidden from all the main streets except Cheapside, which since the Great Fire has offered a glimpse down the length of King Street. Perhaps this is why so many people think that the civic centre is the eighteenth-century Mansion House, which is merely the lord mayor's residence. He did not have one in the Middle Ages, when its site in the heart of the city was shared between St Mary Woolchurch and the Stocks Market, where meat and fish were sold from the time of Edward I.

London's rulers have met in the present Guildhall for over five hundred years and nearby for much longer. A handful of aldermen could use a private house, but a growing bureaucracy must soon have made proper offices essential. 'Land of the Guildhall' was listed about 1130; citizens were meeting at the Guildhall to elect the sheriffs by 1244 and a hundred years later it was 'the hall of the pleas of the city'. By 1400 there was a great chamber (the actual Guildhall), with a cellar underneath, an upper room where the councillors debated and an inner one where trials took place. This building had access to Aldermanbury and stood a little north and west of the present one, although partly overlapping its site. In front, to the south, Guildhall Yard was reached through an inner and an outer gateway from what is now called Gresham Street, after the Elizabethan financier; throughout the Middle Ages this was, more vividly, Cat or Cateaton Street, where cats used to prowl. The Guildhall's enclosure also held two gardens and, on the east side, a chapel which had been founded or rebuilt in 1299; from 1356 the chapel was served by five priests, who formed a college or chantry and lived next door. Facing Cateaton Street, west of the outer gateway, was the church of St Lawrence Jewry, whose closeness inevitably has made it the church of the corporation. East of the gateway, perhaps with a garden backing onto the college and stretching as far as Basinghall Street, stood a large house which the city had bought in 1280 only to sell soon afterwards to the Bankwell or Bakwelle family, which held it for nearly one hundred years.

We know enough of this early Guildhall to disbelieve the early Tudor chronicler Robert Fabyan when he calls it 'an old and little cottage'. He is right, at least, in tracing to 1411 the decision to start work on the 'fair and goodly house' which impressed him in the 1490s and which in part survives today. This was a sensible time to build, now that government and ceremonial were at last crystallizing, and civic pride was stirred. When private gifts ran out in 1413 the common council, bewailing the disgrace which would otherwise engulf 'this, the most noble of cities', increased for six years a series of fees and fines. The levy had to be renewed throughout the 1420s, while business went on in the old Guildhall. In spite of many wellwishers, including the executors of Richard Whittington who paid for glass in the windows and Purbeck slabs on the floor, the main work lasted until 1439. The stone fabric must have been designed by the master mason, John Croxton, although the roof was probably a carpenter's speciality. Croxton worked for over thirty years on the Guildhall and other civic buildings 'and therein spended his young age', in return for a small house and 20s. a year; at last, after a pathetic plea, his wages were doubled and he was reimbursed for paying workmen out of his own pocket.

The surroundings, too, were refashioned. In 1396 the city acquired the Bankwells' property, where a covered market was soon held every week from Thursday morning until Saturday morning. Only here, under the mayor's very nose, could non-citizens store woollen cloth for sale in London, and only here could they sell it; since wool was England's staple product, the place became famous under its corrupted name of Blackwell Hall. Immediately to its north the college and chapel were so ruinous by 1430 that Henry VI allowed them to be pulled down. A library was built by Whittington's executors next to Blackwell Hall and a larger chapel farther north, with the priests' college to the east. The new chapel, like the Guildhall itself, almost proved too ambitious; in 1446, two years after its dedication, the roof was still unfinished.

The Guildhall buildings which stood here at the end of the Middle Ages are represented today only by the hall itself, with a completely different front and a new roof, and the restored Wren church of St Lawrence Jewry. St Lawrence's now faces the Irish Chamber, while Guildhall Yard itself is enclosed on the west by a late Georgian wing, containing the Justice Room, about to be demolished and on the east by an Edwardian range, damaged in the Second World War, which houses the art gallery. Along this eastern side plaques commemorate Blackwell Hall, the library endowed by Whittington, and the chapel. They cannot show us the exact sites (the chapel had two, the earlier one being east of the present Guildhall), nor can the dates tell the full story. The Blackwell Hall thronged by fifteenth-century woolmen was rebuilt under the Tudors and burned in the Great Fire, although it was still a woolmarket when pulled down in 1820. The library did indeed have a short life in its first home, for the Protector Somerset ransacked it, leaving only a storage-place for clothes, but books are said to have been rehoused in 1614 and the present Guildhall library was officially founded, as a London collection, in 1824. In the 1870s this moved to its present site, to the east, where it also houses an extensive reference library. The college of priests who served the chapel of St Mary Magdalen of the Guildhall, next to the old library, disappeared with other chantries at the Reformation. Their property was soon bought from the king by the city but the chapel, damaged in the Great Fire, was pulled down in 1822.

The Guildhall itself had its share of improvements and calamities. The late medieval building reached its most elaborate state in Fabyan's time, for lanterns or louvres for ventilation were added to the roof in 1499 and kitchens to the back in 1501. At last the lord mayor could hold his feast in premises belonging to the city, instead of in a company's hall or in his own home; save in national emergencies, he has done so ever since. People crossing the forecourt saw the south porch adorned with statues of Christ, Aaron and Moses, and of virtues on which civic bodies have always prided themselves—Discipline, Justice, Fortitude and Temperance. The porch was flanked by side-doors leading to the eastern and western porch was flanked by side-doors leading to the eastern and western crypts which lay beneath the hall. This scene lasted until the oak roof timbers burned slowly in the Great Fire 'as if it had been a palace of gold', leaving only the walls and monuments of the hall itself, with its porch and crypts. Everything then changed, for a flat roof was put in, the walls were heightened to take round-headed windows, and the porch was redesigned, although the images were kept. The porch was given its simpler, modern look a hundred years later, and it was left to the Victorians to conjure up the Middle Ages once more with a high hammerbeam roof. In 1940 bombs reduced the interior to walls and monuments again but renovation has broadly followed the medieval dreams of the 1860s.

In spite of everything, to pass through the restored entrance arch is to step back some 360 years, into a vaulted chamber of two bays, with walls of stone panelling. A stone bench runs along the left-hand wall and intricate bosses, repainted and gilded, adorn the roof. The first of the central bosses has the arms of Edward the Confessor (a cross and five doves), familiar from Westminster Abbey and showing that men in the 1420s believed a Guildhall to have existed before the Conquest; the second has the arms of the masons' own king, Henry VI (the lilies of France quartering the leopards of England). Steps on the right lead up to a room over the porch and down to the eastern crypt, where shafts of blue Purbeck marble support vaults of pale Beer stone. This crypt is of roughly the same date as the porch and stairs: at seventy-seven feet by forty-six feet it is the largest in London. The western crypt, which adjoins it, is almost as big but, being criss-crossed with walls to strengthen the floor above, is never open to the public (*Fig. 40*).

If, instead of turning right in the porch, we walk straight ahead, we pass some renovated stonework and through modern oak doors into the great hall itself. The floor is Victorian, relaid in 1954, and, like the ground floor of every ancient building in London, higher than the original. The stone arched roof is modern but no one knows whether this or the wooden hammerbeam roof burned in 1940 comes nearer to the design of 1411; the strong columns against the walls, which divide the hall into eight bays, were presumably meant to bear the weight of masonry, but oak may have been used instead when funds ran short. None of the wood, glass or statuary is medieval, and the minstrels' gallery at the west end is a Victorian idea. The dormer windows high up in the long north and south walls are modern, and the large east and west windows, while

185

Fig. 40 *East crypt of the Guildhall, looking south-west, about 1411–20*
(Crown Copyright)

keeping their old form, have been thoroughly repaired.

These losses seem small when we remember that the walls have outlasted four roofs, although a lighter colour shows where the tops of the columns were rebuilt after the fire of 1666. At first the long walls held a double row of windows, but buildings close outside made the lower row useless, so that all have disappeared except for one in the south wall, left of the main entrance and next to the bronze Royal Fusiliers' Memorial. Here stone window-seats, a latch and hooks for the shutters are genuine survivals from an age which is gallantly evoked all around with banners and painted shields. In general the walls have been so patched and pared that we cannot touch a surface and reflect that someone did the same over five hundred years ago. They do, however, preserve the outline of the hall, allowing us to compare it with the majestic pile at Westminster.

The king's hall, as finally left to us by Richard II, is only a generation older than the city's. The Guildhall is more florid and at the same time more ecclesiastical, because of the stone arches and the columns stretching to the roof. Yet the halls were built for similar purposes and must have looked much more alike when the Guildhall had its hammerbeam roof. At Westminster the king sat in state on a dais to give justice or to feast. At the Guildhall the lord mayor still sits on his dais, today's 'husting', to preside over fortnightly council meetings, at presentations and banquets, and sometimes to entertain his sovereign. The Guildhall put even the richest companies in their place by showing that the city could build better than any of them. Was it also a riposte, to prove that citizens could do as well as the king? His hall was 240 feet long and the span of its open timber roof, 68 feet, was the widest in England. Theirs was 152 feet long and had the second widest roof-span, 49 feet. Comparisons are inevitable but Guildhall, although a showpiece like its rival, has the added distinction of still being in regular use.

By 1400 at least four companies—the Goldsmiths, Merchant Taylors, Skinners and Fishmongers—occupied sites where they remain today. Many more built their own halls while the new Guildhall itself was going up. However, since private owners and their needs more often change, we are lucky to have even one chance of comparing the city's costly premises with those of a livery company.

Threadneedle Street, whose odd name first appears in Stow and probably comes from a children's game, is not just the home of banking. On the south side, opposite the Bank of Montreal, are two doorways leading to the Merchant Taylors' Hall, east of which the company's almshouses once ran as far as the church of St Martin Outwich, on the corner of Threadneedle Street and Bishopsgate. The almshouses were later moved to Tower Hill and then to their present home in Lewisham, and St Martin's was demolished in 1874, but the hall itself has been in the same hands longer than that of any other company. The premises—for the term hall embraces many reception rooms and offices and, in this case, even a garden— contain all that is left of where London's medieval liverymen debated, dined and prayed.

The tailors, strongly organized well before 1300, were one of the first four crafts to receive a royal charter, in 1327. They were then known as Tailors and Linen Armourers, since an important branch of their business was to make lining and padding for armour. Twenty years later trustees acquired for them the property which they have owned ever since, two adjoining houses which can be traced back in the Crepin family to 1281. The tailors probably used the main residence facing Cornhill, on the site of 2 White Lion Court, until they built themselves a dining-hall to the north, leasing off the old quarters but keeping the kitchen and domestic offices. Doorways to Cornhill through White Lion Court and Sun Court (the latter open once a year for the livery to attend St Peter's Church) are reminders of this move. The new hall was ready by 1392, when the guild took it over from its trustees. A chapel, built by 1398 and probably earlier, did not survive the Reformation; it probably stood immediately east of the dining-hall, since part of its crypt lies beneath the hall's eastern end. The great kitchen, first mentioned in 1388, has the longest pedigree of all, since it had belonged to the Crepins' mansion; it was however rebuilt about 1425 and lost its old roof in 1878.

Thanks to the Great Fire and the Second World War there seems to be nothing medieval about the hall itself, which was reopened in 1959. In fact it covers the original area and, behind the restored panelling, the core of the fourteenth-century walls survives roughly to the height of the frieze. In its day the tailors' hall, measuring some ninety-three feet by forty-three feet, had no rival. For over five hundred years the company has dined here on food cooked in the great kitchen, although the chef's ancient spit can no longer be used in a smokeless zone. The kitchen too is unusually large, being thirty-seven and a half feet square. It is entered from the north through three Perpendicular arches, like an arcade in a fifteenth-century church, and much of its painted stonework is obviously old. Unlike the kitchen, exceptional for its long use, the crypt of the chapel is deserted but much closer to its early state. One bay was pulled down in 1853, its space now being a cellar of the Australia and New Zealand Bank, but the other vaults and walls have needed very few repairs.

The Merchant Taylors, like most companies, have treasures which are displayed at their own celebrations and sometimes at exhibitions. A little of their plate belongs to the end of our period and so do two funeral palls, which once covered the coffins of liverymen and are now framed in the cloisters; the earlier pall, of about 1490–1512, miraculously retains the original rich colouring of the embroidered velvet. More stirring than any isolated object is the fact that so many reminders of the past are built into today's premises. Wine is still stored in a long cellar which runs south from beneath the western entrance in Threadneedle Street; the far end has been turned into a ladies' cloakroom, but even here old vaults can be seen among the cream wash and tiles. A wall of the scullery next to the kitchen preserves a piece of rough boundary wall recorded in 1388. Worn pieces of sculpture, some from other sites, are set out in the otherwise empty crypt. Beneath a trap in the parquet floor of the hall itself are sections of three earlier floor levels, the bottom one being fourteenth century, which show more vividly than anywhere else how disasters and renewals have raised the ground on which London stands. Other sites have even longer or more complicated histories, but few have so much to show for it.

The opulence of institutions says nothing about ordinary people. We cannot see where they lived, for the humbler the home the more often was it rebuilt. Even the rich are lucky to be remembered by their names and only one man has left anything by which we can judge his domestic surroundings. This was Sir John Crosby, a wholesale draper who steadily climbed the ladder to become warden of the Grocers' Company, Member of Parliament, alderman and, in the topsy-turvy year 1470, sheriff. Like many great names in business, Crosby did not begin penniless, but with advantages which he exploited. His grandfather had been an alderman and his father, who was in the king's service, left him the Middlesex manor of Hanworth. Crosby took up the popular and profitable Yorkist cause, was knighted for helping to repel the Bastard of Fauconberg in 1471, and afterwards employed in commerce and diplomacy by that Italianate businessman, Edward IV. He never became mayor, perhaps because of other duties, and his only surviving son, born of a second marriage, did not live long enough to continue the line. Otherwise to outward appearances Sir John was an enviable man, more so than most of those who presided at their companies' halls or at the Guildhall itself.

Bishopsgate was the hub of Crosby's life, in spite of his country estate and his warehouse off Poultry. Although first elected alderman for Broad Street, he changed after a year to the larger neighbouring ward of Bishopsgate and represented it until his death. He left money to repair the gate itself and the city wall, to the priory church of St Helen Bishopsgate, and to poor householders in the ward. In the south transept of St Helen's he still lies in effigy beside his first wife, wearing a collar of suns and roses, the emblem of Edward IV. It was from the prioress that in 1466 he leased, or more probably re-leased, property along the east side of Bishopsgate

Street, where he built Crosby Place. His land stretched some 240 feet southward from Great St Helen's as far as the former No. 12 Bishopsgate. The mansion itself was set back like the Merchant Taylors' Hall, hidden from passers-by by humbler houses and reached by passages. Its main entrance is now marked by a covered way next to the Chartered Bank, a little north of Threadneedle Street's junction with Bishopsgate. This is dimly labelled but leads to Crosby Square, once the large inner courtyard of the mansion. To the right of this passage there stood a chapel and behind it two smaller courts, with grand lodgings farther in facing the main court. To the left lay first another small court, leading to a dining parlour or council chamber. Straight ahead, as a plaque still shows us, was the Great Banqueting Hall, entered from a passage way under a minstrels' gallery, which formed an extension to its southern end. This, on a new site and under the name of Crosby Hall, is all that survives of the homes of the medieval Londoners.

It is only a fragment of a quite untypical home—if home is the right word for what was almost a self-contained palace. Crosby Hall, like the Savoy and mansions of an earlier age, had its own brewhouse and bakehouse, as well as gardens, stables, kitchens and plenty of store-rooms, most of them stretching eastward, north of the great courtyard. The public apartments were more than status symbols; they helped Sir John in his career by allowing him to entertain colleagues from the city, courtiers and foreign visitors. So regally did he build that Richard of Gloucester, after escorting the young Edward V to the Tower, made Crosby Place his head-quarters while perfecting his schemes to become Richard III. Perhaps the Crown was offered to him there, for an upper part of the council chamber was later called the throne-room. The duke was only a tenant of Crosby Place, which Shakespeare mentions, for Crosby's executors did not surrender it until 1501. Two years afterwards it housed ambassadors from the Holy Roman Emperor, and later owners included Sir Thomas More. Stow, shortly before Sir Walter Raleigh stayed there, said that it had been the tallest house in London. The inner courtyard had a back entrance onto a lane, which ran east to St Mary Axe and, inevitably, was known for centuries as Crosby Street.

Crosby Place in time went the way of all city buildings. It lay just beyond the reach of the Great Fire, but only the banqueting hall and adjoining council chamber survived a blaze in 1672. These, because of their strength and size, lingered on in various humble roles. After renovation in the 1830s the hall was used for evening-classes, concerts and prayer-meetings, and then for storage of wine. The Chartered Bank of India, Australia and China bought the premises in 1907, demolishing the council chamber but eventually, after a belated public outcry, allowing the hall to be moved.

We must go to what in Crosby's day was the riverside village of Chelsea (*Cealc-hithe*, a landing-place for chalk or limestone) to see the remains of his house. At the corner of Danvers Street and Cheyne Walk, a hundred yards west of the restored parish church, Sir John's hall has given its name to a hostel for the British Federation of University Women. The brick range of the hostel has been designed in scale with the building from Bishopsgate, which has been re-erected on the east side as a dining hall. The hall itself has been refaced in white Portland stone and, inevitably, given a new lantern. It still faces the same way but the approach is quite different: the projecting southern end, by which it was usually entered on its old site, has been rebuilt and the new 'main' doorway at the top of the steps is rarely used, so we must cross the grass and go into the hostel. A corridor on the right leads to the hall through an original doorway north of the oriel, so that we enter as Crosby would have done from his council chamber.

We are in the hall's upper end, where the tall oriel window gave the family some privacy and a view onto the courtyard now covered by the Chartered Bank. Opposite is a stone wall-fireplace, unusual even at the end of the Middle Ages and enormous by modern standards. Farther down lesser people, copying their ancestors, must have warmed themselves at a brazier, for there is an octagonal opening in the fifth of the roof's eight bays, underneath the lantern. Another thing to notice about this top end is that the windows high up in the long walls are comparatively small, probably to make room for tapestries. The narrow end-wall here is modern, like the opposite extension with its gallery, but the windows in the long walls have been reset just as they were. All the walls are plastered, as before, although the oak floor has replaced one of Purbeck marble. The oriel is entirely original and the central boss of its stone vault, with Sir John Crosby's freshly gilded crest, is our only reminder of the hall's builder. Above all, in both senses, is the roof, with its shallow arches and elaborate bosses and pendants. This is the original, intact, with red, blue and gold paint to enable one to pick out its carvings. It seems particularly glorious from the south, where

191

Fig. 41 *Timber roof of the great hall from Crosby Place, looking north,*
about 1470 (National Monuments Record)

there is no distraction from the modern extension (*Fig. 41*).

The design of a hall, the centre of any great man's home, hardly changed from the fourteenth century until Stuart times. Crosby Hall gains in value by reminding us of still earlier buildings, but there is one thing to remember. Halls were communal, relics of a primitive camaraderie, and as the rich became more sophisticated they expected more privacy. Entire households had once used the hall for meals, leisure and, if we go back far enough, sleeping. Private apartments and domestic offices were later added, as parts of a hall or as separate buildings, so that Crosby's hall is merely the grandest reception room of his vanished mansion. It is more precious for allowing us to compare private with public affluence, for Sir John's dining hall covers 69 feet by 27 feet, whereas the Merchant Taylors' Hall, the Guildhall and Westminster Hall are 93 feet, 152 feet and 240 feet long respectively, and correspondingly broader. Crosby Hall does more than show us these differences for ourselves. It shows us, if not how Londoners lived at the end of the Middle Ages, at least how they could aspire to live.

One comparable property has been left by the lawyers. We have seen how law students settled outside the wall, mainly along the western road out of Newgate, and how some moved south to the Templars' land. There, after absorbing many smaller groups or Inns of Chancery, they remain as two of the four Inns of Court, the Inner and Middle Temples. Others stayed in the north, where by the fifteenth century they lived in several societies along Holborn. Thavie's Inn was the house of the fourteenth-century John Thavie, now commemorated in the block on the south side of Holborn Circus. Barnard's Inn, named after Lionel Barnard, its first principal in 1435, lay a little farther west, where it is still the name of an opening on the far side of Fetter Lane. Opposite was Furnival's Inn, where the red-brick Prudential Assurance building covers a site owned by William, Lord Furnival, baron of the Exchequer, who died in 1383. William probably founded the Inn, or at least settled his own clerks there; he was the last male of his line, but in the 1880s the family was commemorated anew, in Furnival Street. The obscurely named Staple Inn, just outside the Bar, is well known to Londoners because its Elizabethan half-timbering is the only picturesque frontage in Holborn. Here, as along the Strand, amalgamations produced two Inns of Court. The leases and in Tudor days the freeholds of Thavie's and Furnival's Inns were bought by Lincoln's Inn, while Staple Inn passed to Gray's Inn. Eventually they were sold, as was Barnard's Inn which had never been owned by its lawyers, and everything save the façade of Staple Inn disappeared.

London is left with her four Inns of Court, of which the Inner and Middle Temples have nothing medieval except the knights' church. Gray's Inn, on the north side of Holborn beyond the city limits, is named after the Lords Grey of Wilton, who by 1308 here held the manor of Portpool (where there was, literally, a pool) from St Paul's. They probably used the manor house until 1370 and retained their interest until 1506, although lawyers may have been there throughout the fifteenth century. Only the family name and that of Portpool Lane, applied in the fifteenth century to Gray's Inn Road instead of to its easterly offshoot, remind us of the Middle Ages. Lincoln's Inn alone has anything more solid to show.

Lincoln's Inn's origins are obscure, for its traditional founder Henry de Lacey, earl of Lincoln (who died in 1312) was displaced by the discovery of another inn, named after Thomas de Lincoln, a serjeant-at-law. The serjeant's property, however, which lay on the south side of Holborn east of Staple Inn, soon passed to the abbot of Malmesbury and was found to have no connexion with the present Lincoln's Inn. Since Henry de Lacey was close to Edward I and just the sort of man to have promoted legal training, he has been cautiously reinstated, although there is no proof that he settled lawyers in his own home in Shoe Lane. Migrants from Thavie's or Furnival's Inn perhaps moved west to form Lincoln's Inn, but this theory is based on later links between the three bodies. All that we know is that in 1422, when its records begin, the society of Lincoln's Inn held most of its present site beyond the Bar, along the west side of Chancery Lane. The northern part had been called Cottrell's Garden and is now covered by the Palladian Stone Buildings; the southern part had been the bishop of Chichester's town house.

The oldest parts of Lincoln's Inn, dating as they do from the very end of the Middle Ages, are not built of stone. They are of red brick, like Mayor Jocelyne's repairs to the city wall and Cardinal Morton's gatehouse at Lambeth. The gatehouse in Chancery Lane, opposite the Sun Alliance and London Assurance office, can best be seen from the corner of Cursitor Street. In its H-plan, an archway with rooms overhead and two cross-wings, and even in its blue-black diaper patterns, it resembles the slightly earlier Morton's Tower. It leads to a quadrangle with barristers' chambers called Old Buildings next to the gateway and along the south, the Old Hall facing us to the west and Inigo Jones's stone-faced chapel to the north. This is Old Square, a piece of pre-Reformation planning until recently almost surrounded by the original buildings, although the range running north from the gateway is obviously Victorian. By crossing the square and passing through the narrow passage south of the hall, or beneath the archway to its north, we find that Old Buildings continue, to form what is nearly a second, smaller, courtyard. Beyond on the left opens the spacious seventeenth-century New Square; on the right lie the gardens of the Inn, dominated by the present hall, begun in the 1840s, with its adjoining library.

Over the main entrance are the arms of Henry de Lacey, of the Tudors, and of Sir Thomas Lovell, a distinguished Speaker of the House of Commons and member of the inn, who died in 1524. The arms have been renewed, so has a scroll beneath them which gives the date of the gatehouse as 1518, and so unhappily has the gatehouse itself. Complete rebuilding of the central block and southern cross-wing in the late 1960s means that we can only pass through a

Fig. 42 *Interior of the Old Hall of Lincoln's Inn, looking south, 1490–2*
(A. F. Kersting)

model of the early Tudor gateway, although the gate itself is ancient. It is a very careful model, reproducing the larger windows inserted in the seventeenth century and the one small window which had been left facing the street on the ground floor of the southern wing. The same fate has befallen the chambers along the south-east and south sides of Old Square, which had been drastically altered in 1609 and later given new windows, except in the polygonal stair-turrets. Beyond the passage south of the Old Hall, which was cut in 1583, we can still see what the whole southern range of Old Buildings looked like a few years ago; this part was built in the 1530s, some ten years later than the original section farther east.

The difference between the Tudor of Henry VIII and that of Elizabeth II is obvious, in the smooth new edging and the pallor of the bricks. We can see at once that the Old Hall still lives up to its name, although the southern end-wall is Stuart and the northern one, like the arch linking it to the chapel, is modern. The lantern is also modern, like most such picturesque but vulnerable structures, as well as the parapet. This hall, finished in 1492, is the most ancient part of the inn. Its original doorway is on the far side and a pointed stone arch has been reset in the north wall, under the modern passage, to remind us of a thirteenth-century building on the same site. The hall, used for lectures and receptions, is now entered from the Tudor passage to the south. It is divided into five bays, the southernmost one being the seventeenth-century extension. West-minster Hall and Guildhall are free-standing and so can have windows in their end-walls but most halls, as here, are joined to other buildings; the extra bay, therefore, although it adds four squared 'oriel' windows to the windows in the intermediate bays, does not make the hall conspicuously light. The roof is not of hammerbeams, although it has been described as such, but of arches and high-up cross beams called collar-beams. It is far plainer than the one put up by Sir John Crosby, but is almost exactly the same length (*Fig. 42*).

The green spaces to the west contrast sharply with the courtyards near Chancery Lane. Even at the end of the Middle Ages the grandest buildings served communal purposes. Great men like Sir John Crosby—and for that matter the king himself—still spent much of their time in public, dining and worshipping in state, continually entertaining and beset by hangers-on. Crosby Place, however, in spite of the bustle and ceremonial, was a private house, and the liverymen who met in their companies' halls also had their own homes. Monks, on the other hand, had always lived in common and so, in their turn, did scholars and lawyers. The monastic houses were all taken over, although a few churches were handed over to the citizens, and London never had any colleges like those of Oxford and Cambridge, but the lawyers' inns survived the Reformation. Only parts of the Charterhouse at Clerkenwell (*see p. 230*) and the early courtyards of Lincoln's Inn now remind us of the intimate, enclosed lives of so many medieval people.

Several medieval residents live on in their names, although most of them were men like Sir John Crosby rather than Henry de Lacey. Barons and prelates are commemorated mainly along the riverside towards Westminster. In the city itself Warwick Lane is so called either because the Beauchamp earls of Warwick held property there in 1368 or because the Kingmaker had a town house there ninety years later; the much darker, narrower Suffolk Lane, north from Upper Thames Street to Lawrence Pountney Hill, reminds us of a still more remarkable family, the De La Poles, who began as Hull merchants and by the fifteenth century, when they bought property here, were dukes of Suffolk. Apart from these and from Queenhithe there is nothing noble or regal, for King William Street, Queen Street and King Edward Street are all named after more recent monarchs.

The family-conscious clique which dominated Fitz Stephen's London is represented by the Basings and the Bukerels. The former, from Basing in Hampshire, were in the city by 1200; they had given their name to the now vanished Basing Lane by 1275 and, perhaps still earlier, to Bassishaw Ward and Basinghall Street. The Bukerels, starting with an Italian pepperer who came over soon after the Conquest, had as their main home the fortified mansion of Bukerel's Burh, which the first Andrew Bukerel gave up when leaving for Jerusalem in 1183, never to return; his heirs remained at the heart of civic life for another hundred years, and by 1343 the street running from the east end of Poultry to Walbrook was called Bucklersbury. More recent than these was the family of William de Farndon, a goldsmith who received from his father-in-law in about 1279 the ward which he passed on forty years later as Farndon or Farringdon; from this ward Farringdon Street, built over the Fleet river in the early nineteenth century, gets its name. Sir John Philipot, the patriotic grocer whose name ironically comes from the French 'Little Philip', lived in what is now Philpot Lane, joining

Eastcheap to Fenchurch Street. Richard Whittington left money for a priests' college and adjoining almshouses in what was first called Bow Lane and later Paternoster Lane; Whittington College, although now at Felbridge where it is still managed by his company, the Mercers', has given its old home the name of College Street. Around the corner, in College Hill, a plaque records Whittington's burial in the old church of St Michael Paternoster Royal; a few yards higher up the hill, another plaque marks the site of his house.

Among lesser families that of William Cosyn, alderman from 1306 to 1315, is commemorated in Cousin Lane, which continues from Dowgate Hill down to the Thames beside Cannon Street station, while the Trigs, fourteenth-century fishmongers, were responsible for Trig Lane, which leads from Upper Thames Street to the water-stairs midway between Queenhithe and Blackfriars. The well-known Little Britain comes from Robert le Bretoun, presumably a native of Brittany, who was left houses in its parish of St Botolph Aldersgate in 1274. Finch Lane, linking Cornhill to Threadneedle Street, may go back even further, to the moneyer Ælfwin Fink, a contemporary of Fitz Stephen and, from his name, an Englishman. Sometimes the original person is more mysterious. An unknown alderman was responsible for Aldermanbury, at first a fortified place rather than a street, and a pre-Conquest citizen called Lotha or Hlothere for Lothbury. A common early surname was Noble, which has given rise to Noble Street, running south from London Wall. Friday Street, which now links Cannon Street to Queen Victoria Street, was so called over eight hundred years ago; it too might record an early citizen, since Friday was a christian or font-name and a surname, although perhaps it simply refers to the sale of fish on Fridays. Mark Lane, from Fenchurch Street to Great Tower Street, was once Mart Lane and, before that, Martha Lane. Another shadowy woman was the Anglo-Saxon or Scandinavian Gudrun, now unromantically recalled in the narrow way north from Cheapside to Gresham Street, Gutter Lane.

Humdrum objects are not cherished, so that the more familiar a thing has been, the harder it is to come by. Thanks to this paradox, and because cheap materials do not last, London boasts medieval architecture in stone, which was expensive, but not in wood and plaster, which were common. It is the same with furniture, clothing and most domestic ware. We can see the oak coronation chair, made for Edward I to hold the stone of Scone which he seized in 1297, but no wooden furnishings from a citizen's house of that time; the London Museum has only an oak cradle, made some two hundred years later and used at Chepstow Castle, and a fifteenth-century cupboard. Apart from seven embroidered funeral palls (owned by the Merchant Taylors, Vintners, Fishmongers, Ironmongers, Brewers and Saddlers), the city companies have kept a surprising amount of plate from the fifteenth century onwards, but these were ceremonial treasures. For everyday things we have to rely on chance finds, often dredged from the Thames or dug from the City Ditch and other refuse pits. An intriguing assortment has nonetheless been built up. Most of this is at present shared between the Guildhall and London Museums. although the British Museum's much wider collection includes a few pieces made or found in London. For the Middle Ages, as for Anglo-Saxon times, the oddest fragments help to chart the capital's growth.

For every ten people who love the stained glass of the Middle Ages, there is probably not one who thinks of medieval pottery. In fact a great deal has been found in London, from the Normans until the Tudors. We can even see a domestic revolution which is still with us, in the arrival of metal for storage and cooking vessels. In Fitz Stephen's time these were normally of earthenware and were coarse and dark, as they had been before the Conquest. Glazing inside, to make them less porous, became common from about 1250. More land was cultivated then than in later, sheep-ridden, years; from this golden age of farming date the finest materials and the widest range of patterns, as well as the biggest specimens, jars nearly two feet high and presumably used for storing grain. Polychrome ware was now imported from south-western France, where the English managed to keep a foothold for three hundred years. Most of this, whiter and more delicate than anything produced at home, has naturally been found in London. Native pottery was not made in the city itself but was fired in kilns up to twenty miles away in the clayey, well-wooded countryside, especially Surrey. In the fourteenth century metal began to take over in the kitchen and the larder, so that pottery became cruder and much less common. By 1500, however, expensive blue and white Italian maiolica ware, and even Spanish pottery, was finding its way to London.

A few pieces must be singled out for their own sake and not just because they are medieval. The London Museum in particular has many jugs and storage jars, the best dating from the thirteenth

199

Fig. 43 *Yellow-glazed pitcher with applied decoration of green trellis and red pellets and rosettes, from Southwark, 13th century* (The Trustees of the London Museum)

Fig. 44 *Fragment of green-glazed anthropomorphic jug from Bishopsgate, about 1300* (The Trustees of the London Museum)

century, attractively glazed in mossy green, yellow or brown. Some of the jugs are squat and bulbous, others are tall and sagging, perhaps because the potters modelled them on leather bottles. Both museums have polychrome jugs, which are quite distinctive with bright green and yellow motifs outlined in very dark brown; an English attempt to copy their 'parrot-beak' spouts can be seen in a yellow jug in the London Museum. The birds, plants, scrolls and shields which adorn this French ware are no more striking than many native designs. Some decorations are painted, others are stuck on or 'applied': the London Museum, for example, has two yellow-glazed pitchers with applied green lines and red pellets and rosettes (*Fig. 43*).

Some objects intrigue us because they have hardly changed, such as the London Museum's pipkin, with its curved side handle for hanging, or a terra-cotta cake-mould, perhaps used at Smithfield fair. Others have become true museum pieces, such as the 'aquamaniles', which held water for rinsing greasy hands at table. The

London Museum has one in the shape of a rather clumsy horse minus its rider, as well as the spouts from two others, which are modelled like rams' heads; the Guildhall Museum has the spout from a third, also made into a ram's head. Potters, like wood-carvers or sculptors, enjoyed modelling men and beasts. Part of a man on horseback, once set in the bottom of a vessel, is in the Guildhall Museum, next to a green glazed jug in the form of a comical human figure like a tall toby jug. The London Museum has the neck of a larger jug, with arms crossed at the wrists and hands clasping the chin of a mask-like face (*Fig. 44*). Outstanding among the plainer work of the late Middle Ages is the Guildhall Museum's black and white unglazed watering pot, with a tiny opening in the top and a perforated base; after it had been filled by submersion, air pressure retained the water so long as the thumb covered the upper hole. No one, after seeing this sprinkler, can say that men in the fifteenth century lacked ingenuity.

Decorated floor-tiles, even more than pottery, show what strides were made in the thirteenth century. The Romans, as is well known, had tessellated (mosaic) pavements, but the Saxons were quite unable to copy them. Like many articles of comparative luxury, medieval floor-tiles first appeared in churches. Gradually they spread to other buildings and from the fourteenth century they became ever more popular in London.

Floor-tiles are usually red or reddish brown, with a creamy yellow design. Sometimes, before firing, the soft squares of clay were impressed with a wooden stamp and the hollows filled with pale pipeclay, to produce inlaid tiles. These, although introduced from northern France, soon reached their perfection in England, thanks perhaps to Henry III's patronage of the tile-wrights. In the fourteenth century shallower patterns were stamped, to save the pipeclay, and eventually the wooden stamp itself was smeared with pipeclay and pressed on the surface like an inked block on paper, producing printed tiles. Although the two main sorts of tile can look very much alike, inlaid designs were usually finer and longer lasting. Their replacement by printed patterns shows that six hundred years ago, as in our own time, artistry and skilled craftsmanship could be squeezed out by mass production.

England's best medieval tiles are where they have always been, on the floor of the Chapter House of Westminster Abbey. It is not always easy to appreciate them there, in their thousands, and these anyway are too early and too well-made to be typical. The London

Museum has a case of twenty-four, among which an inlaid tile showing a queen with a hawk (*Fig. 45*), from the Chapter House, stands out among the later, printed, work. These come from sites in the city and Westminster and are matched by a few others in the Guildhall Museum. Some may actually have been made nearby, for there was a tile-kiln by the bank of the Fleet, close to the present site of Farringdon Street station, but most came from the Buckinghamshire village of Penn and elsewhere in the Chilterns.

Expensive and often beautiful floor-tiles should not make us forget that the tilers' main job was to cover roofs. Every fire and tempest was good for business: Fitz Ailwin's regulations were chiefly concerned with stone walls but in 1245 the mayor ordered that all houses were to be roofed with tiles, shingles or boards. Standard measurements were soon customary and in 1477 they were fixed by Parliament, which insisted on good clay, dug and stored at least a month before it was made into tiles. Bricks, usually smallish and at first called 'wall tiles', because they were useful in fireplaces, became common only at the end of the Middle Ages. Partly because of the snobbish enmity of superior crafts, the Tylers and Bricklayers became a livery company only under Elizabeth, but a few medieval specimens of their basic work are in the Guildhall Museum.

From prehistoric times animal hides have been turned into leather. Ox-, cow- and calf-skins were soaked, cleaned and treated in vats with tannin, an astringent substance from the crushed bark of oak and other trees. A mineral process, whereby the skins of deer, sheep and horses were 'tawed' with alum, was also known before the Conquest, although the most supple leathers of all were oiled. The actual production of leather was a messy business, which did not attract fastidious craftsmen. It needed lime, for removing the hair, and plenty of water; soon after 1300 there were complaints that it polluted the Fleet and in 1311 the white-tawyers, who worked with alum, were forbidden to flay dead horses in the city or its suburbs. Hides were a leading export; they were supposed to lie in their vats for a whole year and, whether raw or tanned, were inspected by those who were to use them. London's tanners passed on their wares to the curriers, who stretched, shaved and greased the skins before, in turn, passing them on to the leathersellers. These did not at first make goods themselves, but they came to control most of the smaller manufacturers. Those who escaped, to form livery companies which survive today, were workers in the tawed soft leathers: the cordwainers, who used the best leather, preferably from Cordoba in Spain, the girdlers, who used many other materials as well, the glovers and the saddlers. Parchment, from sheep-skins, and vellum, from calf-skins, were related to leather; they too were cleaned and smoothed, but were not tanned and so not waterproof. The skinners dealt not in hides but in furs.

Leather in the Middle Ages often took the place of pottery. There were portable bottles or costrels, now as strange as aquamaniles, and large jugs for beer, later called black-jacks. Uses stretched from inkwells and pen-cases in the fifteenth century to leather-covered boats which, a hundred years earlier, Edward III had used against the French. Less surprisingly, there were also saddles and reins, shoes, belts, straps, book-covers and sheaths. Even the humblest of these might be decorated: often they were engraved with a blunt tool, as they had been under the Saxons, later they might be stamped with a metal stamp, cut with a knife, or, occasionally, pushed out from the back and so embossed. The most solid objects are often of *cuir bouilli*, literally 'boiled leather', which was probably steeped in a solution with wax or oil. The most numerous are leather sheaths for daggers.

Among the costrels in the London Museum a miniature one, with a leather stopper, is the sort from which Chaucer's pilgrims might have quenched their thirst (*Fig. 46*). This, a book-cover and a stamped inkwell, with a pen-case in the Guildhall Museum, stand out, although some of the sheathes are finely patterned. The most human items are shoes of the fourteenth or fifteenth century, two of them in the Guildhall Museum and the rest in the London Museum, which also has some shoe-fronts which have lost their soles (*Fig. 47*). Those entirely of leather have no heels and fashion made them more pointed than earlier ones would have been. Such foot-wear was expensive and not very practical for the streets. The poor had 'galoches', either clogs or wooden soles with thongs, or pattens, raised and probably ironshod, as on the arms of the Pattenmakers' Company. The London Museum also displays some early Tudor shoes, broader and with rounded toes.

Bone-work remained popular for spoons, knife-handles, pins, combs and gaming-pieces. Fitz Stephen says that animals' shin-bones were used as skates. It is often impossible to say whether bone objects are medieval or even earlier, since many designs hardly changed. Combs however, although still usually with a double row of teeth, became longer at the end of the Middle Ages. Chessmen,

Fig. 45 *Painted tile showing a queen holding a hawk, from the Chapter House of Westminster Abbey, mid 13th century* (The Trustees of the London Museum)

Fig. 46 *Leather costrel with embossed ribs and scroll design, from the City Ditch, 14th or 15th century* (The Trustees of the London Museum)

Fig. 47 *Leather shoe, late 15th century* (The Trustees of the London Museum)

as can be seen from the cast of the fourteenth- or fifteenth-century one in the Guildhall Museum, grew more elaborate. Ivory, the finest bone, was more likely to be used for religious work, which includes a small panel carved with the Nativity in the London Museum and two figures from crucifixes in the Guildhall Museum.

Many things made in bone could also be made of horn. This called not for carving but for moulding, since the horns of cattle become soft when heated and can be formed into any number of shapes. They could even be pressed into thin, transparent sheets, tougher than glass, which were widely used for lanterns (hence the spelling, lanthorn), and, until Tudor times, for windows. Two inkwells in the London Museum remind us of 'the poor men of the little craft of horners', as they called themselves in 1391 (*Fig. 48*). Theirs was smelly work which, like that of so many craftsmen as opposed to wholesalers, did not bring great profits. In 1476, threatened by newer materials, the horners united with the leather-bottle makers, although later a market was to be found in leaves to protect the pages of children's books, which became known as horn books. The present livery company, whose arms display inkwells and bottles, flourishes from its links with the horners' heir, the plastics industry.

Metal-work, naturally, is more plentiful than anything else and in much the same wide range of tools, ornaments and weapons as from Saxon times. A few pieces rank as plate, being of silver and gold or overlaid with gold, but most are of baser metals—iron, tin, lead, copper and alloys such as pewter (tin and lead), bronze, brass and latten (all based on copper and tin). This distinction, however, can be confusing, since similar articles might be made out of many different materials. The museums in fact display very little plate, since so much has been melted down because of fashion, greed or puritanism; the livery companies and colleges at Oxford and

Cambridge now own most of the oldest pieces. Goldsmiths' wares could be assayed or tested as early as 1300 but it was not until the London company was made liable for sub-standard wares that a date-letter was introduced, in 1478; by using different types of alphabet the letter has been changed every year since then, so that one could find out who was warden when any article was stamped. Most plate from the end of the Middle Ages is thus hall-marked London.

Cutlery became more like our own. Forks were not used at meals until Stuart times—which was why people washed at table after holding the meat and cutting it with a knife—but spoons were always needed. Although normally of wood, bone or horn, they were sometimes of metal: gold was beyond the reach of nearly everyone except the king (the Mercers' Company has four spoons with gilt knobs out of a set left by Whittington to the college which he founded), but spoons of silver were prized as early as the 1250s, and many more were made of pewter or latten. Metal spoons can often be dated from the type of knop, the knob at the end of the stem, but there is a much more obvious change in the shape of the bowl; the early bone spoons have long, narrow, flat bowls, while the metal ones began with wider bowls, like a leaf, and gradually filled out until at the end of the Middle Ages they were pear-shaped.

We can also see the coming of scissors, which have two looped handles and act on a pivot, although they were never so common as the clumsier shears, which even barbers continued to use. Metal purse-frames were another late arrival. These consisted of a bar, hung from two arms below the frame, as is shown by one with a modern purse attached in the Guildhall Museum. They did not quite oust the simple, earlier purses, which were little bags tied with string, nor the big wallets carried by travellers, but they became something of a craze between 1480 and 1520. Keys, too big for purses, were carried separately by anyone who had things worth locking up. Many of them survive, the older ones having long looped handles.

Lighting too shows a change. In Norman times people relied heavily on cresset-lamps, a cresset being a bowl or funnel to hold the wax or oil, which were usually of stone or pottery. Candles, varying from clean wax tapers to rushes steeped in tallow, were also used, and domestic candlesticks of brass in time became quite common; the earlier candlesticks are usually pricket ones, with a spike for the candle, the later ones, of which the Guildhall Museum has two good

Fig. 48 *Horn inkwell with incised, compass-drawn ornament, from Finsbury, probably 15th century* (The Trustees of the London Museum)

Fig. 49 *Bronze door-knocker (ring missing) in the form of a monkey's head, from Thames Street, 15th century* (The Trustees of the London Museum)

Fig. 50 *Pewter brooch in the form of a crowned A, 14th century* (Guildhall Museum)

207

examples, have the more familiar sockets. Cylindrical metal lanterns, later often with panels of glass or horn, also grew popular. The Guildhall Museum has an elaborate bronze hanging-lamp, in three parts, from as early as the twelfth century. Other metal-work includes a square wrought-iron box for alms, with the royal leopards and lilies, and a round bronze door-knocker like a monkey's head, from which the ring is missing (*Fig. 49*); both are in the London Museum.

Although huge circular brooches had been common from pagan times, dress-ornaments multiplied as time went on. By 1200 knotted belts had given way to ones with buckles and metal tag-ends or belt-chapes, usually of bronze. Their story, with that of brooches, belongs to the complicated history of dress. For the rich, fashion in the Middle Ages was every bit as eccentric and fickle as it is today. In the London Museum there are pictures, based on sculpture, brasses and manuscripts, outlining the main changes in men's and women's wear. With these are ranged rings, brooches, hooks, pins, hat badges and other metal objects, all of them worn in the medieval city. Among them is a silver-plated pomander of about 1500, like a perforated globe on a delicate chain, to remind us of the smells which no one could escape. Both base and precious metals were worn. In the Guildhall Museum readers of Chaucer's *Prologue* can single out among the cheap pilgrims' tokens a humbler version of the gold brooch worn by his prioress (*Fig. 50*):

> On which was first i-writ a crowned A,
> And after, *amor vincit omnia* [love conquers all].

Although most early cooking-vessels were earthenware, metal ones had always been known. The London Museum has a flat-bottomed stew-pan, slung from an iron chain, and a skillet, two cauldrons and two ewers, all with three legs for standing over the flames. These are bronze and from the later Middle Ages, but of a type used earlier. Metal jugs, bowls and a mortar also survive. Some wooden eating bowls, displayed near them, are typical of those used widely by the poor. Mazers, now long forgotten but the commonest of late medieval drinking vessels, were bowls often made of wood edged with metal (ordinary ones, of course, were entirely wooden). The British Museum has an excellent late example of maple-wood and silver, hall-marked London 1532, which Robert Pecham gave to his fellow monks at Rochester. Rose-water dishes, for catching the water poured over a diner's hands from an ewer, were also likely to be of precious metal. The London Museum's only piece of secular plate from the Middle Ages is the silver-gilt base of a bowl which was used either for rose-water or drinking.

An enormous amount of metal-work reminds us of the hold of the Church. Plate itself is extremely rare, thanks to the Reformation. This makes all the more precious the silver-gilt 'Pecocke Chalice', although only its hexagonal stem belongs to the monstrance which the haberdasher Sir Stephen Pecocke left to the church of St Martin Ludgate in 1536. Monstrances, raised receptacles for displaying relics or the consecrated Host, were broken and melted down by the Reformers; Pecocke's one, made in 1507, was acceptable only because the top was replaced by a simple bowl which could be used as a communion cup (*Fig. 51*). A plain latten chalice of about the same date, probably made for burial with a priest, stands near it in the London Museum. One of the largest pieces of metal, made later in Italy but found in the Thames at Wapping, is the Guildhall Museum's bronze reliquary in the shape of Christ's head. The humblest but the most moving ones are small mortuary crosses of lead, with which monks were often buried. A hoard unearthed from the grey friars' cemetery at Newgate, now shared between the Guildhall and London Museums, is perhaps a memorial to the Black Death.

Nearly everyone, at some time or another, went on pilgrimage. For most people, this was the only chance of seeing new places, and of travelling fairly safely, in good company. Their journey had the attractions of a packaged tour, although it also had a deeper meaning, raising hopes and soothing fears. The same is true of the badges which they bought at the shrines; to buy was good in itself, but the objects were souvenirs and, for the seasoned pilgrim, advertisements. The pilgrim in the late fourteenth-century *Vision of Piers Plowman* stuck them all over his hat and cloak,

> So that men should know
> And see by his signs
> What shrines he had sought.

People like him collected badges much as modern tourists put stickers on car windows.

There were badges at all sorts of places, from the grave at Windsor of the murdered Henry VI, who was never even canonized, to the famous tomb of Edward the Confessor at Westminster. Some were sold at St Paul's, but most of those found in the city come from

Fig. 51 *Silver-gilt stem of monstrance, 1507, with later cup—'the Pecocke Chalice'* (The Trustees of the London Museum)

Fig. 52 *Hilt of bronze knife-dagger from the Thames at Blackfriars Bridge, mid 15th century* (British Museum)

England's most popular shrines—those of Our Lady of Walsingham, north-west of Norwich, and of the Londoners' own saint, Thomas Becket, at Canterbury. Both the Guildhall and London Museums have a map of the places which the citizens visited, with examples of what they brought back. The badges were of lead, pewter, or, occasionally, brass, and were cast in stone or iron moulds. The Guildhall Museum has a stone mould used at Waltham Abbey, and the British Museum has one of St Thomas. Badges of St Thomas are usually just mitred heads, but bells, initials, crowns (from royal shrines), the sword of St Paul (as on the city's arms) and other, more complicated, designs are also known. So are ampullae, vials for holy water or oil, which could be filled at Canterbury from a well said to be coloured with Becket's blood. Some badges were worn by noblemen's servants or by members of a guild, but most seem to have belonged to pilgrims. The large number left, considering their soft, perishable material, shows how common these religious knick-knacks were.

Horse-trappings too are plentiful—stirrups, spurs, bits, horseshoes, and harness-bosses, pendants and buckles. So are weapons, although it is often not certain if early ones are pre- or post-Conquest. Differences in the pommels of swords and in the cross-pieces known as quillons are used by experts for dating, and one very general change about 1300 was the slow replacement of the wide blade, useful only for cutting, by the more tapered blade for thrusting. Swords were for soldiers but a dagger was carried by every man: quillon daggers, like miniature swords, and rondel daggers, with circular guards, were military, while kidney-daggers, with kidney-shaped bits of wood forming the guard, and baselards, with small pommels balancing the quillons, were for ordinary citizens. The commonest of all civilian weapons can only be called knife-daggers, since they had a single edge and sprang from domestic knives, often having a dual purpose. A fifteenth-century one in the British Museum, not on general display, is inscribed *Pences ben* (think well) and *Wyth al myn hert* (*Fig. 52*). Like another example, in the London Museum, it is decorated with engraved bronze plating, so that the owner could eat or defend himself in style.

CHAPTER SIX

London and the Church

The main difference between a detailed map of London today and one of five hundred years ago is in the amount of land held by the Church. Old street-lines remain but not what lay between. Wide tracts now have nothing but the name of an office-block to remind us that they once belonged to religious houses, while only a handful of crosses could pinpoint the survivors of scores of parish churches. The difference would be still greater if the earlier map could show not just these buildings but the property which was leased out. In all, the Church may have owned two-thirds of the city.

The change can be blamed on Henry VIII who, to justify his marriage to Anne Boleyn, announced in 1534 that he himself was head of the Church in England. So ended over nine hundred years of submission to the Pope and, with it, London's medieval scene, for within six years the monasteries had gone. Their treasures, buildings and estates were forcibly surrendered to the king, who soon gave away or sold much of his spoils; their inmates were pensioned off or, if stubborn, executed. The most sweeping fire or tempest had never done such damage. New owners ensured that not even Henry's Roman Catholic daughter Mary Tudor could undo her father's work. Nothing was to be the same again.

The English Church in the Middle Ages was part of an international body, served by men who owed spiritual obedience, as well as certain payments, to Rome and who for many offences were lightly punished by their own courts. Some were secular clergy, moving in the outside world to serve its needs: men in minor orders (often clerks, who earned a living as such), deacons or sub-deacons, priests, who did not always have their own church, and bishops.

Others were monastic or regular clergy, leading more or less retired lives within their precincts. The secular clergy are fairly straight-forward, since the three major orders of deacon, priest and bishop persist in the Church of England today. There are no longer swarms of clerks whose misbehaviour caused so much trouble between Church and State in the time of Fitz Stephen and Becket. Nor are there chantry priests to sing (French *chanter*) masses for the souls of benefactors; such endowments were common from the fourteenth century, when nobles, merchants and even groups of poor men banded together to pay priests and build special chapels, but chantries soon went the way of the monasteries. The most mis-understood difference is that between rector and vicar. The rector was supported by his parishioners' tithes—payments, originally in kind, which were enforced long before the Conquest; the vicar evolved as a stand-in, often under-paid by the rector or by some religious house to which the tithes had been made over.

More confusing are the varied monastic clergy. Until the Conquest there were only monks or nuns who lived, sometimes rather freely, according to the rule of St Benedict; these Benedictines were sometimes known, from their clothing, as black monks. The Nor-mans introduced Cluniacs and, soon after 1100, when reform was sweeping Europe, the austere Cistercians, who wore undyed wool and so were called white monks. Other orders followed, including the military ones of the Templars and the Hospitallers, whose knights resembled monks in that they lived in common and took vows of poverty, chastity and obedience. A hundred years later came the first friars—preachers who travelled and begged, circulating among the people, as monks could not, yet bound by a rule and free from the possessions of ordinary priests. A rule, however, needed a headquarters, so yet more religious houses sprang up, for Franciscans or grey friars, Dominicans or black friars, Carmelites or white friars, and other mendicant orders. Unlike many monks, the friars were naturally drawn to towns where they could appeal to the crowds. To complicate matters there were groups of canons, some of whom lived like monks (regular canons), while others (secular canons) were so loosely organized that they were more like secular clergy, such as those who served St Paul's. There were also individual holy men and women: hermits, who could move around, and anchorites, who were solemnly walled up with the bishop's blessing in their chosen cells.

This variety means that there are many names for religious houses.

213

'Monastery' and 'convent' are vague terms, particularly as in the Middle Ages convents were not necessarily thought to be only for women. An abbey was a self-governing house, as were all the oldest Benedictine foundations, including Westminster. A priory in theory was still to some extent controlled by its parent-house, which might be overseas; the larger ones in practice soon became independent, so that when in the Hundred Years' War the king decided to seize all alien priories only a few houses suffered. As a guide to wealth and even to antiquity, the distinction between abbeys and priories by the end of the Middle Ages was as unreliable as that between the greater and lesser city companies today. By tradition, however, the heads of the most famous abbeys, mitred abbots, were summoned like bishops to the king's council and in due course to the House of Lords (less in their spiritual capacity than as great landowners). Groups of secular canons or chantry priests may be said to have formed colleges. Sometimes they were brought together to tend the sick, so that hospitals (themselves often indistinguishable from almshouses) should be added to what, for want of a better phrase, can be called London's religious houses.

A sceptical or indifferent age can hardly appreciate the Church's spiritual hold, but at least we can understand her practical value. When government concentrated on war, public order and raising supplies, the clergy were left to provide the nearest approach to the welfare state. Even in London, where citizens banded together for mutual help, the Church was indispensable. A stranger would find the safest and most comfortable lodging with the monks. If he starved, they might feed him. If he fell ill, they might nurse him. If he prospered and wanted his son to be educated, the clergy alone could do it. If he then wanted a haven for his dependents, or for himself in old age, a monastery might supply it. If he committed a felony (a graver crime than a misdemeanour), he could seek sanctuary in a church for forty days, although he would then have to go into exile unless he had reached one of the two places where he might stay for life.

In time religious houses put walls around their property, hindering or even blocking rights of way. Kings and popes often granted judicial and financial exemptions, so that London was dotted with special areas that were not handed over to the city until 1697. There were many wrangles over privileges and property, which the clergy, who could produce or forge better documents, usually won. Sanctuary itself was sometimes violated for private vengeance or, as in the

Peasants' Revolt, in a general frenzy; the cut-throats and political refugees whom it sheltered were always a headache. To read of all the incidents and lawsuits, particularly with some of Chaucer's unkind descriptions in mind, is to imagine a long cold war between Church and laity. Yet sanctuary on the whole was respected. Perhaps every man felt that there was something to be said for it, when the wearing of daggers caused so much unpremeditated bloodshed. London and the south-east welcomed the Reformation more than the backward north and west, but this does not say much. Churchmen under fire from Wyclif may well have felt that the Reformation was round the corner, yet buildings went up and money rolled in for another hundred and fifty years. Attacks on the bishop's officers early in Henry VIII's reign, like the Lollard riots, were mainly by poor men or young apprentices, who could be turned to violence in almost any cause. Solid citizens, the sort of men who spoke for London, were conservative. They liked to spend their money on visible good works. Their favourites might change but even the friars, derided for begging when they no longer needed to, were helped until the end. The wonder is not that there was so much trouble in such a crowded city, but that there was so little.

St Paul's, the source and early mainstay of Christianity in London, has always been unique. From its foundation in 604 it has held the bishop's *cathedra* or throne and so been the centre of a diocese. Older than any other church within the walls, it also became in a sense the parish church of the city, where services of general remembrance or thanksgiving were held. The Roman missionary's dedication was never changed, perhaps because Londoners were proud of its early date, although in many other places a local saint ousted the original one, as did St Swithin at Winchester. St Paul, standing in the middle of the city with a drawn sword in his right hand and the banner of England in his left, still dominates the obverse of the common seal of London, as he has done at least since 1219. It is his sword, not the dagger which struck down Wat Tyler, which fills the first quarter of the ubiquitous city arms (*Figs. 9 and 12.*).

The men who first served this church are obscure. They were not monks but they lived by some kind of rule and escaped drastic reformation after the Conquest. The bishop was of course the nominal head but, though sometimes a keen builder, he was often absorbed in state business. London was a coveted see, embracing

Middlesex, Essex and part of Hertfordshire; before the Reformation seven holders, including Mellitus, St Dunstan, Simon Sudbury and Wolsey's stumbling-block, Warham, became archbishops of Canterbury. The Normans therefore installed a dean who, at the head of thirty major canons, formed the governing body or chapter. These canons had incomes from prebends, estates which included Holborn, Islington and St Pancras, but many later lived elsewhere, partly to escape the cost of entertaining civic dignitaries. Below were a mass of minor canons, vicars and chantry priests. The archdeacon of London (another Norman introduction) was a diocesan figure and the chancellor, a kind of chief secretary, also had outside duties, being in charge of all the city's schools except those of St Mary-le-Bow and St Martin-le-Grand. The cathedral also had a precentor, for the choir, and a treasurer, whose underlings included a sacrist to look after the treasure, vergers, a chamberlain, almoners, and keepers of the bakehouse and brewery.

The canons were in many ways a law unto themselves, favouring the barons against John and later worsting both Henry III, who had ordered the arrest of their treasurer, and the mayor, who carried it out. Disputed boundaries and efforts to keep people out of the cathedral precinct caused much trouble. In 1281 it was agreed that the canons might shut their gates at night but forty years later there were complaints that they were obstructing the way west to Ludgate. Here, as at Westminster, unpopular rights of sanctuary survived the Reformation, to be upheld by Elizabethan judges against the city's claim to make arrests there.

Some of the open views of St Paul's today make it hard to imagine the walled precinct and buildings around the medieval cathedral. In the north-east corner of the churchyard there was a belfry, the Jesus Tower. Also to the north-east, where the folkmoot met, stood Paul's Cross, famous as a site for sermons and proclamations. First recorded in 1241, when it was probably a high stone cross on a platform, this was rebuilt in the 1380s and again, with a pulpit, in about 1450, and was finally pulled down by the Roundheads. It is now recalled by a plaque on the east face of the tall Edwardian memorial. On the north side of the churchyard a large charnel house, for bones, was established in about 1282, with a chapel overhead. Against the north wall of the cathedral, limited on the east by the north transept, lay the cemetery called Pardon Church Yard, which had a library, a chapel and cloisters with wall-paintings of the Dance of Death. West of this, separated only by a path to a door

Fig. 53 *Reconstruction of Old St Paul's from the south-west*
(The Trustees of the London Museum)

in the north wall of the nave, lay the bishops' garden and residence. There had been a palace since Fitz Stephen's day, originally on the south side near a brewery. Bishops came to stay until Tudor times, when their great hall actually touched the north-west corner of the cathedral and their grounds stretched north to Paternoster Row. The south-west angle of the churchyard contained the parish church of St Gregory (another, St Faith's, lay in the crypt of the cathedral) and between the south wall of the nave and the south transept was the octagonal fourteen-century chapter house (*Fig. 53*). A once famous grammar school dwindled into a choir school after 1510, when the present St Paul's School (now in West Kensington) started on the eastern side of the churchyard; its founder was the dean, John Colet, the son of a lord mayor. There were not yet any shops in the churchyard itself, although it was later to become the home of stationers.

Fig. 54 *Interior of the nave of Old St Paul's, looking east, Norman with later vaulting, from a 17th-century etching by Wenceslaus Hollar* (British Museum)

We know nothing about the first churches and little about the one started by Bishop Maurice after the fire of 1086, since his great Norman building was damaged by fire in 1135 and later by lightning. What became known as the 'new work' was started from the east end in 1259 but the central tower, with its spire and cross, was finished only in 1314 and a south aisle added to the Norman nave (*Fig. 54*) twenty years later. Old St Paul's, as it finally emerged, had a Lady Chapel and side chapel, a choir with tall windows, a central lantern tower, north and south transepts, a magnificent nave of twelve bays and two bell-towers at the west end. Although it broods over the city in later prints, they cannot do it justice, for the spire was not rebuilt after being struck by lightning in 1561, when the whole cathedral nearly caught alight. Probably this was 450 feet high, much taller than that of Salisbury Cathedral which is England's pride today. Correspondingly long (585 feet), St Paul's was surpassed only by the cathedrals of Milan, Seville and St Peter's in Rome. Wren's masterpiece, 513 feet long and 363 feet high to the top of the cross on the dome, is slight by comparison and, for all its fame, less of a magnet to the eye. It roughly fills the old site but it does not stretch so far west and its axis points some ten degrees farther north, to avoid coinciding with the medieval foundations.

Old St Paul's, of which there is a model in the London Museum, proclaimed that London was the capital. Throughout the kingdom, even in Ireland and Scotland, the Church sought donations and offered indulgences (remissions of sins) to those who would contribute to the 'new work'. Among the citizens, familiarity bred carelessness, for in 1385 the bishop complained that his cathedral was used as a public market, and that boys threw stones at birds in the churchyard and played ball to the peril of the windows and images. A reforming Elizabethan, depicting the bad old days, sneered that 'the south alley for usury and popery, the north for sorcery, and the horse fair in the midst for all kinds of bargains' were 'so well known to all men as the beggar knows his dish'. When churches were so much bigger than any other buildings, people naturally met here, in the dry, for all kinds of business. Criticisms, however justified, only emphasize St Paul's importance in everyone's life.

The secular canons of St Martin-le-Grand came second only to the canons of St Paul's. One Ingelric and his brother established or perhaps even re-established this collegiate church ten years before the Conquest, so that it was older than any nearby religious house except Barking and Westminster. The saint was Martin, a fourth-century bishop of Tours, famous for having divided his cloak to give half to a beggar. St Michael the Archangel, All Hallows (All Saints) and St Mary the Virgin alone received more medieval dedications in London, although we now have only the successors of St Martin Ludgate, in the city itself, and, outside, St Martin-in-the-Fields. Within a few months of his accession William I granted special privileges: St Martin's became a royal free chapel, under a dean, with rights of permanent sanctuary, rivalled only by Westminster, and freedom from ecclesiastical and civil jurisdiction. The canons' precinct stretched west from Foster Lane to cover most of the site of the recently demolished Central Telegraph Office. St Martin's Lane (now itself called St Martin's-le-Grand) cut the precinct in two; any smaller way could probably have been stopped up but the canons could do nothing about daytime traffic on the main road out through Aldersgate. It was here that the curfew was rung to keep Londoners indoors. The citizens resented this special sanctuary, which was unaffected by royal seizures of their own liberties, and in the fifteenth century they vainly battled to assert themselves. In spite of attempts to control abuses, so traditional a believer as Sir Thomas More complained of the 'rabble of thieves, murderers and heinous traitors, and that in two places specially. The one at the elbow of the city (Westminster), the other in the very bowels'. The end was not very dignified, for St Martin's was granted to the abbots of Westminster from 1503 until the Reformation, when it went to the king and the church itself was soon pulled down. The legal privileges however continued until abolished by Parliament in 1815, when a site was being prepared for the Post Office. A plaque in the wall of Empire House, facing St Martin's-le-Grand, recalls the site of the canons' church.

Neither St Paul's, Westminster Abbey nor St Martin-le-Grand began as offshoots of foreign movements. After the Conquest things changed. Bermondsey Priory, founded in 1089, was dependent for nearly two hundred years on its Cluniac mother house in France, although it finally became an independent abbey. It lay beyond the bounds of Southwark but deserves mention partly as the forerunner of outside influences and partly because its founder was a merchant of London.

The next batch of houses was for Augustinian (more briefly Austin) canons or canonesses. The canons of St Mary Overie, whose church is now Southwark Cathedral, come first, since they were installed there by two Norman knights in 1106. A year later the priory of Holy Trinity or Christchurch was founded by Queen Matilda just inside Aldgate, with the city wall, now Duke's Place, as its north-eastern limit. All the area now bounded, clockwise, by Duke's Place, Aldgate, Leadenhall Street, the south end of Creechurch Lane and Heneage Lane once belonged to the priory; its great court is roughly marked by Creechurch Square and the cloisters, with the canons' church to the south, by Mitre Square, where there is a plaque. Holy Trinity was one of the richest London houses. Its receipt of all the property of the *cnihtengild* in 1125 is our only guide to the wealth of that important citizens' association, and the priors, as we have seen, became aldermen of Portsoken ward, which lay on the other side of the wall. In spite of such a promising start, this house ended up in poverty. It was the first one to be dissolved without the pope's consent, in 1532, when England still owed nominal obedience to Rome. Nothing could have encouraged the general destruction which followed more than the lack of fuss which greeted Holy Trinity's fate.

At Smithfield, as in Southwark, the Austin canons have a solid memorial. In 1123 a hospital was founded by Rahere, a courtier of Henry I and canon of St Paul's, on his recovery from a critical illness; he is also said to have had a vision of being rescued from the jaws of hell by St Bartholomew and, accordingly, to have endowed a priory immediately north-east of the hospital. These both lay within the Bars, although beyond the wall, and were separated by what was once Duck Lane and is now the northern end of Little Britain. There are still two churches, St Bartholomew-the-Less and St Bartholomew-the-Great, to recall the hospital and the priory. The hospital managed to struggle through the Reformation (see p. 228). The priory was among the last to be surrendered to the king, in 1539; most of its buildings were demolished but the choir of the church survives, as a Norman monument unique in London (see (p. 240).

Two more Augustinian houses, of canonesses, were founded in the 1130s or 1140s. One was Haliwell Priory, Shoreditch (where there was a holy well), the other was St Mary's, Clerkenwell. Both of these rich houses lay well beyond the city boundaries, in Middlesex. They have left no remains, but visitors to the priory of the knights of St John may notice the tower of St James's Church, off Clerkenwell Close. This marks the site of the nuns' church, for their property lay immediately north of the knights' headquarters.

The next arrivals were the military orders. The Hospitallers or, to give them their full title, the Knights of the Hospital of St John of Jerusalem, are first mentioned in London some sixteen years later than the Templars (see p. 57), about 1144. They dispensed hospitality, like most religious orders, but did not in fact run a hospital at what became their English centre in Clerkenwell. Their roughly rectangular precinct ran east from the present gatehouse over St John's Lane, then north to the corner of Aylesbury Street, and west to Clerkenwell Green. It would take several volumes to do justice to these knights, as they heroically resisted the Moslem tide which forced them back over the centuries from Palestine to Cyprus, Rhodes and, finally, to Malta. The English medieval branch or *langue* was one of seven in western Europe; although suppressed at the Reformation it was restored in 1831 and is now independent, with the Queen as its Sovereign Head and the title of 'the Grand Priory in the British Realm of the Most Venerable Order of the Hospital of St John of Jerusalem'. The knights, with branches all over the world, still run an ophthalmic hospital in Jerusalem, as well as the St John Ambulance Association for first aid training and the Brigade for practical work. Their headquarters are once again at Clerkenwell, in the remains of the old priory (*see p. 232*).

By 1216 some nuns had taken over the parish church of St Helen Bishopsgate, whose dedication to the mother of Constantine the Great, the first Christian emperor, inevitably led it to claim Roman ancestry. This was the city's only house of Benedictines, the oldest and biggest order. Such a conservative choice was only to be expected, since the founder was a citizen—William, son of William the goldsmith. Perhaps for that very reason St Helen's became a local favourite: the Basings, who provided several nuns and one prioress, soon contributed towards a new church, and Londoners often placed widows or unmarried daughters there, paying an annuity to the house. Edward I helped by arriving on foot, with a train of barons and prelates, to present a piece of the True Cross. In 1432 stricter rules against slack services, fashionable dress, lavish entertainment and 'much coming in and out at unlawful times', show that it had almost become a smart boarding-house. The large priory, later next door to Sir John Crosby, covered Great St Helen's and stretched north over St Helen's Place, where the Leathersellers' Hall occupies the site of the nuns' hall. Their unusual church continued to be used by the parishioners, so it escaped the Reformation. (*See p. 240.*)

When Henry III was a boy and London was recovering from its support for the rebel barons, the friars arrived. First came the disciples of the Spaniard St Dominic, who made Oxford their headquarters but who had settled in Holborn by 1224. Patronage from Hubert de Burgh and then from the king himself, from whose time almost every royal confessor was a black friar, can hardly have pleased the Londoners. The Dominicans were never so popular as the Franciscans who quickly followed them but in 1279, to the dismay of St Paul's, they bought the strategic site of Baynard's Castle. Before they had even sold their Holborn property to the earl of Lincoln, they began their new church, with help from the king and a Dominican archbishop. Edward I allowed them to pull down part of the defences, which the citizens after much prodding rebuilt farther west, and so changed for the last time London's walled outline. On Edward II's fall the Dominicans are said to have fled for their lives, but relations soon improved, to judge from the citizens buried in their precinct. This eventually stretched from the new wall by the Fleet eastward as far as Puddle Dock and from the Thames almost to Ludgate Hill; there is now a commemorative plaque on Broadway Chambers, where Ludgate Broadway becomes Blackfriars Lane. The church itself had a long nave, since the friars were famous preachers; it stood just south of the present Carter Lane, with a cemetery to the north and a cloister farther south, now covered by Playhouse Yard. Great councils met in a hall nearer the river, on the west side of today's Printing House Square. Easy access by water may explain why there were so many state occasions: kings, ambassadors and even Parliaments met here, where the papal legates heard Henry VIII's divorce suit, before fatefully adjourning the case to Rome.

In 1224 nine Franciscans crossed to England, five staying in Canterbury and four moving on to London. These followers of St Francis of Assisi, also called the grey friars or friars minor, clung closest of all to the ideal of poverty, travelling barefoot even in midwinter and living on coarse bread and sour beer. They soon left a hired house in Cornhill for a plot north of Newgate Street, which was vested in the city on their behalf, since they were allowed to have nothing of their own. Nearby was the butchers' quarter, the Shambles, and between the friars' precinct and that of the canons of St Martin-le-Grand ran Stinking Lane, now King Edward Street. This unattractive patch was given by a mercer, John Ilwyn, the first of many Londoners to take the Franciscans under their wing. William Joyner, mayor in 1239, built them a chapel, and soon the friars' simplicity inspired a positive scramble to patronize them: Henry le Waleys paid for the nave, Gregory de Rokesley for the dormitory and another alderman for the chapter house, while the Basings helped to bring them an early supply of piped water. Royal and noble favours followed: in 1306 Edward I's second queen, Margaret, founded a more splendid church, which advanced with gifts from the next two queens and was almost finished before the Black Death. Their precinct, although unwalled by 1340, was reaching its maximum size: from the main street north to the city wall, and from Stinking Lane westward almost to Newgate. The Franciscans in turn won courtly influence and so drew the wrath of Wyclif, but they never quite lost their place in London's heart. Most people left them money, Richard Whittington giving enough for a big library; as late as 1514 the public contributed to paving the nave with marble and the city fathers, as founders, agreed to make a yearly procession there on St Francis's Day. When the end came the grey friars were found to have more treasure than any rival order. Their buildings were turned over to the citizens, as was only just. In 1546 the eastern half of the 300 foot long church was re-opened to serve the new parish of Christ Church, Newgate Street, while the western half was left unroofed for burials. To combat beggary, which grew worse with the fall of the religious houses, other buildings of the priory in 1552 were repaired for poor father-less children, who formed Christ's Hospital or the Bluecoat School. Plaques on the Post Office facing Newgate Street recall the grey friars and the school, which occupied their land until moving to Horsham in 1897. Soon after this date the school buildings were demolished.

The first friars to reach London were the black ones, followed by the grey and the white. The white friars or Carmelites, descended from the ascetic hermits of Mount Carmel in Palestine, did not arrive until 1249. Although never numerous in England, they flourished after their foundation by Sir Richard Grey (of the Gray's Inn family) on the fashionable riverside road to Westminster. (*See p. 56.*) Next came the Augustinian or Austin friars. Royalty apart, they could have had no grander patron than Humphrey de Bohun, earl of Hereford and Essex, who installed them on the west side of Old Broad Street in 1253. This was the order's main English house. It was not particularly popular, feuding with the Franciscans over property and later narrowly escaping attack from a Lollard mob. The huge church was surpassed only by the grey friars', since the nave alone was 153 feet long. Part of the western end survived until the Second World War, for it was given to the Dutch Protestants, whose rebuilt church in Austin Friars now occupies the medieval site.

Two small orders, the Friars of the Holy Cross and the Friars of the Penance, also penetrated thirteenth-century London. The first became known as Crutched Friars, from the cross (Latin *crux*) worn on their habits. Small but not particularly poor, they petered out only to reappear quickly south of Hart Street. The second, called from their sackcloth Friars of the Sack, fell victim to Rome's alarm at the mushrooming of so many groups. In 1274 the pope, who even thought of suppressing the Carmelites and Austin friars, forbade the Friars of the Sack to receive new members and so snuffed out a small group which had settled at Aldersgate and then at Lothbury. The still more obscure Pied Friars and Friars of Areno may also have lasted for a time, the first in London and the second in Westminster.

The friars rejuvenated Christianity as they went from strength to strength. The last wave reached London as late as 1294, when the king's brother Edmund, earl of Lancaster, established the order of St Clare outside the eastern wall. There were not many friaresses; the Clares had only two other houses in England and a similar order, the Dominicanesses, only one. The Clares were a feminine counterpart to the *fratres minores* or friars minor; St Clare of Assisi was a contemporary of St Francis and her disciples were the *sorores minores*, shortened in English to Minoresses. Their London house was thus called the Minories. Special grants meant that even after the Dissolution the five-acre precinct was free from the bishop, until 1730, and separate from the city's Portsoken ward, as it still is. In this drab area nothing can be seen of the abbey buildings, although their foundations lie beneath the desolate southern and eastern sides of Haydon Square.

After 1300 there were very few new houses, for missionary zeal died down and even the friars were tempted away from their ideals. For the next two hundred years rich men preferred to endow chantries. Sometimes the priests were sufficiently well organized to have formed a college, such as those who served the Guildhall chapel or who, for much longer, had served St Thomas Becket's chapel on London Bridge. None was a large foundation, except the college of secular canons which Edward III set up inside his palace at Westminster and dedicated to St. Stephen (*see p. 81*).

Two more monastic foundations, both just outside the Bars, complete the list. In 1348 Edward III founded the Cistercian abbey of St Mary Graces, so called in gratitude for his French victories and for escaping shipwreck. His choice filled a gap, for when the ascetic Cistercians or white monks had swept across the land two centuries earlier they had avoided all towns (England's most famous monastic ruins today are Cistercian ones in secluded Yorkshire dales). East of the postern gate by the Tower, where the land sloped down to the empty marshes of Wapping, Edward found a suitably forbidding plot, which had been intended as an extra cemetery because of the Black Death. Next to the Tower the riverside was already occupied by St Katharine's Hospital, so he settled the white monks to the north, where the Royal Mint now stands, and gave them more land running down to the Thames beyond St Katharine's. Although St Mary Graces was not a hospital, it won such a name for charity that Londoners at the Dissolution linked it with St Bartholomew's and St Mary of Bethlehem as especially deserving to be spared. The Cistercians also lived up to their fame as farmers by draining the land to the east and strengthening the riverbank. The city had every reason to be thankful for the monks' hard work: at their dispersal Nightingale Lane, now Thomas More Street, cut down from their main buildings on the higher ground through market gardens to breweries, wharves and a dock.

Last of all came the London Charterhouse, home of the Carthusians. The very word 'monk' comes from the Greek *monachos*, solitary, but the Carthusians more than any had kept to the original hermit's life, leaving their cells only to worship, to eat in silence, and for limited periods of conversation. From their centre at the Grande Chartreuse, in south-east France, they first reached England in 1178. So severe an order made slow headway, for it offered neither artistic, intellectual nor physical work as a substitute for lonely contemplation, but its example shone brightly as others grew tarnished. In the plague year 1349 one of the king's fellow knights, Sir Walter Manny, bought thirteen acres from St Bartholomew's Hospital as an extra cemetery. The field, Spital Croft, lay north of St Bartholomew's Priory. A chapel was quickly dedicated but Manny's plans for a college of twelve priests expanded, with encouragement from the bishop of London, until in 1371 he founded a new Carthusian house—England's fourth but the first of five more within some forty years. These sprang from a change of policy when the order, which had always shunned crowds, decided to contrast its austerity with urban worldliness. Unimpressed by the nearness of the capital, the Carthusians remained aloof. Sir Thomas More thought wistfully of retiring among them and young men of fashion were attracted to the very end. The Carthusians alone caused Henry VIII serious trouble, many courting martyrdom by refusing to renounce the pope's supremacy, even before the general attack on religious houses had begun.

The Charterhouse was founded so late that we know an unusual amount about it. The whole thirty-acre precinct lay between what are now St John Street and Goswell Road: Manny's cemetery had today's Clerkenwell Road as its northern boundary and stretched irregularly south to cover the south-western part of Charterhouse Square; this area was filled out when the knights of St John conveyed land covering the rest of the square and stretching east along Carthusian Street to Aldersgate. Plots farther north as far as Dallington Street were also added. The vast cloister, 300 feet by 340 feet, lay just north of Charterhouse Square; to its south-west were the church and most other buildings, which were far less important to the self-contained Carthusians than they would have been to most orders. On the other sides lay fields, gardens and parkland stocked with game. The prior and twenty-four monks lived in separate cells, like tiny houses, strung around the cloister and each with its own garden behind. All the donors of these cells are known—they included the mayor Sir William Walworth—and there is even a plan of the waterworks. After the Dissolution most of the cloister was pulled down and the adjacent property turned into a town house, until Sir Thomas Sutton, who made a fortune from coal, founded a school and hospital here in 1611. Like the earlier foundation, Christ's Hospital, Charterhouse School has found more space in the country, but Sutton's Hospital, which we should now call an almshouse, still includes the monastic remains on the west. (*See p. 230.*) The eastern half has gone full circle, since much of it came from St Bartholomew's and has now returned to form that hospital's medical school.

The arrival of the Carthusians meant that every major religious order could be found within sight of London, except the Premonstratensians or white canons. This was not all, for care of the soul was so much more important than care of the body that hospitals, too, were at least semi-religious foundations. Some were regular monasteries, with lay brothers or sisters to specialize in care of the sick. Others were almshouses, with attendant priests or nurses. These became increasingly common, like chantries or small colleges. Many hospitals were for lepers and eventually at least six were run by the city itself. Most of these grim sentinels along the main roads stood well away from the wall, ringing London from Hammersmith to Mile End.

If we ignore the pre-Conquest tradition about St James's at Westminster, the first hospital in the area was St Giles-in-the-Fields. Here in Holborn the bountiful Queen Matilda, who died in 1118, endowed a leper-house; although the city was made overseer, lepers were later in danger of being ousted by decrepit royal servants. The hospital, which was dissolved in 1539, was centred on the triangle now formed by Charing Cross Road, Shaftesbury Avenue and the (much older) St Giles's High Street; its chapel was probably

227

where St Giles's Church stands. Next comes St Bartholomew's, Smithfield, founded by Rahere for poor pilgrims and wayfarers. This escaped control from the neighbouring priory in about 1200 and, although it did not escape Henry VIII, it was so quickly refounded that it can claim to be the oldest surviving hospital, on land held for well over eight hundred years.

Another Matilda, Stephen's wife, founded the Royal Hospital of St Katharine-by-the-Tower in about 1147. Outside the postern gate she bought some empty land running down to a mill by the Thames. Edward I took some of this for his fortress next door, but his beloved Queen Eleanor had already re-endowed the hospital. It survived the Reformation and moved to Regent's Park in 1825 to make way for St Katharine Docks. When the new chapel in turn was dismantled in 1948 its glory, the duke of Exeter's tomb, was taken to St Peter's in the Tower so as to be near its medieval home (*see p. 149*). St James's leper-house at Westminster was at any rate the fourth hospital, for its privileges were confirmed in 1189, and a year later we hear of an obscure almhouse by St Paul's. We also hear of London's most central hospital, dedicated to its favourite martyr Thomas Becket. It was run by the knights of St Thomas of Acon, a small order modelled on the Templars and perhaps founded when Richard the Lionheart captured Acre from the Saracens. This was very much the citizens' hospital, on the site of Becket's birthplace north of Cheapside, which had been given by his sister Agnes and her husband. Londoners loaded it with gifts, and new property was being added until shortly before its suppression. The neighbouring mercers, who had contributed heavily to the hospital of St Thomas of Acon during its last century, then bought the site, where Becket House now contains the company's hall and chapel.

In the next fifty years appeared St Mary without Bishopsgate, St Mary Rouncevall, the House of Converts and St Mary of Bethlehem. The first, known as St Mary Spital, was founded by a citizen and his wife on land provided by an alderman. It had Augustinian canons, whose churchyard is now marked by Spital Square, with lay helpers to look after the sick. Most medieval hospitals were tiny but St Mary's had 180 beds at the Dissolution, when the lord mayor vainly asked Henry VIII to spare it, along with St Mary Graces and St Bartholomew's Hospital. St Mary Rouncevall was at Charing Cross (*see p. 66*).

Henry III's house of refuge for converted Jews, which may be considered a hospital, is chiefly interesting for its later history. A handful of converts, from immigrants, lingered on in Chancery Lane until Stuart times, but in 1377 the property was assigned to the Keeper of the Rolls, who as chief clerk had charge of all the records of the Court of Chancery. This made it an obvious site for the Public Record Office in the 1850s. The house of the order of St Mary of Bethlehem, on land given by a sheriff in 1247, at first came under the bishop of Bethlehem and reminds us that the Holy Land was once in Christian hands. The city took it over and by 1403, with six lunatics and three sick, it was really a lunatic asylum, which made easier its mismanagement by absentee masters and dishonest under-officers. The hospital was much poorer than St Mary Spital, yet no one could do without such a place. After the Reformation it moved to Moorfields and eventually south of the river, where it continues as the Royal Bethlem Hospital. In Broad Street a plaque tells visitors to the Great Eastern Hotel that they would once have been entering the site famous as 'Bedlam'.

Among the many other hospitals was that of the brothers of St Anthony of Vienne, on the site of a former synagogue given by the king in 1243, where the Westminster Bank now stands at the corner of Old Broad Street and Threadneedle Street. This began as a poor offshoot of the French house, in Dauphiné, although it prospered after passing to the Crown as an alien priory, when its cramped quarters were enlarged to include a grammar school. Edward IV attached St Anthony's to St George's, Windsor, so that it survived the Reformation, only to be plundered into extinction by an Elizabethan. The order did much to nurse sufferers from rye-bread poisoning or ergotism, which became known as St Anthony's fire. The saint himself was said to have overcome the demon Gluttony, in the form of a hog, and in London this story was put to good use: the hospital's pigs, with bells around their necks, were allowed to wander freely through the streets, where the charitable helped to fatten them. Inevitably, the boys at the grammar school were nick-named 'Anthony's pigs' by their rivals. A plaque opposite the entrance to Finch Lane records the brethren and the French Protestants who later took over their church.

There was a hospital for blind men called St Mary within Cripplegate or Elsing Spital, founded in 1330 on land given by the first warden William de Elsing. Although this was dissolved in 1536 its church became the parish church of St Alphage London Wall (see p. 233). Another well-known hospital was St Augustine Papey, perhaps so oddly named because St Augustine's relics were at

229

S

Pavia. This house, founded in 1442 by the local clergy for sick priests, died with the chantries, but its church is commemorated by a tablet on the corner of St Mary Axe and Camomile Street. Among the others, Whittington's Hospital comprised thirteen almshouses next to his college, which were eventually moved to Highgate and then to Sussex, where they are still supported by the Mercers' Company. Similar foundations, usually less lavish, continued right through the Reformation. Among the last which can be called medieval were Sir John Milborne's almshouses, built in 1535 and finally closed in 1897, whose endowment still contributes towards pensions paid out by the Drapers' Company.

There is hardly one stone on top of another to remind us of these religious houses. Only where the church became a parish church is there anything to see, except in Clerkenwell. This busy if rather down-at-heel area north of Smithfield Market is extraordinarily neglected by people who work in the city. Although it lies beyond the Bars the Charterhouse, which is one of its glories, is nearer St Paul's than are the Tower of London or the Strand.

To tour the Charterhouse is largely to tour a sprawling Elizabethan mansion. Its earlier history is obvious, however, to anyone who walks along the north side of Charterhouse Square. The lower part of the courtyard wall, with its distinctive squares of flint, comes from the monastery, and so do the stones from which the upper part has been rebuilt. The chequerwork continues around the main entrance arch, to whose massive oak door the arm of the last prior was nailed by order of Henry VIII. Beyond the gateway (where visitors are taken on Wednesdays in the summer, at 2.45 p.m.), is a conduit house which once held the monks' water cistern; the bricks are from the last years of the monastry, although the pagoda-like roof of green copper has been renewed. Through a farther, re-constructed, arch to the right lies the Master's Court, now London's nearest approach to the quadrangle of an Oxford or Cambridge college; it is a post-Reformation enlargement of the Little Cloister but has earlier work along its eastern side. To the west, a narrow entrance leads to the Wash-house Court, part stone and part brick but wholly monastic, except for the windows and minor repairs (*Fig. 55*). This was where the lay brothers lived or worked. The south-west corner of the monks' own cloister, including the prior's cell, was where the Elizabethan Great Hall faces the Master's Court. Part of the western walk was incorporated into a gallery running

Fig. 55 *Wash-house Court in the London Charterhouse, looking north-west, early 16th century* (Copyright Country Life)

north to a tennis-court, so that we can still see the doorway to one of the cells and the opening through which food was passed. By looking out across the courtyard of St Bartholomew's Medical School, we can also see how enormous was the original enclosure. The bombs which so damaged the later mansion revealed much about the medieval plan and proved that the present chapel was once the chapter house. The tower, whose picturesque upper stage and bell-turret date from 1613, had housed the Carthusians' treasure: from the floor of its upper room, still covered with medieval tiles, a shaft was found piercing the south wall in the fashion of a squint, a common device so that outsiders could follow a religious service. This showed where to dig for the tomb of the founder, Sir Walter Manny, who was known to have been laid before the high altar, where there is now a lawn. Manny's corpse, encased in lead for 576 years, was saturated but identifiable. Some painted carvings from his tomb are now in the treasury, while the bones lie, under a simple slab, in their old resting place.

A few hundred yards farther north are two properties from the priory of the Knights of St John, as impressive in their way as the Charterhouse. The former main gatehouse straddling St John's Lane was rebuilt in 1504 by the grand prior Thomas Docwra. It looks very romantic, with its battlements and four-storey flanking towers, from which fly the red and white banner of the order and also, usually, that of the lord prior. The stone facing has in fact been restored, for the gatehouse had a very chequered history until it was regained by the order a hundred years ago. Inside and next door there are valuable relics of the knights' rule in Cyprus, Rhodes and Malta, which can be seen by arrangement with the curator of the museum at St John's Gate. Most of the woodwork and some of the rooms, including the Chapter Hall, are new, but the stonework of the Chancery and the adjoining Council Chamber, which bridges the road, are of Docwra's time. Beyond, the more westerly of the staircases is unique; it is the original turret staircase, spiralling upward to the library, with steps and central (newel) post of oak instead of stone. The library, on the third floor, boasts an illuminated French missal of the fifteenth century and a warrant, signed by Henry VIII, to pull down the knights' church; a French silver processional cross of the early sixteenth century and a chalice brought by Philip of Spain some fifty years later are the oldest pieces in the fine collection of plate, displayed here and in the Chancery. Below again are two rooms housing the museum, with perhaps the finest private coin collection in England (not of English coins) and medieval documents showing the order's estates in many counties.

The knights' church is well beyond the gatehouse, across Clerkenwell Road in a corner of the dingy St John's Square. Here is a perfect example of what treasures can lurk behind the most unlikely walls. The nave is but a whitewashed shell, re-roofed, with some medieval masonry along the north and east, and marks the chancel of the original church, whose circular nave stretched west across the square. A curtain in front of the altar hides two wings of a Flemish triptych, which disappeared at the Reformation and was rescued only in the 1930s, from a Dorset manor house, to grace once more the setting for which it was painted. Below this prize from the end of the Middle Ages is one from the beginning, the vaulted crypt of the early church. To gaze along its length from the west end is to see, more clearly than anywhere else in London, the birth of Gothic architecture: the first vaults were begun perhaps in the 1140s, when arches were rounded, the farther ones were finished before 1185, when they were pointed (*Fig. 56*). The east end broadens out into side-vaults. The southern one has an octagonal Norman font from the knights' church at Hogshaw in Buckinghamshire. In the northern one lies the stone effigy of an emaciated Sir William Weston, the grand prior who died of grief at the suppression of his order.

Other monastic remains are fragmentary. The church of Elsing Spital became the parish church of St Alphage at the Reformation, when the previous St Alphage's was pulled down. Part of its tower has survived the blitz, so the fourteenth-century stones could be left as a striking monument among the new buildings of Route 11. It

Fig. 56 *Crypt of St John's Church, Clerkenwell, looking east, mid and late 12th century* (National Monuments Record)

cannot be reached safely from the ground, because of traffic, but can be studied from the new pedestrian way, St Alphage Highwalk, where there is a helpful notice. An enormous archway from the Chapel of the Rolls has been built against a wall of the Public Record Office in Chancery Lane, where we must walk through the main entrance and look back, to see the curves of honey-coloured stone facing the lawn. The chapel itself has made way for the Public Record Office Museum, with its fine display of medieval documents. It contains the newly painted tomb of Dr John Young, Master of the Rolls, by the Italian Pietro Torrigiani who made Henry VII's monument at Westminster. Young died in 1516 and the classical details, although salvaged from a medieval home, show that the Middle Ages were almost over. Of about the same date, from the chapel of St Thomas of Acon or perhaps from one which the mercers built alongside it, comes a recumbent figure of Christ. This was buried at the Reformation and unearthed in 1954 during clearance for the new Mercers' Hall, where it can now be seen by arrangement. No one knows who the sculptor was, nor where the limestone comes from, nor what has happened to the missing hands and feet. In spite of everything the crucified body, tensed with pain, is a work of art; it lies not on a shroud but on an imperial mantle, once painted purple, and for this reason it is unique.

At least there are plenty of names taken from religious houses. Beyond the Tower St Katharine's Way and St Katharine Docks recall Queen Matilda's hospital, while Spitalfields was once the land of St Mary Spital. Minories, running north from Tower Hill to Aldgate, is the name of the abbey of the sisters of St Clare, who are also commemorated in Clare Street. The nuns of St Helen's have Great St Helen's, leading to their church from Bishopsgate, and the more recently named St Helen's Place. The friars are well represented, with Crutched Friars unromantically passing under Fenchurch Street station, Austin Friars twisting north from Old Broad Street, Blackfriars Lane, station and bridge, and, a little farther west, Carmelite Street and Whitefriars Street among the printing presses. Ironically, the favourite grey friars alone have no memorial. In the north-west Bartholomew Close, Passage and Place, all recall the priory; Cloth Fair, the narrow alley from West Smithfield north of the church, reminds us that the priory was entitled to hold an annual fair every September, to which cloth-sellers flocked. Northward again, Charterhouse Street, Charterhouse Square and Carthusian Street need no explanation. St John Street,

St John's Lane, Square and Place, and Jerusalem Passage of course recall the Hospitallers, as the lawyers' Temples do the Templars. Most dignified of all, foreign envoys are now accredited to the Court of St James's, a reminder of the glorious days of this palace which Henry VIII built over the hospital for leprous virgins.

Familiar as were the religious houses, most Londoners had far more to do with their own parish churches. They went to mass every week and perhaps to wardmoots there, and often ensured that they would at least have a decent burial by modest subscriptions to a parish guild. The very first churches were founded by laymen, who named the priest and whose lands helped to shape the later parishes. Norman reformers soon raised the number of parishes and defined the boundaries but even they could not, in so varied a city, tidy up the administration: thirteen parishes were peculiars of the archbishop of Canterbury and so outside the jurisdiction of the bishop of London, while the dean and chapter of St Paul's claimed special rights in another ten.

Precise numbers are difficult, because of changing names, amalgamations and the question of including Southwark, Westminster and other nearby areas. Throughout the Middle Ages there were over one hundred parish churches in and around London, with some minute parishes in the oldest parts. About 1400 there were ninety-nine crammed within the wall and London's overflow was served by another nine within the Bars, while Southwark had St Margaret's and St Olave's; farther west there were St Clement Danes, St Mary-le-Strand, St Martin-in-the-Fields and St Margaret Westminster, with St Mary's across the river at Lambeth. The Great Fire of 1666 gutted 86 parish churches, of which it was decided to rebuild 51, and later destruction, culminating in the Second World War, left a mere handful. To match these losses, the parishes within the Bars were at last reduced in 1952 from 107 to 24. These still have their own churches, and fifteen more buildings were saved by their conversion into 'Guild Churches', which provide for exhibitions, recitals, lectures and services for the office-workers who pour into the city on weekdays.

Nothing about London is more intriguing than the names of its churches. Even modern buildings are bound to have medieval origins, since the trend has been to unite old parishes, not to create new ones. The actual dedication of every existing church is recorded before 1250, except possibly that of St Katharine Cree. These saints' names, usually chosen by the founder, show how Saxon influence gave way to Viking, and Viking to Norman. There is much more variety than in any newer city, because after the Reformation the only acceptable saints were the Twelve Apostles. What is more, London had so many churches that some topographical or personal description had to be added, although these were colloquial and so apt to change.

Of the twenty-four parish churches which still exist, only All Hallows by-the-Tower has what used to be London's second most common dedication; there were eight of these in the Middle Ages, which is not surprising if we remember that 'All Hallows' would now be expressed as 'All Saints'. St Andrew Undershaft and St Andrew-by-the-Wardrobe commemorate the same apostle, who once had yet another church, in Eastcheap. The first was literally overshadowed by an enormous shaft set up in the middle of what is now Leadenhall Street on Mayday: this maypole, not used after riots in 1517, was later sawn up as a pagan symbol. The second stood just south of the Great Wardrobe, established by Edward III in Carter Lane. St Bartholomew-the-Great and St Bartholomew-the-Less can both be traced to Rahere's dream; neither began as a parish church, although once there was one dedicated to this obscure apostle. St Botolph Aldgate and St Botolph Aldersgate commemorate a seventh-century English saint, popular in Norfolk, who gave his name to Boston in Lincolnshire; Botolph had four London churches, three of them just outside the gates because he was a patron of travellers. St Bride in Fleet Street should really be St Brigid, a still earlier Irish saint. St Clement Eastcheap, like St Clement Danes outside the city, recalls a first-century pope, martyred by the Romans. The following four, like St Bride, have always been solitary dedications. St Edmund the King, in Lombard Street, recalls an East Anglian ruler killed by the Vikings in 869 (the Edmund of Bury St Edmunds). St Giles Cripplegate commemorates the patron of beggars, and St Helen Bishopsgate the mother of the Emperor Constantine. St James Garlickhithe honours St James the Great; garlic was presumably landed nearby from the Thames, and the church's suffix has given its name to Garlick Hill.

St Magnus the Martyr reminds us of early Scandinavian traders, somewhat mysteriously since it was so called by 1067, many years before the martyrdom of Magnus, earl of Orkney. St Margaret Lothbury is dedicated to a probably mythical virgin martyr of Antioch, the Old English street-name being added to distinguish it from three other churches called after her. St Mary-at-Hill and St Mary-le-Bow commemorate the favourite saint of all; 'le Bow' refers to the arches or bows of the crypt, which also explain the title of the archbishop of Canterbury's Court of Arches, which still sits here. St Michael Cornhill commemorates the archangel St Michael, once the third most popular subject, with seven dedications. St Olave Hart Street honours the Norwegian king murdered in 1030, who had two other city churches and one in Southwark (*see p. 90*). St Peter Cornhill and St Peter-ad-Vincula are left from four churches so dedicated; the suffix of the second one, in the Tower, remains puzzling. St Sepulchre Holborn should really be the church of the Holy Sepulchre; it was the only one so named—very fittingly for a church which sounded the knell for condemned prisoners in Newgate. St Vedast Foster Lane is another lone dedication, with an odd history: Vaast was a sixth-century bishop of Arras, whose cult was presumably imported from Northern France after the Conquest; the name was latinized and so became 'Vedast' for the church but was corrupted, through 'Fast' and 'Faster', to 'Foster' for the lane.

The guild churches have also kept their old parish names. All Hallows London Wall, St Andrew Holborn, St Botolph Aldersgate and St Martin Ludgate are easily understood. St Benet Paul's Wharf recalls St Benedict, sixth-century father of the monastic order, who once had three other churches: Paul's Wharf, which still exists, reminds us that the cathedral chapter once owned the quay. St Dunstan-in-the-West commemorates London's bishop, who led the tenth-century revival and became archbishop of Canterbury; the suffix distinguishes it from his other church, off Eastcheap. St Ethelburga Bishopsgate is the only church in England dedicated to St Earconwald's sister, the first abbess of Barking, who died about 675. St Katharine Cree is one of two to another shadowy virgin martyr, the learned St Katharine of Alexandria, who was condemned to torture on a spiked wheel (from which comes the name of the firework). Cree should properly be Creechurch, itself a corruption of Christchurch; this arose because the church was built in the grounds of Holy Trinity Priory, which was sometimes called Christchurch, so that parishioners could worship separately from the monks. St Lawrence Jewry was one of two dedications to a saint said to have been roasted by the Romans on a gridiron (hence the curious shape of Wren's weather-vane). St Margaret Pattens, St Mary Abchurch and St Mary Woolnoth are all interesting in recalling founders or early benefactors: a surname, Patyns, and men called Abe or Abbo, and Wulfnoth. St Mary Aldermary, which Stow thought was older than any other St Mary's, is in fact of obscure origin, although it was known under William the Conqueror. St Michael Paternoster Royal probably records the paternosterers or rosary makers of Paternoster Lane, now College Street, and a group of houses called La Réole, after a town near Bordeaux from which wine merchants came to London. St Nicholas Cole Abbey, in Queen Victoria Street, recalls a fourth-century archbishop of Myra, in Asia Minor, the patron saint of children and the original Santa Claus, after whom four London churches were named; Cole Abbey was once Cold Abbey and originally Cold Harbour, a reference to some nearby shelter.

Many streets are named after churches which are still in use—for example Abchurch Lane and Clement's Lane off Lombard Street, Bow Lane and Lawrence Lane off Cheapside, and St Andrew's Hill and Bennet's Hill off Queen Victoria Street. These need no explanation, but there are many more which come from forgotten churches. The most important today are Fenchurch Street, Gracechurch Street and St Mary Axe. St Gabriel (previously St Mary or All Hallows) Fenchurch, whose suffix literally if obscurely refers to a fen, stood in the middle of the road between the junctions with Rood Lane and Mincing Lane; St Benet Gracechurch was on the south corner of Fenchurch and Gracechurch Streets, by a corn market where grass or hay might also have been sold; St Mary Axe, which claimed to have one of the axes with which St Ursula and her eleven thousand maidens had been chopped to pieces by the Huns, stood on the west side of its street, at the northern end.

From Cannon Street, east of the station, Lawrence Pountney Hill and Lane descend towards Upper Thames Street; between them, half-way down the lane, was the church of St Lawrence Pountney, so called from a college founded by the mayor John de Poulteney in 1344. Just beyond, the parallel Martin Lane recalls St Martin Orgar, which was on its east side. Next was St Michael's Lane, whose top end has been cut off but which still reaches Upper Thames Street as Miles Lane; the church of St Michael Crooked Lane once stood near the Eastcheap end. North of Cannon Street, St Swithin's Lane commemorates a church near London Stone on the west corner (the Guildhall Museum has a marble slab from here, under which was buried the heart of a thirteenth-century sheriff's wife). The parallel Nicholas Lane, now cut by King

William Street, contained the church of St Nicholas Acon by Nicholas Passage. Farther north again St Bartholomew-the-Less, later St Bartholomew-by-the-Exchange, stood on the east corner of Bartholomew Lane and Threadneedle Street. In the eastern part of the city, Botolph Lane runs from Eastcheap to Lower Thames Street, where St Botolph Billingsgate stood just east of St Magnus the Martyr. Farther along, St Dunstan's Hill leads up from Lower Thames Street to the Gothic tower of the ruined St Dunstan-in-the-East. In the west Pancras Lane, once called Needlers Lane, had on its north side the church of St Pancras Soper Lane (Soper Lane is now the northern stretch of Queen Street). Almost next door stood the church of St Sithe, once thought to have been the Anglo-Saxon Osyth but perhaps an Italian saint, Zita of Lucca, worshipped by the Lombards; a truncated Sise Lane still leads south to Queen Victoria Street. Farther west Great and Little Trinity Lanes intersect near the site of Holy Trinity-the-Less. Still farther west, St Peter Paul's Wharf stood at the corner of Upper Thames Street and Peter's Hill.

Out of all these there are three parish churches—St Bartholomew-the-Great, St Helen Bishopsgate, and St Andrew Undershaft—which are essentially medieval. So also is the Roman Catholic church of St Etheldreda Ely Place. All Hallows by-the-Tower and St Bride's have Anglo-Saxon remains (*see p. 19*). St Mary-le-Bow still has its early Norman crypt, recently restored in three parts as a chapel, a common room and a meeting-place for the Court of Arches. The groined vaults are new but much walling is original, notably in the chapel, and a simple spear-head design is one of the earliest examples of Norman decoration on a capital. There is also half of a much smaller crypt, similarly restored and not quite so old, having some typical Norman zigzag or chevron ornament. This belonged to a hermitage near Cripplegate and was bought at the Reformation by William Lambe, a clothworker whose company later moved it to its present home beneath the old churchyard of All Hallows Staining in Mark Lane. It can be seen on application to the nearby Clothworkers' Hall in Dunster Court. Several other parish and guild churches have parts which date back to later in the Middle Ages. Appearances deceive, for the most grandly Gothic looking buildings and especially the tallest, pinnacled towers, are usually much later. Wren, a classical master, sometimes restored and even rebuilt in the pointed Gothic style. In Queen Victoria Street the imposing St

239

Mary Aldermary, with its fan vaults, is basically his work. So are the towers of St Olave Jewry, St Mary Somerset, St Alban Wood Street, St Michael Cornhill and St Dunstan-in-the-East. These, all that remain of their churches, still help to give the city a delightful, mock-medieval air.

St Bartholomew-the-Great, although lopped and battered, is in a class by itself. Since it dwarfs St John's Chapel in the Tower, nothing else in London tells us what great church builders the Normans were. Rahere's priory church was much bigger than anything which served a parish. The gateway from West Smithfield used to be the western doorway (it now has Elizabethan half-timbering overhead) and the churchyard through which the path has been cut was once the nave; the ends of some old columns still project into the pavement. To the right a lawn marks the site of the cloister, whose rebuilt eastern range can be seen under its red-tiled roof. We enter through a Victorian porch where the nave joined the south transept and, to get a central view, should turn left into the gloom and pass under the organ. The rounded east end or apse, typical of the Normans, has been restored and the transepts on either hand have been rebuilt, after centuries of misuse, but the choir has plenty of early work. The new, smoother stone is mainly on the backs of the massive pillars, as we can see by walking around the ambulatory to the Lady Chapel, a restored fourteenth-century addition. There are many fascinating details: one of the very few medieval fonts in London (plain, octagonal, early fifteenth century); the oriel window (*Fig. 57*) built to overlook the choir by William Bolton (the last prior but one, master of the works under Abbot Islip for Henry VII's Chapel at Westminster Abbey); fragments of late Norman carving collected in the cloister; the late medieval tomb-figure of the founder, in his black monastic habit. Above all, St Bartholomew's has atmosphere; it is cool and dim on the most sweltering day and comforting in its simple strength, as only a Norman church can be.

St Helen's, lacking anything taller than an eighteenth-century turret and with a broad, double-featured west front, looks rather strange. It is indeed an oddity, being two churches in one, and also a very great rarity, since it includes a whole monastic church. This is because, unlike St Bartholomew's, it was begun for parishioners. The nuns built a larger church along the north side of the old one, which was then lengthened to match; transepts and later two chapels were added to the south. Some Norman stones may be hidden in the south wall but, as a result of all this rebuilding for rich citizens'

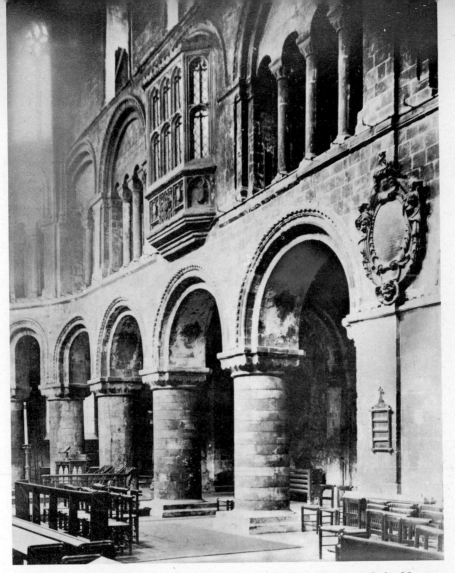

Fig. 57 *Prior Bolton's oriel window, late 15th century, and the Norman chancel of St Bartholomew-the-Great* (National Monuments Record)

daughters, the main walls of the present church are thirteenth century and those of the chapels are fourteenth century. Inside, the two aisles were divided by arches and, until the Reformation, by a screen. The slender arcade, which now gives such an air of space, dates from about 1475. Most of the windows, including the two big eastern ones, are modern, but the roof has some original timbers. Thirteen monastic stalls also survive although they have been moved from the nuns' side, which is now used as an aisle. St Helen's contains more monuments than any other parish church in London, since many were moved here when St Martin Outwich was demolished. They include four brasses of 1514 or earlier and two magnificent pairs of effigies. The older shows Sir John de Oteswich, whose family gave its name to St Martin's, bearded and in a long gown, with a baselard at one side and a purse at the other; he lies in alabaster on a modern tomb beside his wife, so low down in his new home that for once we can pore over the details (*Fig. 58*). Close by, between the Lady Chapel and the high altar, are Sir John Crosby and his wife.

Anglicans now enjoy the churches which were built for Rome, but in 1874 they began to make amends by returning Ely Chapel, which had belonged to the bishop of Ely's house in Holborn. This is now the Roman Catholic church of St Etheldreda Ely Place, set back on the left so that nothing can be seen from the entrance to the cul-de-sac near Holborn Circus. It dates from the very middle of the Middle Ages, about 1300, a sparse period for the capital, where so much was rebuilt in the fifteenth century. After climbing some steps and skirting the south side, we pass through a doorway which once led from the bishop's mansion, to stand beneath the church's soaring west window. Both east and west windows are filled with modern glass but they have fine original tracery and are large enough for a cathedral. St Etheldreda's is a much simpler, more open, structure than any parish church, since it was only a private chapel. It was however an ambitious one, built high up over an undercroft, like St Stephen's at Westminster. This crypt, for which it is well worth requesting a key, is as large as the church itself; the columns are fairly modern but the walls date from 1251, with some rougher stonework which might be Roman. London has nothing like it, except at Lambeth, to show the magnificence of the medieval bishops.

St Andrew Undershaft is a true city church. There is no romantic approach through grass and plane-trees, for it rises directly from the pavement of St Mary Axe at the corner of Leadenhall Street, surrounded by shipping offices. A church was here in Fitz Stephen's time but the present one dates from 1520–32; only the bottom of the tower is older, while the top stage with its pinnacles is Victorian, as we can see from the much whiter stone. Like St Margaret Westminster, St Andrew Undershaft represents the last phase of medieval building, so that the interior is light and rather severe. The wooden aisle roofs are original and so are the bosses of the nave roof, most of them featuring the Tudor rose. The chief contributors were two

Fig. 58 *Alabaster effigies of Sir John de Oteswich and his wife in St Helen Bishopsgate, late 14th century* (National Monuments Record)

merchant taylors, Sir William Fitzwilliam and Sir Stephen Jennings, but many other citizens helped with alms or with manual labour. We know most of this, like so much else about medieval London, from the Elizabethan John Stow. His red-brown marble figure sits in the north-east corner, writing with a quill pen placed there every year by Jennings's successor as lord mayor.

Three other interesting churches lie beyond the eastern limits reached by the Great Fire. It is easy to miss the 550-year-old west front of St Ethelburga's, sandwiched in between the windows of Bishopsgate. The church once had to be entered through two small shops, which were cleared away in the 1930s when an oak door-frame from the original west porch was moved to the London Museum. St Ethelburga's has escaped everything except the restorers. Although nearly every detail inside is modern, it remains a quaint, wholly unexpected retreat, and shows just how small a medieval parish church could be. More typical, perhaps, was St Olave Hart Street, whose small churchyard facing Seething Lane is sheltered by lime trees instead of the usual planes. The church was rebuilt about 1450 and gutted in 1941, but the interior looks very antique since most of it has been pieced together from old materials. The bombs did not destroy the tower and baptistry, but revealed the tall pointed arch between them, previously bricked up. Underneath is a room with late medieval pottery and other finds, and from here we can squeeze down more steps to a crypt some seven hundred years old, where there is a well. The arcades have partly survived in the main body of the church, although we can easily see that much has been renewed. In the far, south-east corner, a good angle from which to view the baptistry, there is a doorway from the earliest stone church. We cannot expect to find so much of the Middle Ages in St Katharine Cree, in Leadenhall Street. This is entirely pre-Fire but only just, since it was built about 1630 in a beguiling but extraordinary mixture of Gothic and classical. The lower part of the tower is from 1504, however, the gift of another lord mayor, and the east end with its round window like a Catherine wheel gives us some idea of that of Old St Paul's.

Close to St Olave's is All Hallows by-the-Tower, gutted in the war but still with enough medieval treasures to be visited for their sake alone. There is the fourteenth-century crypt-chapel of St Francis beneath the east end, where visitors may be escorted. There are the side wings of a triptych in the north aisle; they were probably painted by Jan Provost in 1462 and, like those of the slightly later Flemish triptych at Clerkenwell, disappeared for a long time at the Reformation. Nearby the repaired altar tomb of John Croke lavishly commemorates a fifteenth-century skinner. On the wall behind is a brass to Croke and his family, one of nine which survive in part from 1389 to 1533, forming the finest collection in any London church. On most, when they can be reached by brass-rubbers, we can see that reformers have erased the end of the inscription, which requested prayers for the dead and so was thought superstitious.

In the west there are three other churches with medieval fragments, which could be seen at the same time as St Bartholomew-the-Great and St Etheldreda. Where Newgate Street becomes Holborn Viaduct, just outside the old city gate, is London's largest parish church, St Sepulchre's. The exaggerated pinnacles of its tower and the long Gothic line of the nave, familiar to those who use Holborn Viaduct station or queue outside the Old Bailey, are in fact Victorian. The most striking survival of its fifteenth-century rebuilding is a three-storied porch, refaced outside but with two bays of fan-vaulting, now whitewashed, leading from the pavement into the church itself. Immediately east of St Sepulchre's, Giltspur Street runs north to 'Bart's' hospital, whose chapel is St Bartholomew-the-Less. Traffic rolls through an eighteenth-century gateway and then within inches of the church's west door. Old stone arches lead from the tower into the vestibule and the rebuilt nave. In the vestibule a strip of carpet covers the brass figures of William Markeby, who died in 1439, and Alice his wife; these are early survivals for London, and we can see that reformers about one hundred years later have neatly rubbed out part of the inscription. Lastly there is St Andrew's, at the far end of Holborn Viaduct. This, the biggest Wren church, has been restored since the war, but the bottom of the tower, with pointed arches, doorway and window, is medieval. It is faced all over in a creamy stone, recently cleaned, so that from outside it looks all of a piece. Inside, the stone base of the tower contrasts sharply with the light panelling and cream wash of the nave—a reminder that almost every London church, however classical, has a medieval ancestor.

 *The Price of Growth*

'London, thou art the flower of cities all' declaimed the Scots poet William Dunbar, who with his master the ambassador was feasted at Christmas 1501 by the lord mayor. To us the late medieval scene, although much grander, would seem more sordid than the Norman one. The population was now about 75,000, compared with perhaps 20,000 in Fitz Stephen's day. This was slow growth by modern standards but it had kept London well ahead of every other English town; Bristol had passed York and Norwich to take second place, but with no more than 10,000. Londoners had long been crammed in too small a space and knew special problems, which were to become nightmares as numbers shot up under the Tudors.

More and more regulations were needed. The first mayor's Building Assize, which encouraged stone walls and tiled roofs, had to be strengthened. Thatch was banned altogether in 1213, when all roofs were to be plastered inside, and within a century wood, too, was forbidden for roofs and chimneys. Stone walls never became common, since there were no local quarries, so fire precautions were tightened up. Ladders, and hooks and chains for pulling down houses, were kept in every ward, and by 1381 every house had to have a vessel full of water by its door.

Concern with roads and traffic was another sign of growth. Probably every citizen at first had to repair the stretch between his own house and the middle of the street, but there were specialized paviours by 1300. A 'stone master' was in charge of road cleaning as well as repairs by the 1470s, when householders only needed to look after the narrow footways. From the mid-fourteenth century people often left money for improving the roads, which would otherwise have had to be paid for by tolls. In spite of everything the repairs did not last. Where the Romans had laid solid foundations of large stones, medieval Londoners quickly patched the surfaces. Even if they had known better they could hardly have done otherwise, since they could not afford to hold up the traffic.

Road users themselves had to be rigidly controlled. Iron-rimmed wheels were restricted before 1300; officials were soon measuring them and, from the 1480s, wheels might only be studded with a standard type of nail. London Bridge was by then suffering from vibration, although a kind of highway code had been drawn up perhaps a hundred years earlier, to ensure that carts should be driven no faster when empty than when loaded. Private encroachments on the streets were another menace, for even a doorstep could make all the difference. Spotting and assessing these gave work from Fitz Stephen's time to 'viewers' or (in French) 'veiours', the ancestors of today's borough surveyors. A footbridge over the street, as built by St Thomas of Acon, was one startlingly modern way of relieving congestion. Another way perhaps explains the origin of Knightrider Street, first mentioned in 1322: it was obviously connected with horsemen and may once, when it stretched farther east, have been a kind of express route, uncluttered by stalls.

Another losing battle was fought against rubbish. Every citizen was supposed to keep his own piece of street clean but by the fourteenth century there were 'rakyers' to take the dirt away. Later even the height of the tail-boards on the dust-carts was regulated, so that the loads should not be spilled. This did not help with sewage, which by the 1460s was so bad that the Walbrook had to be cleaned and vaulted over; since then it has always flowed underground. Contractors also agreed to clear the public latrines, some of which were moved from too populous sites. Smoke was not yet such a curse. Coal, as opposed to charcoal, came by sea from Tyneside, hence Seacoal Lane running east from Farringdon Street, where coal was landed from the Fleet. The lime-burners who fouled Southwark under Edward I were followed by plumbers whose smelting was a nuisance in the city itself, but it was not until Elizabeth's time, when brick chimneys grew common and firewood ran short, that coal became London's main fuel.

Piped water helped to fight pollution. Religious houses were usually the first to build conduits, lead pipes to conduct water from nearby springs, but London was rich enough to take the initiative itself. In 1237 a landowner allowed the citizens to lay pipes from the

Tyburn. Eventually water was brought from many sources to the standards, wooden and later stone structures containing cisterns, where the public could help themselves for a small charge. The standard in Cheapside, famous as the site of rabble-rousing speeches and summary executions, stood slightly east of the junction with Bread Street; it was old by 1443, when it was rebuilt in stone. Sixty-five years earlier money had been left to carry the conduit eastward to the crossways at the top of Cornhill, where a plaque facing Gracechurch Street records the second standard. Fleet Street by then had its own supply. Great strides were made in the fifteenth century, when Westminster benefited from the conduit to the palace and even the prisoners in Ludgate and Newgate were allowed the overflow from St Bartholomew's Hospital. These supplies were not meant for industry and as early as 1310 there was a conduit keeper to drive brewers and fishmongers away in Cheapside. Some houses had water from the main but they had to pay special rates. William Campion, guilty of secret tapping in Fleet Street, was led through the city on a November day in 1478 with a miniature conduit on his head, from which he was constantly sprinkled through small pipes. In spite of this, houses had to be searched for illegal supplies twenty years later.

Prisons, oddly enough, were another sign of progress. Primitive societies could do without them by quick sentences and reliance on compensation, banishment or sharp physical penalties. As justice grew more elaborate, there was a demand for safe places which could never be fully satisfied. The city, forced by the flood of national prisoners to develop Newgate as well as the Fleet, was soon looking elsewhere. Perhaps after a short experiment at Temple Bar, a prison was opened at Ludgate about the time of the Peasants' Revolt. London intended this for freemen committed for debt, trespass or other civil offences and, remembering what had happened before, repeatedly insisted that it was not for criminals and outsiders. A citizen's rights must not be swamped, even in gaol, although he might forfeit the freedom and so be sent to rot in Newgate. For those tried before the mayor at the Guildhall, the city prisons known as Counters had by this time been opened by the sheriffs, who had once used their own houses; in the fifteenth century there was one opposite the standard in Cheapside and another in Poultry. These could be quite comfortable, with a tariff for long-term inmates. The Tun, set up by Henry le Waleys on Cornhill, was used for short periods mainly by moral delinquents;

a cage, stocks and pillory later stood nearby. Small lockups were probably dotted all over London by the end of the Middle Ages. Better street-lighting may also be linked with the fight against crime. Lanterns were to be hung outside every house during certain busy seasons in 1406, and later even the size of candle was laid down.

All kinds of personal habits came under scrutiny. In the fifteenth century there were threats against the brothels in Southwark, but it was left to Henry VIII, of all people, finally to close them down. The premises of barbers, as well as stew-keepers, were inspected in case they should be used for immoral purposes, and there were several efforts to ensure that decent women dressed differently from prostitutes. To prevent crime, masks or any other face coverings were repeatedly banned. From 1363 there were many national laws against extravagant dress, until in 1402 fine fur and gold ornaments were restricted to knights, and to those who had been mayors of London, York or Bristol, and their wives. These laws were not aimed at country folk, but at the townsmen whose wealth was in danger of blurring old class distinctions.

We might think that so many restrictions made life unbearable. They did not, because the more personal ones, which we would now find especially odious, could not be enforced. Rules about traffic and dirt, on the other hand, were badly needed. It is most unfair to judge by results, since there were so few mechanical aids. The more that we can see how London tried to cope, the more we should sympathize. The city at the end of the Middle Ages was in as much danger of choking to death as is the Greater London of today. It was the price for having become, in Stow's words, 'the principal storehouse and staple of all commodities within this realm'.

Index